1 7 2014

MY

PARIS

KITCHEN

My Paris Kitchen

RECIPES AND STORIES

David Lebovitz

PHOTOGRAPHY BY ED ANDERSON

TEN SPEED PRESS

Berkeley

SELLE   A OS
COTES   FILET
        PREM ERES
        SECONDES
        DECOUVERTES

EPAULE
COLLET
POITRINE
CARRE   ENTIER

TRIPERIE

FRAICHE OU CONG
FOIE DE VEAU FRAIS
TETE DE VEAU CONG
PIED DE VEAU CONG

Introduction

THE BIGGEST CHALLENGE I FACED WHEN SETTING UP MY FIRST full-scale kitchen in Paris was not calculating where to put the oven in relation to the refrigerator or what kind of fancy counter-tops I should have. It was not deciding what kind of flooring to install or where I would store my pots and pans. Or even whether my oven should be gas or electric. It was the sink.

After a decade of living in France, I had finally made the decision to buy a place to call my own. People always assumed that I had a designer-style expansive chef's kitchen, when I actually worked on a kitchen counter the size of a chessboard. Moving bowls and pots and pans around, I was persistently checkmated by the limited space. Sometimes I would empty the contents of a mixing bowl, then stand there holding the bowl suspended in mid-air, wondering where I would—or even if I could—put it down. (Many times I had no choice but to open the window and put it on the roof.) The temperature in the faltering oven fluctuated haphazardly a hundred degrees in either direction, which required me to stand guard while a batch of cookies baked away, fiddling with the knobs like a crazed person searching for just the right radio station, to make sure my chocolate chip cookies would be perfectly baked. (And it didn't help that sometimes I had to use a chair to hold the door closed, either.) Yet, somehow, in that inevitable way that people adapt to their circumstances, whatever and wherever they are, I made it work. It was hard to complain when many of my friends in Paris had apartments without ovens—or even kitchens. (And some didn't have bathrooms, either, requiring them to use a communal WC shared with neighbors on the same floor. So I guess I got lucky when I rented that first apartment sight unseen.)

How did I end up in this semi-functional kitchen? When I first arrived all those years ago and was searching for a place to live, I saw a listing for a *chambre de bonne* (maid's quarters) that was, admittedly, *très charmante*. And I sent off my deposit. When I arrived, I learned that in the multicultural jargon of real estate, *charmante* meant *charming* (in either language), but it was also quite cozy (i.e., small). I was enthralled by the Eiffel Tower standing majestically in front of me, and I loved being able to see right into the historic Place des Vosges, which was just down the street. However the apartment needed more work than I anticipated (or was alluded to by the photos online).

My first task was removing the gnarled, dead plant vines that crept all the way up the walls and across the ceiling of one of the two rooms. The vines had been stapled firmly in place, even though it was pretty obvious they weren't going anywhere on their own ever again. And the refrigerator was full of leftovers from the previous tenants, who had departed a few months prior to my arrival. But after a couple of months of cleaning it up, I had a tiny but workable kitchen where I would be able to cook and bake to my heart's content.

Shortly after I arrived I discovered that quite a few locals assumed I didn't know anything about food because I'm an American. Many felt it was their duty to set me straight, like the time I was at a press lunch, and a journalist decided to educate *l'américain* about the various greens in our salads. She kept plucking out individual leaves, holding them up, and identifying each one for me. Only after she got the third one in a row wrong did I bother to correct her.

Having moved from San Francisco, where I cooked professionally for several decades, taking part in the farm-to-table renaissance, I was not only well aquainted with the different varieties of lettuce, but I could also rattle off the multiple varieties of peaches, strawberries, plums, figs, and apricots that showed up at our local markets each season. I had worked for thirteen years at Chez Panisse, where farmers raised animals specifically for us, and local gardeners showed up at our back door with paper bags bursting with sunny Meyer lemons or ripe figs picked from their trees that morning, with their sugary juices oozing out through the cracks. Gardeners for the restaurant showed up right before dinner service with tangles of the tiniest salad greens one could imagine, scattered with edible flowers that grew alongside the lettuces. I had friends in the Bay Area who roasted and ground cocoa beans they sourced themselves, turning the liquid chocolate that poured out of the machines into tablets of shiny, bean-to-bar chocolate. And the *pains au levain* that came out of the ovens at Acme Bakery in Berkeley and Tartine in San Francisco were just as good as anything you could get in Paris. So why was I in France?

That's a question I'm frequently asked. And I never have a precise answer. I'd always enjoyed visiting Paris and had taken a couple of vacations here, as well as pastry courses at l'École Lenôtre. But I wasn't one of those people who filled their home with French antiques and rustic Provençal artifacts, dreaming of the day that I'd move to France. My experiences with Parisians, like most visitors, had mostly been with hotel desk clerks, waiters, and shopkeepers. And while these encounters had been pleasant, I hadn't interacted with any Parisians in typical day-to-day affairs. I didn't speak a word of French, and I had only two friends who lived here (who eventually moved away, something I learned to get used to as an émigré). The truth is, I just up and left San Francisco without a plan. And that's my story.

Thanks in part to the Internet, I was able to cross the Atlantic and make the move to Paris with relative ease. However, once I arrived, things weren't as easy as I thought they would be. I learned that banks aren't there to give you your money when you ask for it, and customer service rarely has anything to do with "customers" or "service." For official business, a list of required documents is just a vague idea of things the officials might ask you for, with a few documents invariably omitted, requiring multiple trips (and multiple reams of paper with all the required photocopying). I learned that being a *râleur* (complainer) is not considered a fault in France, but a necessity. In fact, if complaining didn't exist, even French people would admit that there wouldn't be all that much to talk about. And from the bruises on my ribs, I am now well aware that those fragile grandmothers inching to get in front of you at the market are a lot stronger than they look.

As a resident of Paris for more than a decade now, even though I'm not French, I've learned that if I don't nudge people out of the way while in line, I may never get to the front of it. To fit in, I also need to get a little grumpy at times. And for practicality's sake, I make sure my printer has multiple back-ups of ink cartridges and I keep a reserve of cash on hand, just in case my bank tells me they're out of money.

I also learned that Paris is a diverse city and, like the rest of France, it is struggling to hang on to whatever it is that makes it resolutely "French" in the face of globalization. When I sat down to write this book about cooking in Paris today, I honestly wasn't sure what "Parisian food" was. And pondered if French cuisine was even still relevant. In the past few years, French cuisine has suffered some well-documented blows. Fast food has surpassed traditional cuisine in France, the frozen food chain Picard is wildly popular (prompting people to label cafés that serve prepared foods "la cuisine Picard"), and *déception* has become so widespread that an undercover television crew went through the trash bins behind a few well-known Paris restaurants and came up with empty boxes of prepackaged main courses and—*gulp!*—French pastries. (In my mind, there's no better reason than that to bring back the guillotine.)

Coming from Northern California, where you wouldn't dream of buying anything unless you were on a first-name basis with the farmer who grew it or the chicken that laid it, I was dismissed by people in Paris when I mentioned terms like "organic" or "local." "Everything is local in France!" I was told, even after I pointed out the asparagus and garlic that had shipped from Argentina and the strawberries and tomatoes that had arrived in Paris via Morocco in January. (The signs at the markets designating where things are grown are required by the European Union.)

Of the nearly one hundred outdoor markets in Paris, just two are staffed almost entirely by actual farmers selling produce they've grown themselves. The others are *négotiants*, merchants supplied by Rungis, the largest market in the world, which is so vast that it's actually its own city. In Rungis's immense, modern buildings that replaced Les Halles—the glass-and-iron food halls located in the middle of Paris until the 1970s—these merchants buy crates of fruits, vegetables, meats, poultry, and fish to resell back in Paris. But after a visit that started at 2 a.m., on the ride back to Paris with the hazy sun poking up over the still-sleepy city, I thought about how this venerated market modernized the way food is grown, shipped, and distributed in Paris. And how these changes may have had unintended effects on the languishing image of French cuisine, which was rooted in finding the best products and creating something spectacular out of them, no matter how simple and humble the ingredients or the preparation.

In America, we've been forced to confront our food-related issues due to recalls and problems with improperly handled foods. And in spite of many of us being called "flakes" for wanting to improve our food supply, I've been to supermarkets in the good ol' state of Texas with spectacular displays of locally grown tangerines, lemons, and oranges in all hues and colors, familiar varieties as well as the exotic. In Ohio, I remember being pleasantly surprised to find pungent disks of local goat cheeses at a chain grocery store. And in Manhattan, certainly one of the most urban cities in the world, there is a farmers' market where all the produce comes from within a ninety-mile radius of the city. (The market has branched out to nearly sixty stands and markets in the five boroughs of New York City, all of which sell only locally grown produce—including 170 kinds of tomatoes and 350 kinds of peppers. You won't find any garlic from China or Moroccan strawberries.)

It's taken America a few years—and a few scares—to help us get where we are today, but we've made great strides. Now you can buy bars of artisan chocolate at the drugstore or do a tasting of local wines at the airport, farm milk is sold in glass bottles in supermarkets, taco stands have gone regional and organic, and there has been a resurgence of farmers' markets that are thriving across the country.

When I arrived in Paris, people were shocked that I didn't eat most of my meals at McDonald's (I've only been once in France, and like all of them, it was packed—but not with Americans . . .). I think the modern changes of produce shipped from elsewhere

and reliance on frozen foods snuck up on the French. They didn't see what they were in danger of losing, or weren't interested in what had slipped away. The French were mesmerized by modernity, which included increased reliance on refrigeration, cheap foreign imports, working folks having less time to cook, easy access to packaged foods, the proliferation of *chez McDo*, and a touch of Gallic pride, all of which clouded their vision of what was threatening their cuisine.

During the last few years, a lot of silliness started happening as the new wave of Parisian chefs tried to find their footing, fueled by the popularity of cooking competition shows on television, as young chefs were trying to "top chef" each other. I breathed a sigh of relief when I found out that at a culinary festival I couldn't make it to, the main course was braised rabbit stew garnished with Fraises Tagada, lurid-pink buttons of artificially flavored strawberry marshmallows. But I wasn't so fortunate at another event designed to showcase the next generation of chefs, when I was served a whole, unpeeled orange on a skewer (to this day, I still don't know what I was supposed to do with it), as well as raw beets dipped in chocolate sauce (which I did know what to do with, courtesy of the nearest waste can). I never tried the mushrooms served in chocolate sauce at a noted restaurant, and no matter how much fawning the media did, I couldn't bring myself to drink a cup of *chocolat chaud* with fresh oysters floating inside, nor have tuna fish éclairs (sweet) tempted me. To me, talent isn't about using gimmicks or turning to culinary tricks to gain notoriety. It's not about carefully arranged dots of sauce or smears of foam spread across a slate plate; it's simply about knowing how good something will taste when you put the finished plate forward.

Thankfully, over the last few years things have started to change, and today there is a brigade of younger chefs in Paris quietly rebranding French cuisine and, paradoxically, updating it by taking it back to its humbler roots—to *le cuisine du marché* (market cuisine). You won't find thick, creamy sauces or intricately carved mushrooms (with or without chocolate) garnishing their plates. Meats aren't glazed with a thick coat of jellied aspic, but roasted on the bone and served with *légumes oubliés* (forgotten vegetables) like crosnes, small, corkscrew-shaped root vegetables, and *potimarron*, a graceful pumpkin with a chestnut-like flavor and nutty richness.

After the self-assessment that many Americans did, Parisians have started paying more attention to organic foods, shopping in natural food stores where fruits and vegetables aren't shipped from thousands of kilometers away, but presented in wooden

LES PETITES BÊTES

For those of you who like to scan cookbooks looking for inconsistencies, I'm coming clean with a few *petites bêtes* (nit-pickings) you might notice here. I don't like to think of cooking as a one-size-fits-all activity, and I often vary techniques and methods depending on what I'm preparing or how I want the finished dish to taste or look. Most importantly, I want you to have the same results that I do in my Paris kitchen.

So sometimes you'll notice that I call for a specific quantity (i.e., 1 teaspoon) minced garlic versus 1 garlic clove; sometimes I specify thyme by the sprig rather than chopped and measured by the spoonful. Food isn't standardized, and items vary from place to place; sometimes you'll need to use your judgment to decide if a soup needs a little more liquid, or a bit more salt might be needed to get a green salad exactly right to your taste.

crates marked with the name of the local producer on the side (yes, sometimes the first name!); where you can find *tomates à la ancienne* in the summer—when they *should* be available—firm heads of smooth, violet-skinned garlic, and leafy bunches of greens in the winter months. *La Ruche qui dit Oui!* is a country-wide network, set up to bridge the gap between French farmers and customers, which allows Parisians to purchase fruits, vegetables, cheeses, and meats directly from local producers at public "hives" (*les ruches*), located right in their neighborhoods. And even less-affluent people on the outskirts of Paris, who traditionally had little choice but to shop at giant hypermarkets or overpriced convenience stores, can pick up an inexpensive bag of local produce as they step off the RER trains on their way home.

Another change that has affected Parisian dining is that cooks and customers have traveled outside of France and have seen how the rest of the world eats. And while French cuisine can be extraordinary, these travelers have learned the merits of other cuisines and have begun to take them seriously, rather than trying to "Frenchify" them, which is what is usually done. *La cuisine méxicaine* isn't pizza topped with strips of fresh papaya and canned corn. *Le cheeseburger* doesn't have to be a dried-out patty of beef with a slice of orange cheese, wedged in the opening of a cottony supermarket bun, but can (and should) be a slab of juicy Aubrac beef on a toasted bun made by a local bakery with a slice of real *fromage* melting on top. And *tapas* refers to tasty little bits of local ham, cured meat, or perhaps seafood consumed in Spanish bars; it doesn't mean anything that happens to be plopped on a small plate.

Although there isn't a term for *foodies* in French (a moniker that is probably ready to be retired globally), the younger generation that eschewed the old bistros and brasseries (many of which have been taken over by corporate interests) has started seeking out better food and frequenting wine bars, where the food and style of eating are more in line with modern tastes and lifestyles: offering boards of French cheeses and charcuterie for snacking, and perhaps a few salads, along with a vast selection of French wines, often *les vins naturels*. The staff is invariably young, energetic, and friendly, making wine bars perfect for casual dining. So much so that many of the young chefs who have popular restaurants also have opened a *bar à vin* next door, serving great food in more relaxed surroundings.

And—*mon dieu!*—a number of French chefs have trained outside of France. They've returned to their home country and are starting to seek out local produce; they focus on such sustainable fish

as sardines and mackerel; they are making use of techniques like pickling and reviving sous-vide cooking to coax out flavors and experiment with different textures. What these cooks learned outside of France was that in places like America, England, and Australia, we don't need to be bound by any particular tradition to cook or eat a certain way and we often take cues from other cultures and countries. The do-it-yourself movement in America has resurrected ideas from our past, making them the cuisine of the present. In Paris, many are doing that as well, using the time-honored techniques of French cuisine, as well as highlighting outstanding products and embracing the past while moving French cooking forward.

When I moved to Paris, if someone had told me that one day there would be top-quality taquerias and burger joints here, I would have said they were *fou* (crazy). And some Americans can't fathom why anyone would eat a taco or Korean bibambap in Paris, when they don't think it's odd to eat them in New York City or Seattle. Yet tastes and traditions change.

Paris is evolving in a globalized world. The French are not, and should not be, expected to remain firmly fixed in their culinary past. While it's true that "change" is a concept that doesn't come easily to the French (and because they've had such a gloried past, it's hard to blame them), I'm thrilled that young chefs, and diners, are taking French cuisine to the next level.

. . .

My own cooking is influenced by where I've lived, and where I am now. I'm strongly influenced as a cook by my Northern California roots, where the climate and terrain is reminiscent of France. My cooking is replete with aromatic flavors that rely on garlic, fresh herbs, juicy stone fruits, and earthy root vegetables, as well as lots of olive oil. And because San Francisco has a rich tradition of chocolate-making—beginning with Etienne Guittard, a French émigré who founded his company during the Gold Rush in 1868 in downtown San Francisco, to a wave of bean-to-bar chocolate makers practicing the craft today—I tend to go a little overboard with the chocolate, which you'll notice I use in a lot of my desserts. (Without apologies!)

My cooking starts with shopping, usually at my local market, beginning with a quick scan of all the stands to see who has the nicest baskets of fresh strawberries. I peer over the line to see if the elderly twins who grow their own vegetables just outside of Paris, one of whom shares my love of bitter greens, has tight,

7

robust-looking bunches of spiky frisée. Or I scope out if anyone might have salt cod made from fish that's sustainably raised. After seeing everything, I start shopping, picking up sacks of wrinkled, oily olives and stopping at the *fromagerie* for a slice of whatever cheese they recommend that day (they've never steered me wrong and have earned my undying trust). It's not possible to avoid chatting with the swarthy fellow with the smile that lures every woman—and a few men—to his stand, where he offers a selection of smoked and cured meats from the Auvergne. He wisely hands out samples, knowing that it's impossible to resist whatever he offers. (Which is nice of him because, honestly, he could just skip the samples and stand there and smile at me.) The Arab fellows always have produce I can't find elsewhere, like chervil roots and pleated chile peppers they warn me are *"très pimente!"*—which makes me want to buy all they have. And before I head home, I make my last stop back at the jovial twins for bundles of white-tipped radishes and heads of multihued *rougette* lettuce. Needless to say, I invariably come home from the market overloaded with much, much more than I had originally planned to buy.

In France, we're fortunate that so much of what makes this country great is still celebrated and widely available, from beautiful raw milk cheeses and farm-fresh eggs with bright orange yolks to fresh game featured on menus in the winter to fragile, highly perfumed Gariguette strawberries, whose aroma captivates me when they appear at the beginning of each summer.

In the past few years, the strong influence of other cultures has permeated Paris as well, and shopping in multicultural neighborhoods and *épiceries* has guided my cooking in different and unexpected directions, paths I never would have followed if I were living anywhere else. My life is now in Paris, where I find myself cooking with *les richesses* of France, whose variety of cultural and culinary offerings guide my cooking and baking.

· · ·

As a former professional cook, I know that the most important person in the kitchen is the one who washes the dishes, and the sink is the hub of any and all activity. When I sat down to plan my kitchen in Paris, the only thing I knew for sure was that I wanted a sink that was big and generous enough to wash vegetables and large pots and pans in. I had visions of standing over one of those French farmhouse sinks, those gleaming porcelain beauties that you fill with water to take care of the aftermath of a good meal, or an afternoon of cooking.

But a big, wide-open sink was not so easy to find. I learned that the days of the French farmhouse sink in France are over, and if you want one, you'll have to buy the farmhouse that it's mounted in and pull it out yourself. My online searches kept leading me to America or England, and canvassing plumbing stores in Paris only led to blank stares from salesclerks who were perplexed that anyone would want such a massive encumbrance in their kitchen. Yet I persevered.

It wasn't until late one night, as I followed yet another convoluted Internet search, that a combination of search words I had tried by chance landed me on a website where someone was selling exactly the sink I was looking for, slightly used, but in perfect condition. It had two basins and was deep and wide enough to wash baking sheets, enameled Dutch ovens, and lugs of fruit for jam and jelly-making. So I drove up to Lille, in the north of France, one frosty Sunday in January, having fortified myself with the local specialties—*moules frites* and Merveilleux (page 281)— before hauling the massive sink back to Paris in my Citroën wagon.

Although I use my oven a lot (much more now that I can actually close the door), as well as my refrigerator, stand mixer, food processor, spatulas, whisks, scrapers, rolling pin, and mortar and pestle, it's the sink that took me weeks and weeks to find that has seen the beginning, middle, and end of many wonderful meals in Paris. It's the first place I go to run the water for my café au lait when I wake up. Later in the morning, I fill one of the basins for washing the bunches of Swiss chard and French radishes that I bring home from the market. The rest of the day, you'll find me going back and forth to the sink, filling pots and measuring cups, scrubbing cutting boards, and rinsing knives and mixer bowls . . . and sometimes leaning over it, catching the sticky juices running down my arm from a Provençal peach or a ripe French butter pear. Finally, by the end of the night, as I stand at the sink looking out at the darkening windows of my neighbors' apartments in my Paris *quartier*, it's where I finish up the last of the dishes when my guests have all gone home. Before I head off to bed, I give the sink a quick scrub to get it ready for the next day, when I start all over again.

When I began cooking in Paris, I was surprised to see how French recipes differed from their American counterparts. A quick glance and you'll see that they're about half as long, with the number of steps for even the most complex pastry reduced to three or four brief sentences. Pan sizes are never mentioned, and there aren't headnotes, perhaps just a few *astuces* (tips) mentioned in a sidebar. Specifics of techniques aren't explained, nor is there any indication of serving or storage suggestions. (I think because everything gets eaten right away.)

An American recipe to make caramel might read "Spread 1 cup of granulated cane sugar in a large, wide skillet. Over medium heat, let the sugar melt. As it begins to liquefy, it may darken at the edges. If so, using a heatproof utensil gently encourage the melted sugar around the edges to move to the center of the pan, stirring lightly, just enough to make sure the sugar cooks evenly. As the sugar continues to cook, tilt the pan to avoid the sugar lumping into hot spots and burning in place. Once the sugar is smoking and starts to bubble, the caramel is done. Remove the pan from the heat and set aside."

In France, that same recipe would simply read "*Caraméliser une tasse de sucré.*"

(The word *tasse*, which translates to cup, would refer to a coffee cup full, a rather imprecise measure that would send most bakers into fits.)

When I've cooked with French friends, including those who came by to show me recipes for this book, they admonished me while they were cooking to stop taking notes and to watch what they were doing instead. They told me that I needed to cook *au pif*, or "by the nose," a French expression that means to cook by feel, which they'll say—making certain I understand—while tapping the side of their nostril with a finger. (And then I made sure they washed their hands after making the gesture and before continuing to cook.)

The crux of it is that we've become more and more dependent on recipes to tell us each and every detail, so we don't have to think for ourselves. Or we've somehow become afraid to trust our own instincts. Having a recipe website, I'm constantly fielding questions from people wanting to know how much "1 medium banana" weighs (with and without the skin), how to omit sugar from dessert recipes, or what specific adjustments to make when using premium or European-style products like high-fat butter, high-protein flours, and high-percentage chocolate.

There are no right or wrong answers, but it shows how complicated cooking has become to some folks; how people are overthinking the enjoyable process of baking a chocolate cake or tossing together a salad. Some of this, I suppose, we could attribute to analytical magazines and cookbooks that dissect recipes and techniques, which I guiltily confess that I enjoy reading as well. (Although I don't take them as gospel since I don't know if I want food to be reduced to a standardized formula.) And then there are the picture-perfect cookies, dips, and/or roasted meats, styled to look worthy of something meant to be admired from afar, rather than something you actually want to make, and eat, at home.

When I'm in the kitchen, I know I'm going to have to do a little thinking for myself and rely on my senses, no matter how closely I'm following a recipe. No recipe can tell us precisely how long to cook a steak to our liking, or when to add a dash more vinegar to perk up a vinaigrette. It's simply not possible to write one recipe that knows exactly how thick the cut of beef is or takes into account every type of olive oil and the acidity of each vinegar out there. Ovens vary (even professional ones) and cooking times can be more or less than indicated, depending on the material of the cookware or bakeware used, and ingredients change, depending on the season, ripeness, and geography.

Cooking *au pif* means you check things in the oven before the time indicated. If you think a salad dressing needs more garlic, add more. Season with salt to your taste. Recipes are guidelines, starting points for cooks to diverge from. Take them in your own personal direction. As much as I'd like to be in your kitchen, whether in Paris or elsewhere, I can't. So I suggest you adopt the French attitude in the kitchen and cook "by the nose." Just be sure to wash your hands before you do.

11

Ingredients

SHOPPING FOR INGREDIENTS IS NOT JUST THE FIRST PART OF cooking; it's the most important (and fun) part. I spend as much time gathering ingredients as I do preparing them. It's hard to make good food with bad ingredients, but it's easy to make good food with good ingredients, because most of the work is already done for you.

I've never been comfortable with the phrase, "you eat with your eyes." I don't know about you, but me? I eat with my mouth, and I'm not as concerned with how things look as with how they taste. What good is something that looks fancy but doesn't taste so great? A farm chicken doesn't have the overgrown plumpness of a factory bird but is a lot more appealing to me. A blemished heirloom apple that wasn't cultivated to travel around the world is the one I choose over the perfectly symmetrical fruit. I have a deep suspicion of tomatoes that are too round and smooth, especially those hothouse varieties with the stems still attached; they give the appearance of a bunch of real tomatoes but their bland wedges are a reminder that it's better to wait until summer.

I also don't mind rinsing a bit of dirt off my vegetables before I prepare them. And, like the French, I prefer to choose poultry and fish with the heads on because I can see and evaluate their freshness for myself. I like watching the butcher use a razor-sharp knife to cut a few steaks to order for me. And it's impossible to pass the turning rotisserie at the market *volailler* and not come home with a spit-roasted *poulet fermier*, which I devour the moment I get home.

Some say that you shouldn't go shopping for ingredients with a recipe in mind, but rather let what you find at the market determine your menu. I never thought that was a good idea until I moved to France and realized that my choices were a lot more restricted than what I was used to in California. In Paris, even when things are in season, the market may be teeming with figs for weeks, then they strangely disappear the one day you are looking for them, only to reappear the following week at the stands. On market days, I've learned to take it in stride and go with a vague idea of what I want to make and try to be flexible rather than resolute.

Yet globalization has crept into France—and elsewhere—and no matter where you shop, most things are available whenever you want them. I don't want cherries in the winter, or asparagus in the fall. I want tangerines in the winter, asparagus in the spring, peaches in the summer, and pears and apples in the fall. Even things that we don't normally think of as "seasonal" produce, such as garlic, leeks, and potatoes, do have seasons, and it's good to do your best to respect them.

I don't get as attached to the label "organic" as much as I focus on shopping from local producers at my market and in my neighborhood. At the market, I search out the stands where people are selling produce that they grew and picked. I may be naïve, but I refuse to believe that people presiding over bushels of home-grown fruits and vegetables are thoughtlessly dousing pesticides on everything. I feel better buying from people who are personally invested in what they are growing and selling, and it makes me all warm and fuzzy inside to support people who are part of the same community that I'm in. I do insist on organic or unsprayed citrus when using the zest in recipes, and suggest that you do as well.

Yet I get uncomfortable when people get too preachy about ingredients, because everyone has a different budget, and the availability of ingredients varies from place to place. Handcrafted bean-to-bar chocolate is great for snacking, but it isn't going to shine when melted and mixed with butter, eggs, and flour for a cake. I don't believe that a $39 bottle of wine should be reduced for the sauce in *coq au vin* (page 177). I did a blind tasting a few years back with a panel of the best bakers in San Francisco, and the butter that came in second was the supermarket brand. (First was an imported French brand.) So even if you're not baking in Paris with French butter, you can do very well by using what's available where you live.

Here are some of the ingredients I use when I cook. Although these are the recipes and foods that I prepare and serve in Paris, there is nothing that shouldn't be available in an average well-stocked supermarket—most carry Dijon mustard, shallots, and thick-cut bacon. If you're stumped trying to find things like fleur de sel or an elusive spice, there is the Internet, where everything is only a few clicks away. You can check the Sources (page 339) for a list of places where some of the ingredients are available.

Anchovies

Most people were introduced to anchovies when they appeared as unwelcome guests on a pizza. These anchovies are usually of the lowest quality, mushy, and strong-tasting. They are nothing like good anchovies, which can be found in shops that specialize in French, Italian, or Spanish products. It's hard to recommend a particular brand to buy, so ask for a recommendation at the shop. Price can be an indication of quality. Some argue that salt-packed anchovies are better than oil-packed, but there are good and not-so-good brands in both categories. Choosing anchovies mostly comes down to what is available and your budget.

Good-quality, oil-packed anchovies are widely available in France so I tend to use those. They can be used right from the jar. Salt-packed anchovies are sold whole and should be rinsed of salt and deboned before you use them. To prepare them, soak the anchovies in cool water for about ten minutes. (If they're very salty, you can soak them in milk in the refrigerator for twice as long.) Once softened, insert your thumb into the center of the anchovy and slide it down lengthwise, opening up the fish and releasing the backbone from one side of the flesh. At this point, you can pull out the backbone entirely. Pluck off any fins and rinse under cool water.

Bacon

Bacon is available in France either **smoked** (*fumé*) or **unsmoked**. You'll notice it's used in a number of my recipes because I like it as much as the French (and Americans) do. However, bacon is more often used as a seasoning in French cooking rather than crisped up and served on the side. I like to use it to flavor a braise, as with the Buckwheat polenta with braised greens, sausage, and poached eggs (page 158) and Chicken with mustard (page 169).

French bacon is almost always cut into *lardons* for cooking—rectangular batons made by slicing thick-cut bacon crosswise into strips about 1/2 inch (1.5cm) wide or in cubes.

I tend to avoid commercial bacon, which has a lot of water added, and buy bacon from a butcher or at a farmers' market. Fortunately, good bacon can be found in many supermarkets as well. The recipes in this book specify whether to use smoked or unsmoked bacon. Where unsmoked bacon is called for, you can also use pancetta, which most butcher shops and well-stocked supermarkets carry.

Butter

There are two kinds of butter in France: the good kind, and the great kind. But kidding aside, the French use both **salted** (*demi-sel*) butter and **unsalted** (*doux*) butter. During the past few years salted butter has become a lot more prevalent due to the popularity of salted butter caramel sauce (page 334), which originated in Brittany. This region of France has an almost unnatural devotion to butter (which is why I love visiting), and the butter is salted to preserve its freshness. I've taken to it as much as everyone else has.

Many commercial brands of butter in France offer salted butter *aux gros cristaux de sel*, with big crystals of salt kneaded into the butter—just enough so they're incorporated but not enough so that

15

they melt during storage. That's my butter of choice for my morning toast, with a swipe of rugged buckwheat honey on top. You can make your own by kneading ¼ to ½ teaspoon of large flake sea salt into a stick (4 ounces/115g) of softened unsalted butter, then rechilling it.

For baking, however, I generally use unsalted butter mainly because that's what people expect in a recipe for a cake or cookies. Previous wisdom dictated that unsalted butter was fresher. Nowadays, however, that's not really an issue, and I'll often use salted butter—even in desserts—and simply decrease or omit any salt in the recipe. (For those who want to do some math, there is approximately ¼ teaspoon of salt in 4 ounces, or 115 grams, of salted butter.) If there is just a small quantity of butter in a recipe, such as 2 to 3 tablespoons, salted and unsalted butter can be used interchangeably unless noted.

Cheese

Cheese isn't a luxury; it is considered a vital part of French life. Along with wine, cheese is the most direct expression of *terroir*, the concept that a product takes on certain attributes of the climate, soil, weather, and terrain where it is produced. And those attributes make a certain cheese, or other product, distinct from any others. I was leading a wine tasting with a sommelier friend and when someone asked him if *terroir* was a bunch of bullsh*t, he reacted as if his soul had been yanked out and crushed. In America, we do have the concept of *terroir*, but it's not identified the same way as it is in France. If you don't believe me, try a California chardonnay alongside one that was produced in France, and taste the difference.

When it comes to French cheeses, as far as I'm concerned they have never been—and will never be—successfully duplicated anywhere else, although there are a lot of great cheeses made elsewhere in the world. Be aware that such popular cheeses as Brie and Camembert sold elsewhere (and even in France) aren't always the real deal. Those names were never trademarked, so unless it's labeled as *Brie de Meaux* or *Camembert de Normandie*, it's not the same as the authentic cheese with its geographic appellation in the name.

There are hundreds of French cheeses and most are meant to be eaten as is (see The Cheese Course, page 247). Some cheeses, though, are frequently used in cooking. **Comté** is one of the most popular cheeses in France, and I use it frequently in recipes. It's a nutty raw milk mountain cheese from the Jura; **Emmenthal**, **Gruyère**, and **Jarlsberg** are comparable and can be substituted. In America, similar

cheeses are generically called "Swiss cheese" and can be used in recipes that call for Comté; try to find the best-quality ones.

Blue cheeses are made by introducing spores and mold into cheese and letting it ripen, creating the rippled blue or blue-green veins that run through them. Most have the taste of sweet butterfat with a mildly acidic afterbite. **Roquefort** is a very specific blue cheese made from sheep's milk and inoculated with spores from moldy rye bread. There are only seven producers of Roquefort, and its flavor is like none of the other blue cheeses. I use it in Winter salad (page 98) because its particular flavor makes a difference there, although it can be used in place of blue cheese in other recipes. There are very good blue cheeses made elsewhere, including the United States, Denmark, and the United Kingdom.

Goat cheese is widely popular in France. Soft, fresh goat cheeses have a texture similar to cream cheese and are ideal for spreading. The ones exported from France are usually called Montrachet, and there are many fine goat cheeses made in other countries. Goat cheeses that have been aged have a more assertive, pungent flavor and develop a chewy crust. While delicious for eating, their flavor is too strong to use as a substitute for the fresh stuff, especially in desserts like cheesecake (page 302).

Many cities have cheese shops and those are good places to taste, learn about, and purchase cheese. Local farmers' markets are excellent places to explore and learn, too.

Chocolate and Cocoa Powder

I am frequently asked, "What country makes the best chocolate?" which is an odd question, because cacao beans are harvested all over the world, then shipped far away from where they are grown, where they're made into chocolate. So it seems peculiar to think that any one particular country has a special *je ne sais quoi* for turning cacao beans into chocolate. While it's true that Switzerland, Belgium, and France have long histories of making the stuff, the United States has made up for lost time with an American "revolution" in chocolate-making, which has broadened the way many of us think about chocolate. And now you can find high-quality chocolate makers in various countries around the world, in addition to the well-known places. That said, there has long been an appreciation (and market) for fine chocolate in France, so naturally a lot of good chocolates have been produced in this country. In Europe, I use European chocolate, though there are many brands produced elsewhere that are excellent.

For baking, I recommend sticking with **bittersweet** or **semisweet chocolate**, which have between 55 and 70 percent cacao

17

solids. Higher percentage chocolates, with more than 70 percent cacao solids, are very acidic and can react unpredictably in recipes. In the United States, the terms "bittersweet" and "semisweet" are interchangeable and neither is necessarily sweeter or more bitter than the other.

Unsweetened chocolate is often referred to as bitter chocolate; since it has no added sugar or cocoa butter, it should not be used in recipes that call for bittersweet chocolate.

Whatever chocolate you like, if you bake frequently, try to buy it in bulk so you have it on hand. It's not only more convenient, but more economical, too. Dark chocolate will keep for several years (if you can keep your hands off it), stored in a cool dark place—but not the refrigerator, where the humidity can encourage spoilage.

Cocoa powder is made from pressing pure unsweetened chocolate paste (called chocolate liquor) to remove a percentage of the fat. Dutched cocoa has been acid-neutralized and is usually darker than natural cocoa powder. I've never seen natural cocoa powder in Europe, but most supermarket brands in America are natural cocoa powders, unless specified otherwise. If unsure, check the list of ingredients and see if there is an alkalizing agent in it.

Pure cocoa powder, whether Dutch-process or natural, is always unsweetened. (Some people get confused when they see "hot cocoa mix," which has milk and sugar added, or "powdered chocolate," which is ground up chocolate and contains sugar.) In the recipes in this book, you can use either natural or Dutch-process unsweetened cocoa powder.

Although I don't specify any particular brands of chocolate, I am a fan of Valrhona cocoa powder (Dutch-process), because the flavor and color are a lot more intense than other brands. It's more expensive, but I find it gives baked goods a noticeable boost of deep chocolate flavor and color.

Cream, Milk, Crème Fraîche, and Yogurt

One of the benefits of living in a country whose agricultural achievements are celebrated (such as at the annual Salon d'Agriculture in Paris, which has almost three-quarters of a million visitors, in a city with population of just over two million) is the selection of high-quality dairy products. And many of the classic dishes of French cuisine make good use of the bounty, from cream-rich gratins to chocolate ganache used to fill chocolates.

For most baking and cooking, I use **whole milk** or **heavy cream**, and in some instances **half-and-half**. (For folks outside the United States, half-and-half is a product made with approximately half heavy cream and half whole milk.) In the ingredient lists for recipes, where applicable, I list when it's okay to use milk instead of cream, or if there are other options. But if one is specifically listed, I don't recommend making substitutions, because you won't be as satisfied with the results.

Heavy cream and its cousin whipping cream usually vary by a few percentages of fat and can be used interchangeably. If you can, avoid using ultra-pasteurized cream, which doesn't taste very good and will be stubborn to whip. When whipping cream, chilling the bowl and the whisk beforehand will help it whip faster, which is especially useful if you are doing it by hand.

Crème fraîche is one of the glories of France and is available in every supermarket. If you find yourself in France, I very much recommend that you go to a good *fromagerie* and try their crème fraîche. Tasting it is a life-altering experience. Crème fraîche in France leaves a clean, slippery taste of fresh butterfat when you lick it off the spoon and it is so unbelievably rich you may want to apply for French citizenship. (Well, at least until you see the paperwork.) In the United States and elsewhere, cheesemakers are producing their own crème fraîche, and you can find it in well-stocked supermarkets, natural food stores, and even online. If you can't get it, you can make a version at home (page 327).

For all recipes that call for **yogurt**, use plain, full-fat varieties, or Greek-style where noted.

Eggs

I often joke that I am one of the largest consumers of eggs in Paris because I can go through dozens and dozens (and dozens) a week. And it always astonishes vendors and cashiers when I arrive at the checkout carrying so many cartons of eggs. In addition to being concerned about how I'm perceived by French salespeople, I've also become more sensitive about how chickens are raised and eggs are produced. In France, each egg is stamped with a number: 0 or 1 means that the eggs are free-range; 2 denotes the eggs are from chickens allowed to roam in a specified area; and 3s are eggs from caged chickens. Some supermarkets have started to ban eggs from battery-raised chickens, and I've made a concerted effort to buy free-range eggs as well.

Whenever people who live elsewhere see a French egg, with its brilliant sunny-yellow yolk, they always exclaim, "Why don't we get eggs like that where we live?" Luckily, fresh farm eggs are becoming more and more available. If you want good eggs, head to the farmers' market or natural foods store, especially if you are making Shakshuka (page 154), Baked eggs with kale and smoked salmon (page 151), or *œufs mayo* (page 103), where eggs star as a prominent ingredient. If using eggs raw, for *le grand aïoli* (page 145) or a chocolate terrine (page 287), purchase eggs from a trusted source. (People who have compromised immune systems or are pregnant should avoid raw eggs.)

Fish

Over the past decade, I've become very aware of the effect that overfishing has had on the earth's supply of certain fish. And although the displays of fish heaped up on glistening flakes of ice at the outdoor markets in Paris continue to tempt, I can't ignore the guilty feeling I'd have facing a plate of bluefin tuna, no matter how much I want it. So I look for sustainable varieties of fish, such as tuna from the Basque region, as well as sardines and mackerel, which are tastier, healthier, and more affordable as well.

In places where I mention the use of fish, such as Baked eggs with kale and smoked salmon (page 151) or *brandade de morue* (page 144), I recommend trying to find a wild or sustainable variety. Note that many varieties of salt cod are made from other kinds of fish that are more sustainable than Atlantic cod, including haddock, pollock, and Norwegian or Arctic cod.

Flour

All the recipes in this book that call for flour use **all-purpose flour**, unless otherwise noted, and were tested with French flour (type 65) as well as American all-purpose flour. **Cake flour** is a finely milled, slightly acidic flour, and makes for a finer texture. Most supermarkets carry it. You can make a reasonable substitute by replacing 2 tablespoons of the flour in a cup (140g) of all-purpose flour with cornstarch and sifting them together three times.

Bread flour is a stronger, high-protein flour, designed for bread-baking, and I use it when making Multigrain bread (page 241). If you don't have access to bread flour and plan to bake bread frequently, you can add 1 teaspoon of vital wheat gluten (available in natural food stores and online, see page 339) to 1 cup (140g) of all-purpose flour.

Chickpea flour (also called garbanzo flour) is made of ground chickpeas and is used in Panisse puffs (page 245). It's gluten-free and can be found in natural food stores and online (page 339), as well as in shops that specialize in Indian and Middle Eastern foods.

Garlic

There is a misconception that all the French love garlic. True, in the south, garlic is used liberally. But Parisians tend to curl their lips up at the smell of it cooking, nor are they fond of smelling like it afterward. And the few times I serve anything with raw garlic in it, people often look hesitant. But in the end, everyone seems to have no trouble wiping his or her plate clean. Like *les provençaux*, Americans like lots of garlic; we cook with it in liberal amounts and we enjoy it raw.

Garlic has a season, and it's spring. That's when the garlic is sweetest and most flavorful. The first mild heads of garlic that show up at the market have moist, white skin, which isn't papery or dried, but smooth and resistant to peeling (it's worth the extra effort). Soon afterward, violet-skinned aromatic garlic appears, and that's when I tend to use the most garlic in my cooking— when garlic is at its best.

When buying garlic, look for rock-hard cloves, which indicate freshness. If I can, I give the heads a hard squeeze before buying them to make sure I'm getting very fresh garlic. I avoid garlic shipped long distances for a variety of reasons, but mostly because it often isn't very garlicky. (You can often tell by checking the root end; if it's overly smooth, with every trace of root and grit buffed away, it's usually garlic shipped from far away.) As with other produce, I do stress that you keep in mind the seasons and that even though garlic is available all year round, it's best in the spring and remains at its peak through early fall.

I use garlic two ways: thinly sliced and minced. Garlic that is sliced doesn't burn quickly, whereas minced garlic cooks quickly and explodes in flavor (and tends to color) almost immediately. To prepare fresh garlic, separate the cloves by hand then trim off the tough stem ends. Set the blade of a chef's knife or cleaver over the clove of garlic so the blade is parallel to the cutting board (with the sharp edge facing away from you) and rap the side of the blade with your fist until the clove bursts a little, loosening the skin.

Remove the skin and slice the clove in half lengthwise; if there is a green germ, remove it, and thinly slice the garlic, or mince it, with a chef's knife. (Some folks like to smash the garlic clove with the side of a cleaver to "mince" it, but that method can release some bitter elements, so I prefer to chop it with a knife.) For dressings like Garlic vinaigrette (see variation on page 96) that use raw garlic, if you have a rasp-style zester, you can grate the garlic against the sharp blades of the zester, which makes very fine pieces and saves a cutting board from smelling garlicky.

Herbs

French cooks use herbs liberally. The most commonly used herbs are **thyme**, **bay leaf**, **flat-leaf parsley**, **cilantro**, **chervil**, **mint**, and **chives**, which are always available at market stands and in grocery stores. **Rosemary**, **tarragon**, **dill**, **sage**, and **savory** are less frequently used by Parisian cooks, but have their place. (For some reason, oregano and marjoram remain elusive.) In the summer, **basil** makes an appearance in small, leafy bunches and whenever I find it for sale in large bundles, I buy as much as I can and gorge myself on pesto and *soupe au pistou* (page 92).

Fresh herbs should be rinsed to remove any grit, but I avoid rinsing thyme, sage, and rosemary, since some of the oils (i.e., flavor) get washed away. However, running your fingers through them should give you an indication as to whether they need to be rinsed or not. Basil leaves should be picked from the stems and washed in a bowl of cool water, then dried thoroughly. I use a salad spinner.

I can't say I've seen a French cook measure herbs, but in most instances, I give precise quantities. Feel free to add more or less, *au pif* (see page 11).

Because French cooking is more dependent on the flavors of herbs than other cuisines, I almost always use fresh herbs. If you want to substitute dried herbs, use half the quantity indicated. Dried herbs vary in quality and strength, so if using dried herbs, buy good-quality ones. I once did a dried herb sampling with a spice company and was stunned by the differences among brands. Use dried herbs within a year of opening the container and store them in a cabinet, away from the light.

Meat

Invariably, you will fall hard for a butcher if you live in France. Yes, even if you are a vegetarian. There is something relentlessly sexy about them. Is it the cotton butcher aprons slouching off just one shoulder? Their swagger hefting a lamb shoulder for your inspection? Or the way they wield those razor-sharp knives with pinpoint precision as they daintily extract *un petit filet* just for you from the soft, juicy meat of the tenderloin? I don't eat a lot of beef, but still find excuses to go to my butcher more often than I should. French women seem to have a special connection with butchers; I think they are the only men they feel comfortable openly flirting with. And to tell you the truth, I don't have a problem with it either.

French people eat a lot of beef, believing that iron-rich red meat is imperative for good health. (Horsemeat is popular as well, although I haven't been able to leap that hurdle yet.) In France,

"meat" (*viande*) is beef, and visiting vegetarians are often surprised when they order a meatless meal and get served something with lamb or bacon in it. For many years, the idea of not eating meat was unthinkable to the French, but the concept has begun to enter the mainstream—although the French aren't as creative with vegetarian cooking as other cultures, because it isn't viewed as a palette for creativity.

I was a vegetarian for a number of years; but nowadays, I find myself digging into a plate of *steak frites* (page 206) at home every now and then or will head to a bistro that I know does it right. When I accompany non-French friends to a bistro, I have to struggle to explain what the equivalents are to American cuts of meat. I finally realized that it's really not possible because the beef is butchered differently. So I've started handing out pictures of a cow, with dotted lines denoting how and where it's butchered, and let my friends fend for themselves.

While steaks are popular, the French will gladly make use of cheaper cuts of meat, which are more flavorful than tenderloins and other choice cuts. Same with lamb and pork, where the shoulders, shins, and ribs are as popular as other cuts—if not more so.

I'm not an expert on meat, so like the French I rely on the expertise of my local butcher. A good butcher will cut meat to order, and with a bit of advance notice can get you anything you want. For less glamorous cuts, Asian and Mexican markets carry meats intended for stewing and braising.

Mustard

Dijon mustard, ground from a mix of spices and vinegar, is the indispensable seasoning and condiment found in every French kitchen and on every bistro table. A dab is invariably added to vinaigrette (page 335) and is the seasoning for such dishes as Chicken with mustard (page 169) and *carbonade flamande* (page 198). Although it seems to keep for a long time, Dijon mustard quickly loses its oomph after the jar has been opened. Mustard should be stored in the refrigerator, and for the best flavor make sure your mustard is fresh. Note that some brands of Dijon mustard aren't actually made in Dijon; the name refers to a style of mustard that's highly seasoned and often made with white wine.

Oil

Every few years, there seems to be some study dispelling what a previous study conclusively proved a few years prior, demonizing one oil and anointing another one as loaded with health benefits. Then, a few years later, the next study comes along to prove the complete opposite. I don't know about you, but I can't keep up!

For years I used olive oil exclusively, until I worked for a restaurateur who insisted that I replicate the taste of a salad dressing that his previous restaurant was famous for. It took me a few weeks of tinkering (yes, really, for a seemingly simple salad dressing) until I realized that the olive oil I was using was overwhelming the taste of the other ingredients. When I made a batch of dressing with regular salad oil, his face immediately lit up, and I heard the magic words: "You got it."

I've tasted a lot of excellent dressings using neutral-tasting oils in Paris. And I've taken a cue from them and often make my vinaigrette (page 335) with **sunflower**, **safflower**, or **colza (canola) oil**, pressed from the mustard-like plants that grow just outside of Paris. I buy them from local producers who cold-press them.

I keep a minimum of two extra-virgin **olive oils** on hand; one for cooking—a relatively inexpensive one—and another for drizzling and adding to dressings and dips. The best way to judge an olive oil? Taste it. Disregard the country of origin, the fancy bottle, or the sticker that noted it won a "blue ribbon" somewhere. (Some of those competitions are less about giving a nod to the best product and more about marketing.) In spite of all the hoopla, the best olive oil is the one that *you* like. And the best way to ensure you're getting good-quality, unadulterated olive oil is to buy it directly from a producer or reputable source. I always use extra-virgin olive oil.

Olive oils, as well as sunflower, safflower, and canola oil, should be kept in a cool, dark place. Avoid keeping them near the stove or oven since the heat will cause them to deteriorate rapidly.

Occasionally, I use **nut oils**, such as walnut and hazelnut oils. A simple drizzle of either on a mound of spinach with a few sprinkles of flaky salt makes a perfect, quick salad. Buy nut oils in small bottles from a place that turns over their stock frequently, since they are prone to spoilage. A very good brand is J. Leblanc, produced in Burgundy and pressed in small batches (see page 339). Store nut oils in the refrigerator and try to use them within 6 months of opening.

Pepper

Black pepper should always be bought in peppercorn form and freshly ground right before using. If I'm doing a lot of cooking I'll grind up a small handful in my mortar and pestle and reach for it as needed.

There are a myriad of black peppers to choose from, and I suggest you do as I do, and head to a spice shop to give them a sniff for yourself.

Admittedly, I use a lot more **dried red pepper** than most French cooks do because I like the little bit of fire that it adds to food. It's something I learned from an Italian cook who uses it in place of black pepper. (She told me it is a holdover from the days when imported spices, like peppercorns, were heavily taxed whereas red peppers were grown locally and dried.) If used in discreet amounts, it adds a subtle kick and the contrast augments other flavors nicely.

The nomenclature can be a bit confusing; chili powder is made of dried ground chiles and sometimes contains other spices. **Red chile powder** is made only of ground chiles and can vary in degrees of spiciness and smokiness, depending on the chile used. **Cayenne pepper** powder is the best known, and is made from one kind of pepper—and it's quite hot. Although they're decidedly not French, I often swap out ancho or chipotle chile powder for cayenne pepper when I want something to taste a bit smoky, such as Smoky barbecue-style pork (page 190). Red pepper flakes are also known as dried crushed chiles (with seeds).

Closer to home, **piment d'Espelette**, a dried pepper powder from the Basque region, is one I like to use. It's excellent, yet expensive—even in France. Used in Basque cuisine, it's not overwhelmingly spicy but is quite flavorful. The color and taste tend to fade within a few months of opening the jar, so it should be used quickly.

Chile powders vary by brand and by the variety of chile used. I use several different varieties; some I buy at spice shops in France, others I bring home from travels to places like Spain, Mexico, and California. Some are smoky-sweet, others are *très piquant*. I call for cayenne pepper in most recipes because it's widely available, but feel free to use as much of whatever suits your taste.

White pepper is something most people don't stock in their spice cabinets. I have grown to like it because it has a sharper bite than black pepper and works well in light-colored foods, such as mashed potatoes (page 216) and celery root soup (page 106). I buy white peppercorns in small quantities, grinding them as needed, as I don't use them too often. White pepper from Penja, Cameroon, is worth seeking out.

Pomegranate Molasses

Pomegranate molasses is made by reducing the tart juice of pomegranate fruits to a thick, tangy syrup. I use a touch of it in Beet hummus (page 58) and Wheat berry salad with radicchio, root vegetables, and pomegranate (page 240) to add a sly but noticeable sweet note. It sometimes goes by the name of pomegranate syrup, and you can find it in shops specializing in Middle Eastern foods, or at Kalustyan's (see page 339). It's also wonderful drizzled over the top of *moutabal* (page 64), Hummus (page 60), and—perhaps surprisingly, Apricot kernel ice cream (page 312).

Salt

When I started cooking, if someone told me that I would someday be paying more than 39 cents for a box of salt, I would have said they were nuts. Nowadays, you'll find at least six types of salt on the counter where I cook, and at least a dozen more in my cupboard, collected from my travels.

The first time I "got" what makes one salt better than another was when I was in the kitchen of my friend Susan Loomis, who lives in Normandy and teaches cooking classes. She had us taste a few delicate flakes of fleur de sel from the Guérande, then a few crystals of ordinary table salt, the stuff that sits in salt shakers on restaurant tables. My mouth was so overtaken by the taste of bitterness and chemicals in the table salt that it's one of the few things I can no longer eat or use.

Though I am overloaded with salt, normal people really only need to have two kinds of salt: one for cooking and another for seasoning.

I use **sea salt** for cooking. In France, we have gray salt, which is mineral rich and comes in coarse or fine crystals. Although it's not quite the same, **kosher salt** is good for cooking.

I use finishing salt to sprinkle over salads, vegetables, and even chocolate (as a snack with a bit of olive oil). **Flaky sea salt**, such as Maldon from England, is very popular in France; it comes in boxes of irregular flat crystals. I use it, but not nearly as frequently as **fleur de sel**. This highly prized salt is harvested by hand, carefully skimmed off the surface of salt marshes when the tide is low. The best is *fleur de sel de Guérande*, harvested off the coast of the Atlantic when the weather conditions are just right. Other countries have adopted the "fleur de sel" moniker, and you can find similar salts from Portugal, Spain, and elsewhere.

It's tough getting people to spend more than they are used to on salt. But I cook a lot, and my salt budget for the year is less than the price of a few *cafés crèmes*.

CUISINE SURGELÉE

Perhaps the most frequently asked question I get about recipes is, "Can that be frozen?" Even though there are frozen-food (*cuisine surgelée*) stores in Paris, it's almost unheard of to find people freezing food at home. (A friend's mother looked at me in disbelief when I told her that bread could be frozen.) With few exceptions, when you're having a dinner party, everything is made the same day. And I don't know anyone who would make anything more than a day—at most—in advance that they were planning to serve to themselves or guests.

There are very few things that improve after spending time in the freezer, so I tend to do as the French and rely less on my freezer and more on serving food as fresh as possible. However we're often time-pressed and not everyone has the luxury of spending as much time preparing a meal as they'd like to. So I've noted where things can be prepared in advance and, in some cases, when they can be frozen.

29

I suggest that you get familiar with the kinds of salts that you have on hand and that you taste the food and salt it to your taste. When in doubt, add less salt than the recipe calls for—you can always add more later, but it's hard to pick all those little crystals out once they're mixed in.

Shallots and Leeks

The French use shallots frequently and every kitchen has a tiny *filet* (mesh bag) of shallots hanging somewhere. Most French shallots are tiny; usually no larger than a prune. Shallots have a juicy sweetness and contribute a subtle onion flavor to foods without the harshness of onions so they can be used raw. A typical shallot weighs about 3/4 ounce (20g)—so if you can only get larger shallots, use that as a guideline for the recipes in this book. Shallots should always be peeled, sliced, and finely minced, unless otherwise indicated.

Leeks are the foundation of many classic French soups and stews. They are often sweated in butter and provide a fuller, more rounded flavor than onions. The most famous French leek dish is *poireaux vinaigrette* (page 88), which is a platter of steamed (or poached) leeks drenched in mustardy sauce. It is one of the most emblematic dishes of French cuisine.

To wash and prepare leeks, trim away the roots to where they just meet the base, leaving the leek intact. Cut off the dark green leaves and any tough lighter green leaves. To clean the leeks, make four incisions down the sides, lengthwise, cutting through just about to the center but leaving the leek whole and the root intact. Soak the leeks in cold water for about 15 minutes, swirling them around from time to time to remove any dirt and sand. Rinse under running water and then pat dry.

Stock

Newcomers to Paris invariably ask, "Where can I find canned stock?" to which I reply, "You can't!" The French either make their own stock or turn to bouillon cubes.

I've never been able to make the transition to *le cube*, which makes everything taste like ramen soup mix, so I've taken to making my own stock (page 326), which is very easy and can be frozen for future use.

If you don't have good stock, water is a better substitute than most canned brands. Although I've not used them, some swear by boxed brands (packed in aseptic cartons), and I've found Better Than Bouillon, a *fond blanc* (reduced stock) sold in American supermarkets, to be *pas mal*.

Sugar

In recipes where sugar is called for, it means **granulated sugar**. The equivalent outside the United States is castor (or caster) sugar, which is slightly finer. **Powdered** or **confectioners' sugar** (known as icing sugar outside of the United States) is ground to a fine powder and has a small amount of cornstarch added to keep it from clumping. **Brown sugar** comes in light or dark varieties, and you should use whichever is specified. Brown sugar should be firmly packed into a graduated measuring cup to properly measure it, or weighed.

Vinegar

Vinegar is just as important to a good vinaigrette (page 335) as the oil. The quality of olive oil gets much of the press, yet vinegar gets short shrift. Fortunately, unlike olive oil, even very good vinegar is inexpensive and using good-quality vinegar will dramatically improve your cooking.

The vinegar I use most often in salad dressings is **sherry vinegar**. Made by our neighbors in Spain and aged in oak casks for at least 6 months, it's reportedly the most popular vinegar in France. It's a bit milder than red wine vinegar, with a pleasant, woody smoothness. For every day, it's not necessary to use one that's extensively aged.

The other bottle I reach for is **red wine vinegar**. It has a sharper acidity than sherry vinegar, and its bracing flavor makes a more assertive dressing. A spoonful can also liven up a stew, such as *coq au vin* (page 177), acting as a counterpoint to a hearty sauce.

When I want a bit of fruity flavor, I'll use **cider vinegar**. There are quite a few apple farms around Paris, and I always buy my vinegar from the apple stand at my market.

I've come to dislike the viscous, sweet taste of "balsamic" vinegar, which has become a repetitious base in too many salads, even in France. Most of the cheap brands are artificially colored and flavored. Real **balsamic vinegar** must be aged a minimum of 12 years and the price will cause you to make sure you have an extra-secure grip on that tiny bottle. I normally stay away from the supermarket stuff but will occasionally add it to sauces where I want a little body and a touch of tartness, as in Buckwheat polenta with braised greens, sausage, and poached eggs (page 158).

Equipment

Yᴏᴜ ᴅᴏɴ'ᴛ ɴᴇᴇᴅ ᴀɴ ᴀʀsᴇɴᴀʟ ᴏғ ᴄᴏᴏᴋᴡᴀʀᴇ ᴛᴏ ᴄᴏᴏᴋ ғʀᴇɴᴄʜ food, but you can easily put together a workable *batterie* of it. Fortunately, most of the items you need are probably already in your kitchen. Here are the items I stock in my Paris kitchen—the pots, pans, and equipment I've used for the recipes in this book.

Baking Dishes

Baking dishes are shallow, wide, and heatproof with sides that are at least 2 inches (5cm) high. Many that are sold worldwide are French brands, such as Le Creuset, Emile Henry, and Staub. Pyrex and CorningWare are American companies that make suitable baking dishes, and there are others. Baking dishes come in a variety of materials: ceramic, earthenware, enameled cast-iron (*fonte*), porcelain, and glass. It's always preferable to use baking dishes with high sides, and wider ones ensure you'll have more nicely browned toppings. Setting the baking dish on a baking sheet lined with aluminum foil is also a good idea to avoid spillovers that might occur during baking.

Some materials heat faster than others, so keep in mind that baking times can vary depending on the material. Use whatever size is indicated in the recipe and check the manufacturer's recommendations for maximum temperature settings.

Baking Sheets

My baking sheets are 13 by 18 inches (33 by 45cm), which are considered standard "half-sheet pans" to bakers in America. I brought my own to France and like them so much I had to buy a larger-than-normal European oven so they'd fit! For most baking applications, such as cookies and biscuits, you can use whatever size you have. One exception is *bûche de Noël* (page 319), where the cake layer calls for a certain size. To keep cookies and other baked goods from sticking, line baking sheets with parchment paper or silicone baking mats, as indicated by the recipe.

Cake Pans

For cake recipes, I call for springform cake pans, which are good for releasing delicate cakes, such as French cheesecake (page 302). Standard springform pans range from 9 to 10 inches (22 to 25cm). My favorites have glass bottoms, which make serving a breeze, since you don't have to coerce the cake off the bottom. Disregard instructions that may have come with a "leakproof" springform pan; many are prone to leaking no matter how much we want to believe they're not. I advise wrapping the bottom and sides of springform pans securely with a large sheet of aluminum foil (or two) when using them.

Dutch Oven

Every French kitchen has a large *cocotte*, or Dutch oven–style casserole. (They are sometimes called "French ovens" outside of France.) I recommend using a large one that holds at least 6 quarts. The best are made of heavy-duty stainless steel or enameled cast iron. Copper works well, too, but is a sizable investment and requires a certain amount of maintenance, especially when the lining begins to wear down.

Make sure pots and pans are made of nonreactive materials; I avoid aluminum pans except those that are anodized (with a dark interior and exterior finish), since nonanodized aluminum will react unfavorably with certain foods, most notably citrus, tomatoes, vinegar, wine, and other acidic ingredients.

Electric Blender

I most often use a hand blender (also called a stick or immersion blender) for pureeing soups. They've been popular in Europe for years, although less so in the United States. I also have a conventional blender that does a very good job of creating an utterly smooth texture. The hand blender is easier to use and you can puree right in the saucepan, so there is less cleanup. Still, I find it hard to match the smoothness you can obtain in a conventional blender. When using a conventional blender, never fill the jar more than half full with hot ingredients, such as a soup mixture; the steam can force the lid off the closed container and cause injury (and a mess).

Food Processor

I use my food processor frequently for making purees, such as Hummus (page 60) and Eggplant caviar (page 66). I find it important to keep the blade sharp; replacing it when it gets dull is a cost-effective way to pretend you were given a brand-new food processor!

Knives

There are three essential knives to have in your kitchen: a long chef's knife, a small paring knife, and a serrated bread knife. If you don't have a good bread knife, you will get kicked out of France. Good-quality knives will make cooking a lot more enjoyable, and safer, since a sharp blade is less likely to slide off food when chopping or slicing. You can bring your knives to a professional sharpener when they get dull or keep them sharp by using a steel or another home sharpening tool.

Choose knives that have comfortable handles and never, ever put knives in the dishwasher. Anyone who does that in my kitchen gets booted out for good.

Mortar and Pestle

A mortar and pestle is an almost essential tool for making the best *pistou* (page 92) and is the classic implement for producing aïoli (page 145) and tapenade (page 57). They're also excellent for grinding spices. The best mortars are made of thick, heavy stone, such as marble or granite, which keeps them stable while you are wildly pounding away in them. You can pick up an inexpensive Thai mortar and pestle at an Asian market.

Pastry Blender

A pastry blender is a handy little tool made up of wires that will quickly cut butter into flour when making pastry dough. They're not commonly used in France, but I use one when I want to make pastry dough by hand.

Ramekins and Custard Cups

These are used for baking Individual chocolate cakes with dulce de leche and fleur de sel (page 261) as well as Cheese, bacon, and arugula soufflés (page 139). I use the classic white porcelain ramekins with a 4-ounce (125ml) capacity, though any ovenproof custard cups with similar capacity will work. In a pinch, I've used thick, heatproof coffee cups for baking custards and individual cakes.

Ramekins have typically been used to make crème brûlée, though I've taken to the French version, which is served in shallow, individual baking dishes (round or oval) whose wide surface area allows for more crackly caramel in proportion to the custard, which I like.

Saucepans and Skillets

I've been through a lot of cookware in my life, and living in Paris, transitioning from a professional kitchen to a small domestic one, I've learned to home in on what I truly need. (Moving a few times, especially internationally, also makes you rethink what you really need.) No matter how you choose to outfit your kitchen, buy the best-quality cookware that you can afford. Your pots and pans will perform better, last longer, make cleanup easier, and save you money in the long run. And they'll also make cooking and baking a lot more pleasurable.

Traditionally, good French cooks have used copper or enameled cast-iron cookware. And while both of those perform well and I have several pieces in my kitchen, they require a certain amount of upkeep. Multi-ply cookware, such as All-Clad, performs well, and the handles stay cool on the stovetop. For the recipes in this book, a small saucepan has a capacity of 1 to 2 quarts (1 to 2l), a medium will hold 2 to 4 quarts (2 to 4l), and a large saucepan is more than 4 quarts (4l).

I use skillets for sautéing on the stovetop. A medium skillet is 10 to 12 inches (25 to 30cm) in diameter and a large skillet is anything larger than that. You can use regular or nonstick skillets, unless otherwise indicated. If you decide to buy a "green" or "earth-friendly" skillet, look for one that's heavy-duty; those made from flimsy metal will warp, which will quickly damage the finish.

Stand Mixer

In my first apartment in Paris, with the tiny kitchen, I tried living without a stand mixer. After a year, I realized that no matter how precious space was, I had to give up a corner of it for one.

The three attachments that come with most stand mixers are a paddle (for beating and creaming), a bread hook (for bread doughs), and a whip (for whipping eggs). When a recipe also could be made by hand, I indicate that.

Appetizers

MIS-EN-BOUCHE

MY VERY FAVORITE TIME OF THE DAY IS WHEN *L'HEURE DE l'apéro* begins. This is no fixed *heure* (hour), but signifies when the day is winding down and you're ready to relax with something to drink, and perhaps a few nibbles, before sitting down to dinner.

The host of the first dinner party I was invited to in Paris told me the party would start at 8 p.m. However, he followed with, "You know, in Paris you're never supposed to arrive on time. That's *très impolite*. You should always be twenty minutes late." For someone who'd spent his life baking professionally, fixating over a timer, it was hard to adjust to *not* arriving exactly on the dot. And to this day, I can't tell you how many times I've paced around the block in Paris, waiting for the twenty-minute minimum to pass so I could finally ring the doorbell.

Having lived in Paris for a decade, I've collected many Parisian friends and entertained often. And in terms of lateness, I've learned that twenty minutes is actually considered the absolute minimum. I have several friends who are so habitually tardy to the extreme that I now say, "We're sitting down to eat at 9 p.m.," because I get so unraveled watching food sit in the oven, waiting for my late arrivals. In some instances, *l'heure* has turned into *les heures*, during which a few too many glasses of *les apéritifs* are consumed. And by the time everyone finally arrives, I am no longer fit to serve anyone anything.

The selection of drinks served during *l'heure de l'apéro* may be wine, beer, or an apéritif. Parisians sometimes drink white port as a before-dinner drink, and *le whisky* has become quite popular, in addition to Cinzano and Martini & Rossi, just called "Martini," which surprises visitors who get served a squat glass of red vermouth rather than a chilled, neat cocktail. Beer has made considerable inroads into café culture, and it's far more common to see foam-topped glasses on café tables in the early evening hours than wine, especially with the younger set. My choice remains wine, often chilled glasses of rosé in the summer, and a white wine from the Loire or a not-too-challenging red wine the rest of the year. Champagne, of course, is appropriate any time of the year, as is Crémant d'Alsace, a French sparkling wine that is affordable enough to turn even the most casual get-together into a festive event.

As a café barman once told me, pushing a bowl of half-eaten pretzels down the bar my way, "*Violà* . . . it's nice to have something to snack on with your drink." I appreciated the gesture, but prefer to serve my guests something a little spiffier. True, if I'm busy, it might be a bowl of pretzels (from a freshly opened bag) or some salted nuts. Other times I will serve sliced dried sausage with some Lucques olives. Or I'll put out a plate of radishes, fleur de sel, and thin-sliced country ham. Because France isn't necessarily a "snacking" culture (I remember a French friend's father being shocked when he caught me eating between meals!), many of the dips and spreads in this chapter are adapted from the other cultures that have settled in France and that tend to like to nibble as much as I do.

When I'm feeling a little exotic, I'll mix some of the dukkah (page 81) I keep on hand with olive oil to make an instant dip to serve with slices of baguette or carrot sticks and cucumber spears. If I've planned ahead (or kept some in the freezer), there might be little rounds of buttery Comté and ham wafers (page 45) or Salted olive crisps (page 42).

When friends are gathered at my kitchen counter, I'll roll out Indian cheese bread (page 50), cheese-filled breads that are best served hot off the griddle; or *pissaladière* (page 69), an onion, olive, and anchovy pizza that can be served warm or at room temperature. The little bit of salt from the anchovies—and the wine required to quench the thirst that it encourages—helps facilitate conversation and may encourage latecomers to arrive on time in the future to see what they missed.

Salted olive crisps

CROQUETS SALÉS AUX OLIVES

Makes 40 crisps

I brought my bread knife with me when I moved to Paris because I knew I would be lost without it. A good bread knife is something everyone should own, especially if you live in a country where bread is a religion. But be careful how you obtain one; it's considered bad luck in France to give someone a knife. Folk wisdom says that the knife cuts the friendship, and the only way to prevent that is for the recipient to give a bit of money to the knife-giver, usually a coin or two. Although the practice hasn't quite been a windfall for me, I give a lot of people bread knives because it drives me nuts to see people hacking away at bread with dull knives.

In the South of France, a glass of wine is usually accompanied by something like these olive crisps, which have a slight saltiness that encourages pouring another glass (and another). To create nice-looking *croquets*, use a bread knife to cleanly slice through the almonds and olives. If you furiously hack away in short back-and-forth motions the edges will crumble. It's not *le fin du monde*, but still, it's not a good use of your awesome bread knife.

In addition to a good bread knife, it's also worth investing in good olives for this recipe. I use the wrinkly, dry-cured olives from Nyons, which magically carry the scent of Provence to these *croquets*. But any olive that's not too damp will work, including kalamatas. If your olives have brine or moisture on the outside, wipe them dry with a paper towel.

½ cup (70g) all-purpose flour

½ cup (70g) whole wheat flour

1 tablespoon granulated sugar

1 teaspoon herbes de Provence, or ½ teaspoon dried thyme

½ teaspoon sea salt or kosher salt

½ teaspoon baking soda

½ teaspoon freshly ground black pepper

1 cup (250ml) buttermilk

⅓ cup (45g) almonds (untoasted), very coarsely chopped

⅓ cup (60g) packed, coarsely chopped pitted olives (about 20 olives)

1   Preheat the oven to 350°F (180°C). Spray a 9-inch (23cm) loaf pan with nonstick spray or oil it lightly. Line the bottom with a piece of parchment paper.

2   In a bowl, whisk together the all-purpose and whole wheat flours, sugar, dried herbs, salt, baking soda, and black pepper. Stir in the buttermilk with a spatula; mix in the almonds and olives. Scrape the batter into the prepared pan and bake for 30 minutes, until it feels set in the center.

3   Remove from the oven and let cool for 5 minutes. Run a knife around the edge of the loaf to loosen it, remove from the pan, and set the loaf on a wire rack to cool.

4   Decrease the oven temperature to 325°F (160°C). Line two baking sheets with parchment paper or silicone baking mats.

5   Holding the outside edges of the cake firmly with your hand to keep the edges from crumbling, slice the loaf crosswise as thinly as possible, no thicker than ¹/₄ inch (.75cm) thick. Lay the slices cut-side down on the baking sheets, and bake for 30 to 35 minutes, flipping the slices and rotating the baking sheets on the racks of the oven midway through baking so they brown evenly. Watch them carefully during the last 10 minutes of baking; you want them to be a deep golden brown, so they'll crisp up nicely when cool. If some *croquets* brown faster than others, transfer those to a cooling rack while the rest of the crisps toast.

6   Remove from the oven and let cool completely before serving. The crisps can be stored for up to 1 week in an airtight container at room temperature.

Cheese to (Almost) Die For

ONE OF THE GREAT THINGS ABOUT LIVING IN France is the opportunity to visit places where food is produced, and I never pass up a chance to go. My friend Jean-Louis, who works with Comté producers, invited me to go on a midwinter trip to the Jura to watch the entire production of the famous cheese.

It was particularly snowy and cold when we went, giving us plenty of excuses to indulge in the rich foods of the region. Those included Mont d'Or, the holy grail of raw milk cheeses, which is so runny it's served with a spoon from the spruce basket that it's ripened in. Someone once asked me to describe how it smelled, and when I said it was "like a cross between a barnyard and well-worn underwear," for some reason, I don't think they were so keen to taste it. But it's better to try it when you come to France, as my descriptions aren't always as enticing as I hope they might be.

Being surrounded by an overload of cheese, the people in the Jura eat a lot of it, and during our last day I was so stuffed with cheese that at lunch in a local café, I ordered fish. However, a woman we were dining with, who works for the cheese cooperative, ordered the *tartine au fromage*, an open-faced cheese sandwich that arrived as tall as a triple-decker burger: two thick layers of hearty toasted country bread with a heap of melted cheese on top, in between, and spilling down the sides. Because her waistline looked like I could completely encircle it with my two hands, I was sure she would take a few bites and beg off, but somehow she managed to eat the whole thing— and then had dessert!

But I'd been dying to see how those cheeses were made, and my dreams almost came too true when the last night, on our way home from a mountain-top ripening cave, our car went sliding off the icy road and tumbled down a small, snowy cliff.

Fortunately, we both survived and some locals (who later told us it was *normale* to rescue people whose cars had gone off the side of the mountain) invited us into their home for a dinner composed of—what else?—slabs of Comté, a luscious Mont d'Or, and a few well-merited glasses of *vin du Jura*. Jura wines are underrepresented everywhere else, but are exactly the right pairing for the local cheeses.

Now, whenever I slice into a chunk of Comté, I think of that night on the snowy mountain: being pulled out of the car, taken in by locals, and restored with the local cheese and wine while sitting near a crackling fire that was almost as warming as their hospitality (and rescue skills).

Comté and ham wafers

SABLÉS AU COMTÉ ET AU JAMBON

Makes 55 wafers

8 tablespoons (4 ounces/115g) unsalted butter, at room temperature

1 teaspoon freshly ground black pepper

1/2 teaspoon sea salt or kosher salt

2 tablespoons chopped fresh chives, or 2 teaspoons chopped fresh thyme

2 1/2 cups (7 ounces/210g) coarsely grated Comté cheese, or another sharp, firm cheese, such as aged Gouda or Cheddar

1 cup (140g) all-purpose flour

1/4 cup (45g) cornmeal or fine polenta

1/2 cup (50g) crumbled or finely chopped ham chips (page 106), from about 2 slices

I remember the time I told some Parisian friends that in America, we cube cheese and serve it before dinner (I didn't tell them about the colored frills on the toothpicks), and they absolutely couldn't believe it. But Parisians often serve something themselves that I find rather cheesy: little store-bought cheese-filled crackers, sold in the *apéro* aisle, alongside a few other questionable party snacks. I've never quite been able to figure out why they're so popular, but in my kitchen, I make my own cheese sablés, buttery wafers that get their name for their sandy (*sablé*) texture.

These wafers are savory and a bit salty, which makes them ideal to serve with drinks before dinner. A baker once confided in me that restaurant owners requested that he increase the quantity of salt in his bread because it prompted the customers to drink more. You didn't hear it from me, but because of the ham and cheese, you might want to plan on having plenty of beverages to accompany these.

1   In the bowl of a stand mixer fitted with the paddle attachment (or in a large bowl, by hand), beat the butter, pepper, salt, and chives on medium speed until smooth.

2   With a chef's knife, chop the grated cheese into small bits; add them to the butter mixture. Stir in the flour and cornmeal. Add the ham, and mix until the dough comes together. (For a vegetarian version, omit the ham.)

3   Divide the dough in half and roll each half on a lightly floured surface into a 7-inch (18cm) log. Wrap in plastic wrap and chill for 1 hour. The unbaked dough can be refrigerated for up to 1 week, or frozen for up to 2 months.

4   To bake the sablés, preheat the oven to 350°F (180°C). Line two baking sheets with parchment paper or silicone baking mats.

5   With a sharp chef's knife, slice the sablés 1/4-inch (.75cm) thick and place them cut-side down on the baking sheets evenly spaced. Bake for 12 minutes, rotating the baking sheets on the racks of the oven midway through baking, until the sablés are golden brown on top. Let cool and serve. The sablés can be kept in an airtight container at room temperature for up to 3 days.

French Crêpes, California-Style

Having a far-reaching and enthusiastic readership has taught me to be careful what I write about. After I discovered the *crêperie* of my dreams in Paris, the Breizh Café, I immediately wanted to share my excitement about what I assumed was simply another corner *crêperie* in a town filled with corner *crêperies* that happened to serve perfectly executed buckwheat crêpes (called *galettes*). The original café was conceived in Japan, which is evident when you see the appealing simplicity of the food and its focus on the best ingredients. So when you take a bite of a hot-off-the griddle *galette complète* basted in Bordier butter (a product from Brittany that has achieved cult-like status in France and around the world) and folded up with wisps of Savoy ham and a farm egg with a quivering yolk—a brilliant-orange sphere

so perfect you're reluctant to pierce it with your fork—it's easy to see why seats in this café have become highly coveted. Once word got out, the little place got so packed that I could no longer get a seat myself.

So I decided that I had to learn how to make the *galette* on my own. As Jean-Luc Corbel, who runs the Breizh Café, explained to me, the secret to turning out a true buckwheat *galette*, which is made from a batter with just two ingredients—buckwheat flour and water—is to "attack" the *galette* while you're cooking it. My first lesson was standing in front of one of the *billigs* (griddles) with Jean-Luc, who invited me into the kitchen after the lunch rush to give me a lesson. Fortunately, there were no customers waiting for their meals because it certainly wasn't as easy as the expert *billig*-boys there make it look. As soon as my batter hit the grill, it spread like a soupy wildfire as I tried my best to rake it smoothly over the top, creating a perfect circle, like those professional crêpe-makers do. But as the batter spread quickly in any and all directions, I panicked, trying to curb the flow with the flat wooden rake. Unfortunately I only succeeded in pushing the batter that was beginning to overflow off one end of the griddle toward the other. By the time I managed to get the *galette* partially under control, it made me homesick for the state of California. Not because I was frustrated and wanted to go back home, but because my *galette* was long and shaped like my previous state of residence . . . with a big, fearsome fissure also running down the length of it.

Jean-Luc assured me that it takes at least a week of daily practice to begin to get it, but I was never able to master the art of the pure buck-wheat *galette*. So now I add eggs, which keeps my *galettes* and my sanity—and any edible *hommages* to my home state that might slide my way—together.

Buckwheat rolls with seaweed butter

GALETTES AU SARRASIN AU BEURRE AUX ALGUES

Makes 12 rolls

The Japanese roots of Breizh Café are obvious in their first courses, which are galettes *façon sushi*—rolled up buckwheat galettes fried in butter from Brittany, seasoned with different fillings, then sliced into rounds like you'd find in a sushi bar.

A good crêpe, or *galette*, should be thin and lacy. The batter is best made a few hours before you plan to use it and should have the consistency of heavy cream. As it hits the griddle, it should be thick enough to coat the bottom, but not too thick, or the galette will be rubbery. The griddle must be hot enough so that almost immediately lots of little holes will form on the surface of the *galette*. That's the moment of satisfaction, when you know that you've got it just right, and then it's a pleasure to just keep going.

The first one (or in my case, two) is/are usually a dud, so don't worry. This recipe makes two extra *galettes*, which I'm allotting as your practice ones.

BUCKWHEAT GALETTES

1¹/₂ cups (210g) buckwheat flour

¹/₂ teaspoon sea salt or kosher salt

2¹/₄ cups (530ml) water, plus more if needed

2 large eggs

SEAWEED BUTTER

1¹/₂ sheets (6g) nori (Japanese seaweed)

8 tablespoons (4 ounces/115g) unsalted butter, at room temperature

¹/₂ teaspoon sea salt or kosher salt

Butter, preferably clarified (page 327), for frying

Flaky sea salt, such as fleur de sel, to serve

1   To make the *galettes*, put the buckwheat flour in a bowl and add the salt, water, and eggs. Whisk well, then cover and chill the batter for at least 1 hour. (The batter can be refrigerated overnight.) Remove the batter from the refrigerator and give it a few brisk stirs. It should have the consistency of heavy cream. If not, whisk in a tablespoon or two of water, until it's the right consistency.

2   Wipe the bottom of a 10-inch (25cm) nonstick skillet or crêpe pan with a small amount of melted butter or oil (I keep a saucer of it next to the stove, with a wadded up paper towel for applying it) and heat it over medium or high heat.

3   Pour ¹/₄ cup (60ml) of the batter into the hot pan, lifting and turning the pan (steeply, if necessary) to get the batter into an even layer. When the underside is a dark golden brown, about 1 minute, flip the *galette* and cook it 30 seconds more, then slide it out onto a dinner plate. Fry the other *galettes* the same way, stacking them up on the plate. If they start to stick to the pan, wipe a bit more butter or oil around the insides of the pan in between frying. If you're not planning to use the *galettes* right away, they can be wrapped and refrigerated for up to 2 days.

continued

4   To make the seaweed butter, wave each sheet of seaweed over a low gas flame, holding it with a pair of tongs, until it darkens a little and shrivels up, about 15 seconds at the most. Let cool. (If you don't have a gas stove, you can crisp them under the oven broiler directly on the rack for a similar amount of time, watching them carefully.)

5   With your hands, crumble the nori into a bowl. Add the butter and salt and mash everything together with a fork until well mixed.

6   Smear a thin layer of the nori butter on the underside (the less attractive side) of a *galette*, using about 2 teaspoons per *galette*. Starting at one edge, roll up the *galette*, pressing down as you fold so it's flattened, not round.

7   Add some butter to a hot skillet and heat as many of the folded-up *galettes* as will fit in a single layer. Cook the *galettes* on one side until crisp, then flip them over and cook until the other side is crisp. It will take a few minutes on each side—and it's worth being patient to get them right. Slide the fried *galettes* onto a cutting board and sprinkle with a few extra flecks of salt, then cut them crosswise into four pieces and serve on the cutting board.

VARIATION: If using a 12-inch (30cm) skillet, use a generous 1/3 cup (80ml) of batter for each *galette*, which will yield 6 to 8 larger *galettes*.

A CONFUSION OF CRÊPES

When shopping at the outdoor markets in Paris, there is invariably someone there tempting shoppers with the smell of warm, buttery crêpes being fried to order on a hot griddle. I prefer those made with buckwheat, called *galettes au sarrasin* in French, so I recently ordered one. The young woman standing over the griddle looked a bit startled. And when I asked why, she replied, "Because Americans never order the buckwheat ones."

Just so you know, a crêpe is almost always made with white flour (*farine de blé*), which is also called a *crêpe de froment*. If you want buckwheat, you ask for a *galette au sarrasin*, which is often shortened to *galette* in crêpe-maker speak. But in case you're not quite confused yet, a *crêpe au blé noir* is also a buckwheat crêpe—just like a *galette*, but called something completely different. Got that?

Even though you can get a *galette au sarrasin* (or a *crêpe au blé noir*) for a main course at any *crêperie* in France, it's practically unheard of to order one made of buckwheat for dessert. Which I do, in spite of the funny looks I get. But now that I've mastered the lingo, I get fewer and fewer of those looks. And I hope you do (or is it—don't?), too.

48

A Passage to India—via Paris

IT MAY SOUND UNLIKELY, BUT MY INTRODUCTION to Indian food happened in Paris. There's a sizable Indian *quartier* up behind the Gare du Nord train station where most visitors don't venture. In addition to being the headquarters of the Hell's Angels of Paris—which may or may not mean the area is safe—there are streets lined with shops and restaurants offering all sorts of Indian foods, many featuring things I couldn't identify if my life depended on it. (So maybe the Hell's Angels are there to protect the uninitiated?) It was here that I learned about *dosa*, a cricket bat–sized, rolled-up crêpe filled with spiced potatoes and served with a lavish assortment of sauces and dips, and perhaps not-so-curiously, where I could find British products like baking soda, golden syrup, and oatmeal. And it was also where I had my first naan.

Traditional naan is a blistered flatbread, quickly rolled out and cooked on the walls of an extremely hot oven, where it puffs up, then settles down into warm chewiness. It's brushed with butter before being ripped apart and devoured communally. I always order *naan fromage*, because I like the warm cheese tucked in the center. And I always order my own, because I don't like to share.

Naan fromage doesn't exist in Indian cooking. At least according to Beena Paradin, to whom I wrote an impassioned plea after I tried to re-create naan at home, with varying degrees of success. Beena was schooled in Paris and teaches cooking classes, writes books, and even had a television series on Indian food in France. So if anyone knows how to prepare Indian food in this city, it's Beena.

I was a bit embarrassed to bring Laughing Cow cheese into her kitchen, but a little sleuthing on my part led to the discovery of which cheese the Indian restaurants in Paris use to melt quickly and smoothly inside the pockets of naan. It may

seem sacrilegious in the land of cheese to use a processed cheese product (even though no one could argue that *La vache qui rit* is anything but French), but with the extravagant lashings of butter added at the end, there's little doubt why this is so popular in Paris.

After a few clunkers in my own kitchen, I was humbled as Beena worked the dough with her beautiful fingers, chatting away while effortlessly baking off a few naan in a cast-iron wok, whose shape she told me mimics traditional tandoori ovens. But happily they worked well in the cast-iron skillet that I lugged across Paris. (And previously, the Atlantic Ocean.) I realized that a big part of Indian cooking, which often yields exciting results—such as pan-fried breads—is to relax and enjoy the process of preparation as much as the result.

One thing Beena explained to me is that India is a country made up of hundreds of different cultures living closely with each other. So people are forgiving of variations and adaptations. While the French are often guilty of "French-izing" (not always successfully) other cuisines, this is a delicious instance of Indians adapting their own cuisine successfully to French tastes, and to mine as well.

Indian cheese bread

NAAN AU FROMAGE

Makes 6 flatbreads

Naan, like Indian cooks, are very forgiving, so even novice bread-makers will be thrilled to learn that it's easy to turn out blistered, irregular rounds of bread with nothing but an ordinary wok or a cast-iron skillet.

If you don't have a stand mixer, the dough, which I adapted from Beena's recipe, is very easy to make by hand because it doesn't require vigorous or lengthy kneading. I usually roll out one naan as another is frying, but this technique requires a bit of multitasking. You can also roll them all out at once beforehand, put them on baking sheets lined with parchment paper, and then fry them off one right after the other. Naan should be eaten hot off the griddle. Made without the cheese, this naan can be served as dipping bread for Eggplant caviar (page 66) or Beet hummus (page 58). Although Laughing Cow cheese is commonly used in Paris, you can use a Swiss-style cheese instead.

One final word of advice: If you have a hood fan, use it, or keep a window open nearby. Frying the breads can create some smoke.

²/₃ cup (160ml) tepid water

Pinch of granulated sugar

1 packet (7g) active dry yeast

1³/₄ cups (250g) all-purpose flour, plus more if needed

³/₄ teaspoon baking powder (preferably aluminum-free)

2 tablespoons plain yogurt (whole or low-fat)

5 tablespoons (75ml) melted clarified butter (page 327), plus more for frying and serving

³/₄ teaspoon sea salt or kosher salt

12 wedges (21g each) plain Laughing Cow cheese

1 In the bowl of a stand mixer fitted with the dough hook, combine the water, sugar, yeast, and ³/₄ cup (110g) of the flour. Let stand 30 minutes; the mixture will become frothy.

2 Add the remaining 1 cup (140g) of flour along with the baking powder, yogurt, 3 tablespoons of the clarified butter, and the salt; knead on medium speed for 5 minutes. The dough will be soft, but if it sticks to your fingers when you touch it, add another tablespoon or two of flour. (You can also make the dough by hand, kneading it on a lightly floured surface for 5 minutes.) Cover the bowl with a kitchen towel and let the dough rest for 30 minutes.

3 Heat a cast-iron skillet or wok over high heat and cover it with a lid, preferably domed.

4 Divide the dough into six pieces. Sprinkle the countertop with a light dusting of flour and knead each piece in a little bit of flour until it no longer sticks to your hands. Working one at a time, roll each piece of dough into a 4-inch (10cm) disk. Starting with one round of dough, place two unwrapped wedges (42g) of cheese side by side in the center. Fold over the four rounded

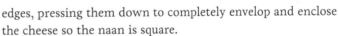

edges, pressing them down to completely envelop and enclose the cheese so the naan is square.

5 Turn the naan over, seam side down, and roll it out with a rolling pin on the floured countertop until it's about 6 inches (15cm) square.

6 Brush a thin layer of clarified butter over the bottom of the hot skillet. Lay one naan on the hot surface, replace the lid, and cook for about 1 minute, until it puffs up unevenly and the underside is browned. Use a spatula to flip the naan and replace the lid, continuing to cook the naan until the other side is browned, about 1 minute. A few black, blistered spots are normal, and encouraged.

7 Slide the cheese-filled naan out onto a plate, brush it with a bit of clarified butter. Repeat the same process with the other rounds of dough, and serve.

VARIATION: Add freshly chopped garlic to some warm clarified butter and use that to brush the finished naan.

The Olive Râleur

FOLKS MISTAKENLY THINK THAT TAPENADE IS just any kind of olive paste, but tapenade gets its name from *tapeno*, the word for "capers" in the Provençal language. Although the term is sometimes used to describe anything made with mashed olives, in order to be authentic tapenade, it must have capers in it. I don't want to get grouchy about it, but it's like a beef burger must be made of beef and a fruit salad needs to contain fruit. If it doesn't have capers, it's not tapenade.

For years the olive guy at my market was Jacques, an even grumpier fellow than me, who hailed from Provence. Not only did I become his best customer, but before I knew it, we were practically best friends. Whenever I stopped at his stall to get olives, he would bend my ear about everything that was bothering him. And rarely was it about olives.

He complained so much that I nicknamed him the *râleur*, because he would rail so much. (Complaining isn't considered a fault in France, but a normal reaction to life, where the odds always seem to be stacked against you.) But when it came to olives, there was nothing to complain about at his stand. Each olive he plucked from his brine-filled bins was the meatiest and juiciest specimen of an olive one could imagine. I never knew that olives could be so good.

Once back in my kitchen, I'd extract the pits from the olives, pressing each one with my thumb, sending a spritz of juice flying forth (I learned to wear a *tablier*, or kitchen apron), then pound them in my mortar into an oily, olivey paste. It took a bit of moxie and after a while—and a lot of pounding—I realized that the tapenades that he also sold were nearly as good as any that I could make at home, without all the pitting and pounding. (And olive-stained shirts.) When he eventually retired, I was surprised by how much I missed him—and his complaining. And, of course, his olives.

Although I miss my twice-weekly visits with Jacques, I don't miss pitting all those olives. Yet because old habits die hard, every once in a while I haul out my mortar and pestle, buy a small sack of olives, and get to work pitting them. And I make sure to complain under my breath about each and every one as I go, in his honor.

Artichoke tapenade with rosemary oil

TAPENADE D'ARTICHAUT, HUILE D'OLIVE
AROMATISÉE AU ROMARIN

Serves 6 to 8

One 14-ounce (400g) can artichoke hearts (2 cups), drained and quartered

1/2 cup (60g) pitted green olives

1/3 cup (80ml) olive oil

1 tablespoon (10g) capers, rinsed, squeezed dry, and chopped

1 tablespoon freshly squeezed lemon juice

2 cloves garlic, peeled and minced

1/8 teaspoon cayenne pepper

Sea salt or kosher salt

Rosemary oil (see page 332)

Toasted sliced baguette or crackers, to serve

For those who complain about pitting olives, easier to make is an artichoke tapenade, another spread that Jacques sold from bins. It can be made quickly with canned artichokes and capers, everything easily whirled up in a food processor with no pitting required. Who can *râle* about that?

1 In the bowl of a food processor, puree the artichokes, olives, olive oil, capers, lemon juice, garlic, and cayenne pepper until smooth. Taste, and season with a bit of salt if necessary.

2 Serve drizzled with a liberal amount of rosemary oil, along with toasted slices of baguette or crackers for dipping. The tapenade will keep for up to 4 days in the refrigerator.

Green olive, basil, and almond tapenade

TAPENADE D'OLIVES VERTES AU BASILIC ET AUX AMANDES

Serves 6 to 8

When I started my website back in 1999, I never intended to focus on recipes. It was meant to complement my cookbooks by providing additional information, stories, and a way to be in touch with readers. But then I moved to Paris. And as I shopped and hit the markets, I got so excited to share all the great things I was tasting and learning about that I couldn't resist posting those recipes right after I made them. However, I soon realized that I had to respond to an onslaught of recipe requests if I posted a snapshot of a basket of croissants or a gilded *gâteau Saint-Honoré* I had admired in a bakery. (Unfortunately, recipes for fancy Parisian pastries cannot be condensed into 140 characters, nor am I very good at tapping out instructions for rolling puff pastry while riding home on the métro using those itty bitty keys on my smartphone.)

I also realized that no matter what I wrote about on my blog, the ingredients that were available in Birmingham weren't necessarily

continued

available in Brisbane or Bangkok, and every recipe I posted would be followed by a number of requests for substitutions. I had to learn to cover every conceivable base when writing recipes for a global audience because something common in France or America, like olives or canned artichokes, might not be available in Fiji or Argentina. Not to mention folks have various food preferences, allergies, and likes and dislikes, such as my fear of squid, which scare the bejeezus out of me (so I understand them 100 percent).

Fortunately I am pretty sure that anyone just about anywhere can make this recipe and there's certainly nothing scary about it. Olives are hardy souls and are available jarred or canned. I don't think I've ever been to a country where almonds aren't available. (But if you can't get almonds, pistachios make a great substitute.) And basil is grown in greenhouses in places where the climate doesn't welcome outdoor cultivation. So I think I covered everything and there's no excuse not to make this—unless, of course, you don't like olives, are allegic to nuts, or have an aversion to garlic. Then I can't help you.

1   Put the olives, almonds, garlic, lemon juice, and capers in the bowl of a food processor. (I don't use a mortar and pestle for this because I like the slightly chunky bits of almonds in the finished tapenade.)

2   Coarsely chop the basil leaves, add them to the processor, and pulse the machine a few times to start breaking them down.

3   Add the olive oil and a sprinkle of salt. Pulse the food processor until the mixture forms a coarse paste, one that still has a little texture provided by the not-entirely-broken-down almonds. The tapenade will keep for up to 1 week in the refrigerator.

Green olive, basil, and almond tapenade, continued

2 cups (260g) green olives, pitted

1/3 cup (35g) whole untoasted almonds

1 small clove garlic, peeled and minced

1 1/2 tablespoons freshly squeezed lemon juice

1 tablespoon capers, rinsed and squeezed dry

1/2 cup (15g) loosely packed fresh basil leaves

1/2 cup (125ml) olive oil

Sea salt or kosher salt

Man versus Machine

MORE THAN ANY OTHER CULINARY DEVICE in our time, the food processor revolutionized French cuisine. Julia Child was an early adopter who discovered this machine could replace some of the laborious kitchen tasks that many classical French dishes relied on, such as turning vegetables into smooth purees and whizzing up a velvety sauce in no time flat. The first French food processor was called a Robot Coupe, or "cutting machine," and the concept was introduced to Americans under the name Cuisinart by a man who was so impressed by the one he saw in France that he decided to take a gamble and develop his own model for the American market. The Cuisinart took a while to catch on—until such luminaries as Julia Child praised it, and the influential Craig Claiborne of the *New York Times* called it "the best food invention since toothpicks." Shortly after, sales took off, and today food processors are widely available in a number of different makes and models around the world.

I have one, too. But I will admit that for many years it languished in the back of a kitchen cabinet, with the unwieldy cord trailing behind. Then one day, I used it for a project and didn't feel like hefting it back into the cabinet. I left it on the counter, and found myself using it a lot more often.

Sure, it's tough to give precious kitchen real estate to an appliance that you likely don't use on a daily basis, but I came to realize how handy it was to have it there to use within a moment. And now I use my food processor more than ever; though I'm still not giving up my mortar and pestle, which yields a different result.

Hand-pounding *pistou* (page 92) produces a paste that is different from handfuls of chopped basil suspended in olive oil. I want to see chunks of avocado in my guacamole, rather than dipping into a bowl of nondescript green puree. And I love the smell that rises from the mortar and pestle when smashing garlic with salt, the first step in making aïoli (page 145). Mashing releases the aroma and flavor from the garlic, both of which will permeate an entire batch of creamy mayonnaise that will eventually be built up as you pound and pound (and pound) away.

Black olive tapenade

TAPENADE NOIRE

Serves 6 to 8

1¹/₂ cups (210g) black olives, pitted

2 cloves garlic, peeled and minced

1 tablespoon capers, rinsed and squeezed dry

1 teaspoon finely chopped fresh thyme, or ¹/₂ teaspoon dried

2 anchovy fillets

1 tablespoon freshly squeezed lemon juice

1 teaspoon Dijon mustard

¹/₃ cup (80ml) olive oil

Sea salt or kosher salt (optional)

This was the first tapenade I ever made, and it is still my go-to recipe. The best olives to use are the slightly wrinkled black olives from Nyons; or, if you have the patience for pitting teensy Niçoise olives, they're marvelously oily and are the base for a wonderful bowl of tapenade. Other olives work well, too, but if they're very salty, rinse them in cold water and pat them dry before using them.

One way to pit olives is to squish them under your thumb or use the side of a broad knife blade, with the blade held parallel to the table (i.e., not facing up), and rap it down briskly to release the pit from the olive meat. Be sure to wear a dark shirt or kitchen apron since the pits like to celebrate their *liberté* in a very "far-reaching" way.

Tapenade can be spread on Herbed goat cheese toasts (page 121). Pastis is the classic accompaniment, although I never developed a taste for the anise-scented elixir that mysteriously turns cloudy when water is added to dilute its high-test taste and strength. I opt for chilled rosé.

1   In the bowl of a food processor, pulse the olives, garlic, capers, thyme, anchovies, lemon juice, and mustard a few times to start breaking them down.

2   Add the olive oil and run the food processor until the mixture forms a slightly chunky paste. The tapenade shouldn't need any salt, but taste and add a sprinkle if necessary. The tapenade will keep for up to 1 week in the refrigerator.

Une Bonne Adresse

THE FIRST TIME I HEARD OF HUMMUS, I WAS working in a vegetarian restaurant in upstate New York. Because it was so popular, we made a big batch daily, grinding up the chickpeas—somewhat incongruously—in an old meat grinder clamped to the kitchen counter. Customers ordered a lot of it, although it always brought down the kitchen staff when a waiter would tell us that a customer mispronounced it, and wanted humus (i.e., decomposed matter used to improve the structure of soil) on their sandwich.

But I should talk, because I've made my share of language gaffes, including confusing the Virgin Mary with a sex organ (*vierge* vs. *verge*—I'll let you look them up). And for years, I had trouble pronouncing my own street name: a number of cab drivers were surprised to hear that I lived at the Bon Marché (pronounced *bomarchay*), a fabulously chic Left Bank department store that's considered a *bonne adresse* in Paris, rather than my little maid's quarters on the boulevard Beaumarchais (pronounced *beaumarchay*). If only!

Although there's not a lot of humus in Paris, one can unearth hummus at a number of Arabic *épiceries* and even in the supermarket, sold in little plastic containers. But I always make my own (page 60). And just as surprising as it is to be taken "home" to Le Bon Marché, adding beets to hummus makes a bright red paste, especially welcome in the middle of a Parisian winter when beets are the most colorful thing at the market. It's especially good spread on toasts accompanied by a glass of Lillet, an orange apéritif wine that never fails to cheer me up, no matter what side of town I live on.

Beet hummus

HOUMOUS DE BETTERAVES

Serves 6 to 8

The secret ingredient in this hummus is pomegranate molasses, a tart-sweet syrup made from reduced pomegranate juice that has now become an indispensable part of my international condiment cabinet—holding its own among American barbecue sauce, Lebanese sesame paste (tahini), Spanish vinegar, and French olive oil. Its fruity tang complements the earthy (or earthly) beets while providing a bit of contrast to their richness. If you don't have it, try a touch of balsamic vinegar. A little drizzled over the top is nice along with za'atar, a thyme-based seasoning available in Arabic markets. This is a good dip for accompanying a platter of raw vegetables, such as carrots, kohlrabi, cherry tomatoes, or other favorites.

1   Put all the ingredients in the bowl of a food processor and process until the hummus is nearly smooth. Taste and add more salt or lemon juice, if desired. Beet hummus can be stored in the refrigerator for up to 4 days; it tastes best the day after you make it.

12 ounces (340g) cooked beets, peeled and diced (you can use canned, drained)

2/3 cup (115g) cooked or canned chickpeas, drained

2 large cloves garlic, peeled and minced

6 tablespoons (120g) tahini

2 teaspoons sea salt or kosher salt, plus more if needed

1/4 cup (60ml) freshly squeezed lemon juice, plus more if needed

Generous pinch of cayenne pepper or smoked chile powder

1 1/2 tablespoons pomegranate molasses

Chiles and Chickpeas

FOLKS DON'T NECESSARILY THINK OF PARIS AS a hotbed of multicultural cooking. I offer two reasons for that: One is that France hasn't traditionally encouraged a "melting pot" culture, and immigrants are expected to adapt to local traditions. And, two, the French palate favors balance and moderation of flavors, which often sideline such spicy or highly seasoned food as Thai, Szechuan, Korean, and Mexican cuisines. French people aren't known to be adventurous eaters and will wave away anything even remotely spicy. Or for those hearty souls willing to give it a try, one cautious bite can provoke a bout of dramatic gesticulating, including the frantic fanning of open mouths and urgent mopping up of the one or two beads of never-before seen sweat that emerges from their foreheads.

However non-French foods are making inroads and even if the foods are sometimes toned down for local tastes, Parisians are starting to appreciate carne asada tacos, Indian curries, and even kimchi. And I applaud those who have been trying out a Szechuan restaurant that opened near me where the food is so hot, even I can barely eat a few mouthfuls without my eyes watering and my throat burning in rebellion. But there they are, their *visages* turning bright red, gulping beer to cool to heat, right along with the best of them.

Cuisines that have a recent history with modern-day France are those from North Africa and the Middle East. I've had my share of some pretty good Middle Eastern food in Paris, but it wasn't until I went to Jerusalem, where eating hummus is like a second religion (or third, or

fourth, or . . .) that I tasted the most astoundingly good hummus. In a country racked with conflict, it's no wonder that determining who makes the best hummus has become yet another point of contention, like just about everything else discussed in the country.

While in Israel, I went to a hummus factory, where tons and tons of chickpeas are processed daily to meet the insatiable taste the Israelis have for it. As I peered in for a closer look, workers lifted a handful of smooth chickpeas from a sorting bin, void of any skins, and told me they were a variety from Bulgaria. While I was tempted to pocket as many handfuls of the skinless beauties as I could, if I planned on having more than one batch of outstanding hummus in my future, I had to replicate it at home. And that involves . . . removing the skins. I know, I know. It sounds like a tedious task, but for a normal batch of hummus, it shouldn't take you more than 10 concentrated minutes. (No wonder with all the chickpeas they cook at the factory, they hunted down a skinless variety.) During a few experiments at home, I did discover that if you drain the warm chickpeas, then run them under cold running water in a mesh colander while moving them around with your hands, many of the skins will slide right off. Another technique is to let them soak in a bowl of cool water; many of the skins will rise to the top where they can be skimmed off. It's not imperative that you remove the skins, but the more you pluck out, the smoother your hummus will be. And once you taste the fruits—or chickpeas—of your labor, you'll realize the difference. Hunger for hummus makes the task go faster.

Hummus

HOUMOUS

Serves 6 to 8

In Jerusalem, I didn't see a single bowl of hummus that wasn't dressed with an unrestrained pour of olive oil and either additional whole chickpeas, pomegranate molasses, a scattering of spices, chopped almonds, or (my favorite) a heap of toasted pine nuts glistening in a puddle of oil cratering in the center of the hummus, waiting to be dug into.

Like many things in Israel, the storage of hummus also becomes a great source of contention. Some say it should never be refrigerated, as that is the surest way to ruin it. Others say to chill it and let it sit at least an hour before you eat it. I've done both and will claim the middle ground. But if you do chill it, take it out in time to serve it at room temperature.

1   Rinse the dried chickpeas and sort them for debris. Put them in a large saucepan, cover with cold water, and soak overnight. (Soaking them overnight will make them cook faster the following day.) The next day, drain the chickpeas and put them back in the saucepan with three times their volume of water. Add the baking soda and set the pan over medium-low heat.

2   Cook at a low boil for 1 to 2 hours with a lid ajar, until the chickpeas are very tender. Remove from the heat and pour them into a mesh colander set over a bowl to reserve the cooking liquid. Run the chickpeas under cold running water, moving them around with your hands to loosen and dislodge the skins. Pick out the loose skins and discard them.

3   In a food processor, puree the tahini, lemon juice, garlic, and salt until smooth. (You can also use a blender, adding ⅓ cup [80ml] of chickpea cooking liquid along with the tahini.) Reserve a handful of the chickpeas for garnishing, then add the remaining chickpeas to the food processor and puree until the hummus is completely, utterly smooth. Taste and add additional lemon juice or salt, if desired. If it's too thick, add some of the reserved cooking liquid until it's a scoopable consistency.

4   Scrape the hummus into a bowl and smooth the top. To serve, use the back of a spoon to make some depressions in the top. Scatter the reserved chickpeas over the hummus along with a generous sprinkling of dukkah or toasted nuts. Dust with the sumac and dribble olive oil everywhere.

1 cup (150g) dried chickpeas, or 2 cups (350g) canned chickpeas (drained and liquid reserved)

½ teaspoon baking soda

9 tablespoons (90g) tahini

4 teaspoons freshly squeezed lemon juice, plus more if needed

2 cloves garlic, peeled and minced

1½ teaspoons sea salt or kosher salt, plus more if needed

Dukkah (page 81) or toasted nuts or seeds, for garnish

Ground sumac or paprika, for garnish

Olive oil, for garnish

Eggplant Égalité

HAVING A BLOG IS LIKE HAVING HUNDREDS, sometimes thousands, of proofreaders, scrutinizing your words, looking for errors or inconsistencies. Some like to reach far, far back into my past, forgetting that people and their tastes (and favorite bakeries) change over time. I have heard from folks compiling spreadsheets to document which bakeries in Paris made my favorite croissant, baguette, or *tarte au chocolat*, or which butter I have chosen for spreading over my breakfast baguette. While it's flattering that people think my taste is a reasonable barometer of what's good in Paris, I'm only human, I have my faults, and I engage in a little (culinary) infidelity every now and then.

Aside from writing about Paris and sharing French recipes, I often veer into other cuisines because, as an American, I come from a multicultural country, and I need a bowl of Korean bibimbap every once in a while or a pot of pork carnitas for tacos, which I might later write about. And as the writer, editor, copy editor, proofreader, translator, fact-checker, art director, photographer, food stylist, prop stylist, photo editor, coding whiz, publisher, cultural ambassador, and often, referee, I can't tell you how long my finger hovers before I hit the "Publish" button. But in spite of my best efforts, no matter how thorough I've tried to be, no matter how much

I've researched exactly what breed of pig is used to make carnitas in the region of Mexico where carnitas originated, I am certain to get called out by someone that I've used the wrong pork and how dare I call it carnitas if it's not made with *puerco de*-wherever, or that the salt must be harvested by certified virgins in some remote marsh that is overseen and blessed by the ancient gods of Michoacán, if I want to call it carnitas.

The upside to being so closely monitored on an international scale are the people who are happy that you're enjoying their particular cuisine and are also kind enough to let you know (nicely) that, um, perhaps you've misnamed something.

Take baba ganoush, which is what in America is used to describe eggplant puree mixed with tahini (sesame seed paste). It's something familiar to anyone who was a vegetarian in the 1970s or 1980s, as I was. But even though I'm firmly an omnivore again, I like to roast up a few eggplants from my local market, charring them over the gas burner of my stove, then finishing them in the oven before blending them to a smooth paste with tahini—a mixture that, unbeknownst to me, is actually a spread known as *moutabal*. Yet like many things in the Middle East, and online, there's a bit of *inégalité* about what makes *moutabal* different from baba ganoush. Me? I'd rather eat than argue.

Baba ganoush

MOUTABAL

Serves 6 to 8

And now that I know this is actually called *moutabal* (with thanks to the reader who pointed that out to me—nicely), I don't get any more odd looks when presenting guests with a bowl of something I sometimes still refer to as baba ganoush.

You can certainly customize this recipe with a bit of whatever spices you like. Cenk Sonmezsoy, a Turkish blogger (cafefernando .com), gifted me with a goodie bag when he came to Paris; it included *isot*, a flaky, dark pepper powder, also called Aleppo pepper, with a curiously sweet-smoky aftertaste that I love in this recipe. Smoked paprika, Basque piment d'Espelette, or even smoked salt used in place of the regular salt can tweak the flavor in a variety of directions.

While it's tempting to use slender Japanese eggplants, the larger, plump globe eggplants work better because of their moisture content.

2 globe eggplants (2½ pounds/1.25kg)

½ cup (130g) tahini (sesame seed paste)

1¼ teaspoons sea salt or kosher salt

3 tablespoons freshly squeezed lemon juice

3 cloves garlic, peeled and minced

⅛ teaspoon cayenne pepper, or another smoked or dried chile powder

⅛ teaspoon ground cumin

1 tablespoon olive oil, plus more for drizzling

2 tablespoons finely chopped fresh flat-leaf parsley

Coarsely chopped fresh herbs or seeds, for garnish

1   Preheat the oven to 375°F (190°C). Line a baking sheet with parchment paper, brush it with olive oil, and sprinkle it with salt.

2   Use a sharp knife to prick each eggplant a few times. Place each eggplant directly over the flame of a gas burner or a grill, turning them as needed, to char the outside evenly. Depending on how smoky you want them to taste, cook them, rotating, for 5 to 10 minutes.

3   When cool enough to handle, trim off the stems of the eggplants and split them lengthwise. Lay the eggplants cut-side down on the baking sheet and roast in the oven until they feel completely soft, 30 to 40 minutes. Remove from the oven and let cool.

4   Scrape the pulp into the bowl of a food processor. Add the tahini, salt, lemon juice, garlic, cayenne, cumin, olive oil, and parsley and puree until smooth. (You can also mash the eggplants by hand with a fork in a large bowl with the other ingredients.) Serve in a shallow bowl, drizzled with olive oil and sprinkled with fresh herbs or seeds. *Moutabal* will keep for up to 4 days in the refrigerator.

La Stresse du Supermarché

Every time I go into a supermarket in Paris, I steel myself first, because I know something is going to go wrong in there. Supermarkets in France seem to do whatever they can to make it as difficult as possible to shop there. It is, I think, in part because the French have traditionally done their food shopping either at outdoor markets or at *vergers*, vegetable and fruit stands, and the impersonal nature of supermarkets lends itself to combative behavior between the shoppers (who don't want to be there) and the workers (who don't want to be there, either). So it's not uncommon to find aisles barricaded so you can't pass, and shelves empty of seemingly everyday products like sugar, flour, or orange juice. And heaven help you if you don't have exact change, because even if the cashier has a drawer full of coins, it is a herculean struggle for them to fish any of them out to give to you.

My first major supermarket kerfuffle happened when my carton of orange juice didn't ring up at the sale price, and the cashier refused to believe that it was *en promotion*. So after some bickering, I went over to the juice display, pulled the sign down from the wall, and set it in front of her. I got the reduction, but I also got a stern reprimand from both her and the manager for doubting their word (which struck me as odd, because for some reason, I thought they were the ones who were in the wrong). At the same supermarket a few months later, I asked for five 1-euro coins instead of the 5-euro note I was handed back as change so I could use their photo machine to get some official photos I needed for a government document. The cashier told me she didn't have any change and slammed her drawer (full of change) shut. Even the Parisian fellow behind me rolled his eyes. Sometimes you just have to laugh at the ridiculousness of it

all. Hence, I've learned to hold on to any and all change, because I just never know when I might need to buy something and I hate to bother the cashier.

One big change—no pun intended—that has made the supermarket experience more pleasant is the automated checkout counter, which means you don't have to suffer the wrath of the cashiers. These counters are also ideal places to break the dreaded 50-euro notes that the ATMs dole out, and which cashiers like seeing about as much as they like admitting to customers that they were wrong. My sense is that cashiers like taking money, but they don't like giving any back.

Although most people who work 9-to-5 jobs in Paris don't have the luxury of going to the outdoor markets to do their daily shopping, I'm fortunate that I can go at my leisure and without any fear of being scolded for buying things.

Once you become a regular at a market, you get to know the vendors and they become like friends and, in some cases, valuable confidants. If you want to know what's going on with any of the other stand owners, or your neighbors, or any other gossip (especially when it comes to fruits and vegetables), the market vendors are the ones to ask.

The only problem is that all this chatting really slows down my shopping. If I just want one thing, like a couple of oranges or two eggplants, I need to dart around carefully to avoid the gaze of some of the vendors, since I don't have time for a lengthy chat about what's new in the potato business or how no one seems to be buying cauliflower anymore. These may not seem like such urgent topics of discussion, but considering the alternatives (for instance, bickering over 7 centimes), I'll stick to doing my shopping at the markets.

Eggplant caviar

CAVIAR D'AUBERGINES

Serves 6 to 8

One of my dreams is that someday, someone will open a smoke-house in Paris. (And no, I don't mean the terraces of the cafés that are packed with people puffing away. We've already got plenty of those.) It's not really such a radical idea. In the Middle Ages, there were communal *fours* in Paris where people brought their food to be baked, such as on the aptly named Rue du Four (Oven Street) in the 6th *arrondissement*. I think some enterprising person should open a place where residents can bring fish, meats (ribs!), and vegetables that we want smoked.

Until that day, I'll continue to roast eggplants on the flame of my gas stove, which gives them a nice char and permeates the eggplant with the smoky flavor that I crave.

Caviar d'aubergines is a popular appetizer in Parisian restaurants served with toasts to spread it on.

1 Preheat the oven to 375°F (190°C). Line a baking sheet with parchment paper, brush it with olive oil, and sprinkle it with salt.

2 Use a sharp knife to prick each eggplant a few times. Place each eggplant over the flame of a gas burner or a grill, turning them as needed, to char the outside evenly. Depending on how smoky you want them to taste, cook them for 5 to 10 minutes.

3 Trim off the stems of the eggplants and split them lengthwise. Lay the eggplants cut-side down on the baking sheet and roast in the oven until they feel completely soft, 30 to 40 minutes. Remove from the oven and let cool.

4 Scrape the pulp into the bowl of a food processor. Add the olive oil, lemon juice, garlic, salt, paprika, and some pepper. Pulse the food processor a few times, until the mixture is almost smooth. Add the herbs and pulse a few more times. (Alternatively, mash the eggplants with the other ingredients by hand with a fork.) Taste and add additional lemon juice or salt as desired.

5 Serve in a bowl, making a shallow crater in the middle and adding a pour of olive oil and a sprinkle of paprika over the top. The eggplant caviar will keep for up to 4 days in the refrigerator. Bring to room temperature before serving.

2 globe eggplants (2½ pounds/1.25kg)

1 tablespoon olive oil, plus more for serving

2 tablespoons freshly squeezed lemon juice, plus more if needed

2 cloves garlic, peeled and minced

1½ teaspoons sea salt or kosher salt, plus more if needed

½ teaspoon smoked paprika or smoked chile powder, plus more for serving

Freshly ground black pepper

2 tablespoons chopped fresh mint, flat-leaf parsley, cilantro, or basil

Ice is Nice

CURIOUSLY, AMERICANS SEEM TO ENJOY THE foods of Provence more than Parisians do. Perhaps it is because Provence offers rugged beauty, quirky customs (described in a number of best-selling books, in English), a temperate climate, and most importantly, freestyle dining with foods that appeal to us, seasoned with the lusty flavors of olive oil, thyme, and lots of garlic. The anchovy thing still eludes a number of people, but not me. I love them, especially the beautiful little fillets from Collioure by the Mediterranean. I get irked when people tell me that I *have* to try something, even though I know I already don't like it, but I'll just put the information out there that these anchovies will change the way you think about them, and leave it at that.

Rosé wine is another thing that took some people a while to love, both in Paris and elsewhere. (I am an anomaly because I took to it right away.) But during the time I've lived in France, sales of rosé have surpassed white wine in the country. Although some of the credit for that belongs to the people in Provence who serve it in big pitchers and carafes filled with ice, I'll take credit for doing my part in Paris.

However, when I drop cubes of ice in my rosé in Paris, I get looks of disbelief, as if people want to say, "How dare he defile wine?" But as my friend Rosa Jackson, who lives in Nice, says, "Rosé isn't considered wine down here. It's a drink." (Elsewhere in France, iced drinks are considered to be responsible for a host of maladies, including something called *ventre congéle*, or "frozen stomach.") In spite of the risks, it goes perfectly with the Provençal snacks, like *pissaladière*, a thin tart smeared with long-cooked onions, thyme, anchovies, and, of course, a good dose of garlic.

Since I seem to have a knack for cultivating disapproving looks, I serve *pissaladière* with iced rosé as an appetizer and can see Parisians' apprehension about both a tart loaded with garlic and onions and iced rosé, which requires some convincing. I say that that's how it's served in rough-and-tumble Marseilles, which seems to put a bit of a scare into them. But all approve when they take their first skeptical bite of the tart. The ice part? Well, let's just say that it still gets a chilly reception . . . and leave it at that.

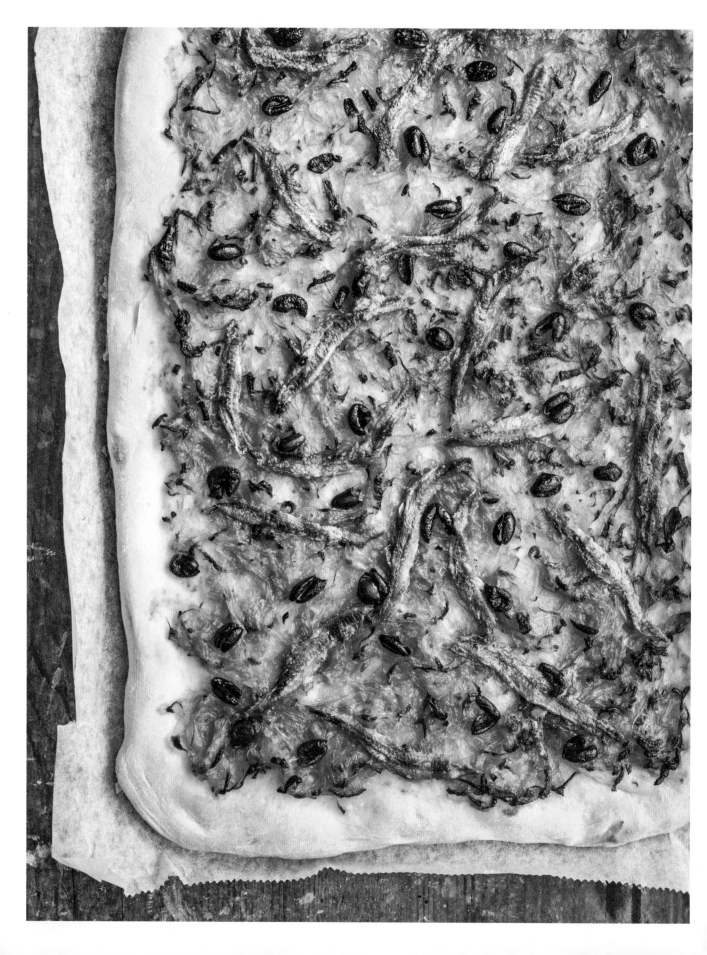

Onion tart

PISSALADIÈRE

Serves 8 to 10

Pissaladière should be crisp and very thin, not thick and bready. Full-flavored onions are strewn over the top along with strips of anchovies and Niçoise olives, which are worth tracking down. If you can't find them, another oily French olive will do, or even chopped kalamatas—although don't tell the people in Provence that you are using Greek olives on their beloved onion tart. They probably also don't want to know that most of the Niçoise olives are now cultivated in Spain, either. The French don't normally pit olives, and indeed, pitting tiny Niçoise olives can make them dry out during baking. So feel free to leave them whole—and alert unsuspecting guests to watch out for pits (and ice, if you serve this with iced rosé, as you should).

CRUST

¾ cup (180ml) tepid water

1 teaspoon active dry yeast

2 cups (280g) all-purpose flour

3 tablespoons olive oil

1 teaspoon sea salt or kosher salt

TOPPING

4 tablespoons (60ml) olive oil, plus more if needed

3 pounds (1.25kg) onions, peeled and thinly sliced

10 sprigs thyme

4 cloves garlic, peeled and thinly sliced

½ teaspoon sea salt or kosher salt

½ teaspoon granulated sugar

Freshly ground black pepper

30 Niçoise olives, or 20 larger olives, pitted or unpitted

16 good-quality oil-packed anchovy fillets

1 To make the crust, in the bowl of a stand mixer fitted with the dough hook (or in a large bowl, by hand), combine the water, yeast, and ½ cup (70g) of the flour. Let stand 15 minutes, until little bubbles appear on the surface.

2 Stir in the remaining 1½ cups (210g) of flour, the olive oil, and the salt. Knead on medium speed for 5 minutes, until the dough is a smooth ball. Oil a bowl, drop in the dough, and turn it so the oiled side is up. Drape a kitchen towel over the top and let the dough rise in a warm place for about an hour, or until the dough has doubled in volume.

3 Meanwhile, make the topping by heating 3 tablespoons of the olive oil in a large skillet or Dutch oven over medium heat. Add the onions, thyme, garlic, salt, and sugar. Cook, stirring infrequently during the first half hour, then, as the onions cook down, stir more often, until the onions are deep golden-brown, about 1 hour. (If they start to burn on the bottom, add more olive oil.) Stir in a few grinds of pepper and remove from the heat. Once cool, pluck out the thyme.

continued

4   To assemble and bake the *pissaladière*, preheat the oven to 400°F (200°C) and line a (13 by 18-inch/33 by 45cm) baking sheet with parchment paper.

5   Turn the dough out onto a lightly floured surface and stretch the dough with your hands into an oval about 12 inches (30cm) long. Let rest for 15 minutes.

6   Transfer the dough to the baking sheet. Pull the dough with your hands until it reaches the sides of the pan. Spread the caramelized onions over the dough, leaving a very narrow rim around the edges. Dot with the olives, lay the anchovies over the top either haphazardly or in a decorative crisscross pattern, and drizzle with the remaining 1 tablespoon of olive oil. Bake for 20 minutes, until the crust is lightly browned. Remove from the oven and slide the tart off the baking sheet and parchment paper onto a cooling rack. Brush a little olive oil over the crust and cut into squares or rectangles. Serve warm or at room temperature with glasses of rosé, iced, of course.

70

Fish Sticks and les Nuggets

I CAN'T SAY I'VE ACTUALLY EATEN A MEAL IN A French elementary school, though every so often there seems to be a story on American television showing the delicacies that discerning French toddlers enjoy, such as sea snails and *les poissons panés*. Those of you with kids are probably amazed French kids will eat sea snails, or *bulots*, although I think fish sticks *(poissons panés)* are, indeed, universally loved by kids everywhere. Especially if they're served with tartar sauce.

How do I know when these programs are aired? Because I get messages and links from people elsewhere, mesmerized that French kids enjoy such grand repasts every day in their school cafeterias. But when I ask my French friends how the food was in their schools, their faces start contorting into sour expressions, and I realize that I had brought back a particularly unpleasant memory when one recounted how he had been forced to eat cow's tongue served in gloppy, thick tomato sauce, which I don't think sounds very good to Americans, young or old.

I didn't grow up in France, but we had pretty good lunches back in New England, from what I remember, which (fortunately) never included tongue. But we did have a lot of seafood, including codfish puffs—light balls of local cod, fried crisp and served with tartar sauce. I remember standing in the queue at the cafeteria, seeing them down the line, and almost not being able to wait until it was my turn to grab a dish off the warmed stainless-steel shelf and put it onto my lunch tray, which I held onto tightly until I got to the table, lest any roll off.

When I discovered *brandade de morue* (page 144), a French dish made of gratinéed creamed salt cod puree, it brought back tasty memories of those codfish puffs, which are sold in Paris by vendors from the Antilles, although I prefer the *accras de morue* I make at home, which taste a lot better than any sold at the market stands.

Fortunately, things may be looking up for the students in Paris. When I pass a school, I check out the lunch menus they post outside, which now feature organic fruits, fresh vegetable salads, French cheeses . . . and, well, *un poulet pané* (chicken nugget) every now and then, because kids will be kids, no matter where they live.

Salt cod fritters with tartar sauce

ACCRAS DE MORUE À LA SAUCE TARTARE

Makes 18 fritters

Les accras are a popular snack during *les happy hours* at cafés, where Parisians gather after work to unwind over glasses of wine or beer and perhaps a little bite to eat. They also make a nice lunch with a green salad. Note that the filling can be molten-hot, even if the shells don't feel that way. I recommend advising guests to be careful when eating them.

SALT COD BALLS

1/2 recipe brandade de morue (page 144), about 2 cups (370g)

1/4 cup (30g) bread crumbs, fresh or dried

TARTAR SAUCE

3/4 cup (180g) mayonnaise, homemade (page 331) or store-bought

2 tablespoons chopped cornichons

2 tablespoons minced shallots

1 1/2 tablespoons capers, rinsed, squeezed dry, and chopped

1 tablespoon finely chopped fresh flat-leaf parsley

1 teaspoon freshly squeezed lemon juice or white wine vinegar, plus more if needed

Sea salt or kosher salt and freshly ground black pepper

Pinch of granulated sugar

FRITTER BATTER

1/2 cup (70g) all-purpose flour

3 tablespoons (25g) cornstarch

2 teaspoons baking powder (preferably aluminum-free)

3/4 teaspoon sea salt or kosher salt

1/2 teaspoon freshly ground black pepper

1/2 teaspoon cayenne pepper

3/4 cup (180ml) beer

1 tablespoon finely chopped fresh flat-leaf parsley

1 tablespoon finely chopped fresh cilantro or chives

1 To make the salt cod balls, mix the brandade with the bread crumbs, then roll the mixture into tight balls about 1 inch (3cm) in diameter. Chill until firm, at least 1 hour. (They can rest in the refrigerator for up 24 hours.)

2 To make the tartar sauce, mix all the ingredients together. Taste and add more salt, pepper, and lemon juice, if desired.

3 About 30 minutes before you plan to fry the fritters, make the batter by mixing the flour, cornstarch, baking powder, salt, pepper, and cayenne pepper in a bowl. Stir in the beer, parsley, and cilantro. Stir just until there are no large lumps of batter remaining, but don't overmix (small lumps are fine). Cover and let sit at room temperature for 30 minutes.

4 Attach a deep-fry/candy thermometer to the side of a large, heavy-duty pot or saucepan and add peanut oil to a depth of 3 inches (8cm). Heat the oil to 365°F (185°C). Line a dinner plate with a few layers of paper towels.

5 When the oil is hot, working with about six salt cod balls at a time (or whatever you think your pot will hold without crowding), remove the quantity you'll be frying for the first batch from the refrigerator. Dip each ball in the batter and roll it around gently to coat. (They don't need to look perfect, and working quickly trumps perfection.) After you dip each one, drop it into the hot oil.

6 Fry the fritters for 2 to 3 minutes, turning them frequently so they brown evenly. Once well browned all over, use a slotted spoon or mesh strainer to transfer the fritters to the paper towel–lined plate to drain. Replenish the fryer oil, as needed, waiting for it to heat up before you fry more fritters.

7 Serve the fritters with the tartar sauce for dipping.

Spiced meatballs with Sriracha sauce

BOULETTES DE MERGUEZ À LA SAUCE SRIRACHA

Makes 20 meatballs

Over a decade ago, a friend said, "You are not Parisian until you've have a merguez sandwich, stuffed with sausage and *frites*, at 3 a.m. . . . eaten on the sidewalk." Well, more than ten years have passed, and I haven't had this late-night experience, which may explain the ten-year (and counting) holdup on my residence card. But I have had plenty of merguez.

Because of the large influx of North Africans in Paris, there are lots of couscous shops and sidewalk stands in the various neighborhoods, serving grilled meat wrapped in warm pita bread. You'll also find such variations on those sandwiches as *l'américain*, filled with grilled meat and stuffed with fries (which I've never seen in America) or one I saw being served over in the Latin Quarter, topped with a tangle of unsauced spaghetti (which I kind of wish I hadn't seen).

One thing that North African restaurants and sidewalk stands share are merguez sausages, which are a fiery red color that should be taken as a warning that those sausage links are going to pack a little bit—or quite a bit—of spice. I love them, and to me, it isn't a proper couscous unless there are a few merguez sausages languishing alongside roasted lamb and lamb brochettes, and a bowl of harissa (page 330) on the side to liven things up.

I like merguez so much that I came up with a way to make them at home, where I serve them as an appetizer. They're normally made in the traditional elongated sausage shape, but when hand rolled, they bear an unfortunate resemblance to something else found on the sidewalks of Paris. So I form them into *boulettes*, or meatballs, which are very easy to assemble and can be cooked at the last minute and served with a dipping sauce.

Sriracha sauce has become almost de rigueur on American tables, and we will squirt it on anything. In Paris, I keep a bottle on hand because my French partner became addicted to the stuff, too, in spite of his patriotic reluctance to consume anything *trop piquante*. But the French seem just as helpless against the power of the rooster, which festoons the plastic bottle of hot sauce. And since *le chanteclair* is the unofficial mascot of France, perhaps that has something to do with its appeal?

Merguez can be made with either ground beef or lamb, and it's important to use meat that isn't too lean, or your merguez will be dry. Sumac is an intriguing seasoning that adds a fruity tang and gives merguez an exotic little lift, although it can be omitted.

I've included two of my favorite dipping sauces. One is a simple mayonnaise mixed with Sriracha hot sauce (you can also use harissa, page 330), and the other (see variation below) is a blend of tangy yogurt mixed with tahini and fresh garlic. You can serve one or the other, or both.

MERGUEZ MEATBALLS

1½ teaspoons fennel seeds

1 teaspoon coriander seeds

1 teaspoon cumin seeds

2 tablespoons minced cilantro leaves

3 cloves garlic, peeled and minced

2 teaspoons sweet paprika

2 teaspoons harissa (page 330), Sriracha, or Asian chile paste

1½ teaspoons sea salt or kosher salt

¼ teaspoon ground cinnamon

¼ teaspoon ground allspice

½ teaspoon ground sumac (optional)

1 pound (450g) ground beef or lamb (not lean), or a mix of the two

SRIRACHA MAYONNAISE

¾ cup (180g) mayonnaise, homemade (page 331) or store-bought

1 tablespoon Sriracha sauce or harissa (page 330), or to taste

1 To make the meatballs, in a hot skillet, toast the fennel, coriander, and cumin seeds for a minute or so, until they smell fragrant. Remove from the heat and let cool, then grind to a powder in a spice mill or mortar and pestle, or crush in a sturdy plastic bag with a hammer.

2 Combine the crushed spices in a bowl with the cilantro, garlic, paprika, harissa, salt, cinnamon, allspice, and sumac. Add the ground beef and mix well. (The meatball mixture can be refrigerated for up to 3 days before rolling and using.)

3 Pinch off pieces of the sausage mixture and roll them into meatballs the size of unshelled walnuts. Heat a tablespoon of olive oil in a large skillet, preferably nonstick, over medium-high heat. Add the meatballs and fry for 8 to 10 minutes, shaking the pan to cook them evenly. (They may need a bit more oil if you aren't using a nonstick skillet.) If you have a grill, you can cook them over a fire as well, or they can be baked on a greased baking sheet in a 350°F/180°C oven for 12 to 15 minutes.

4 To make the Sriracha mayonnaise, combine the mayonnaise and the Sriracha in a small bowl. (The mayonnaise can be made up to 3 days ahead and refrigerated.)

5 Serve the meatballs warm with the Sriracha mayonnaise.

VARIATION: You can also make a cooling yogurt-tahini sauce to serve with the meatballs. Mix ½ cup (120g) of plain whole-milk yogurt, ¼ cup (60g) of tahini (sesame seed paste), 2 teaspoons of minced garlic, 2 teaspoons of finely chopped fresh flat-leaf parsley, 4 teaspoons of freshly squeezed lemon juice, 1½ teaspoons of water, and ½ teaspoon of sea salt or kosher salt until well blended. Taste and add additional seasonings, if desired.

THE BATTLE OF
THE BEURRES

———————

For years, we've all been told to use unsalted butter for cooking, especially baking. And for years, that's what I did, and even preached. But after living in France, where the salted butter comes with *cristaux* of crunchy sea salt embedded in the golden-yellow bars and is so good you can't believe it's just butter, I've become a convert to *le beurre salé*.

I wasn't the first to hop on the salted butter bandwagon. Pastry chef Pierre Hermé's rich chocolate Korova cookies are flecked with shiny bits of fleur de sel, hand-harvested salt from the Atlantic coast. But Henri Le Roux, a confectioner from Brittany who finally opened shops in Paris, uses salted butter in his C.B.S. (*caramel-beurre-salé*) caramels and was the one to define the genre that was to take over the country—and the world. Nowadays, if you scan any dessert menu in Paris, you will invariably find at least one item with the words *caramel-beurre-salé* on the menu, whether it is a sauce, a soufflé, or an ice cream.

My spiral toward saltiness started with me buying salted butter for my morning toast. But there's only so much butter one can eat in the morning. And since I always had a big block on hand, well, why not use it for cooking?

Its flavor is more assertive, especially in baking, and I like getting caught by surprise by little sparks of salt in something, especially caramel or chocolate, where it provides a little contrast and enhances the taste of the other ingredients.

If you buy regular salted butter, it's likely that the salt has been dissolved so that it's not so obvious, but there is a discernable flavor difference you'll probably start to appreciate if you use it often. Salted butter just tastes more, well, buttery to me. Since we naturally have salt in our mouths, eating something with salt is less of a jolt, and goes down easier.

In the old days, salt was said to be added to butter to disguise off flavors, hence the previously held wisdom that unsalted butter was better. But in my experience buying butter (and believe me, I have a lot of experience with that), I've found both salted and unsalted butter to be of equal freshness. Regardless of where you live, next time you cook or bake something, try swapping out unsalted butter for salted. I use them interchangeably, and even the Land O'Lakes butter website says don't worry about compensating for the additional salt in a recipe. So we're both in good company.

LE BEURRE BORDIER
Esprit de Beurre
Beurre de Baratte aux Algues

LE BEURRE BORDIER
Esprit de Beurre
Beurre de Baratte aux Algues

LE BEURRE BORDIER
Esprit de Beurre
Beurre de Baratte Demi-Sel

LE BEURRE BORDIER

LE BEURRE BORDIER
Esprit de Beurre
Beurre de Baratte au Piment d'Espelette

LE BEURRE BORDIER

Sardine spread

RILLETTES DE SARDINES

Serves 6 to 8

One thing about French doctors is their thoroughness, how they leave no question unanswered. Or unasked. Unlike in America where they try to get you in and out as fast as possible, my doctor in Paris spends a lot of time with me, no matter how many people are in her waiting room, asking me everything from a good recipe for *le cheesecake* to which sexual positions I prefer.

My last medical test revealed everything was okay, and my doctor nodded with approval, which was a relief since she had a call-in show on the radio for a number of years giving advice about sex. That is, until she got to the vitamin D levels—she scowled and shook her head back and forth, saying, "We need to do something about this."

She recommended I spend more time in the sun with my face and arms exposed. When I reminded her that Paris is gray and overcast most of the year, she agreed and prescribed tiny glass vials of vitamin D. So I went to the pharmacy to pick them up and mentioned the deficiency to the pharmarcist (I spared him details of the rest of my office visit). He said that everyone—*toutes les personnes*—in Paris had a vitamin D deficiency. So all those Parisians that you see strolling along the Seine aren't doing it to take in the fabulous scenery, or scope out make-out spots, they're enriching their stockpile of vitamin D.

Because I'm an indoor kinda guy (for a number of activities), I've started eating a lot more small fish, namely mackerel and sardines, both of which are high in vitamin D. Fresh sardines are readily available at the fish markets, but the canned ones make very good rillettes, and using them, you can prepare this in less than 10 minutes.

Traditionally, spreads like this in France are made with butter. But I was having dinner at West Country Girl *crêperie*, and the owner brought out a ramekin of house-made sardine rillettes. I smeared a bit on the end of a baguette, and it tasted different from others, yet there was something familiar in it. She was surprised I detected her secret, which was cream cheese. I liked it so much that in this spread I now use both butter and *la fromage à tartiner*— or as they say in French, *le Philadelphia*.

¼ cup (110g) cream cheese, regular or low-fat, at room temperature

3 tablespoons salted or unsalted butter, at room temperature

2 (3¾-ounce/115g) cans sardines

2 scallions, white and tender green parts, minced

1 tablespoon capers, rinsed, squeezed dry, and chopped

1 tablespoon freshly squeezed lime or lemon juice

¾ teaspoon sea salt or kosher salt

Freshly ground black pepper

⅛ teaspoon cayenne pepper

Crackers, baguette, thin-sliced toasted country or rye bread, to serve

1   Mash together the cream cheese and butter with a fork until smooth. Drain the sardines. Run your thumb lengthwise down the bottom of each (there is usually an open seam there) and pluck out the bones. Add the filleted sardines to the cream cheese mixture, mashing them to combine.

2   Add the scallions to the sardine mixture along with the capers, lime juice, salt, a few grinds of black pepper, and the cayenne pepper. Taste and add more salt or citrus juice, if desired.

3   The rillettes can be refrigerated for up to 4 days. Let come to room temperature before serving with crackers, a baguette, or thin slices of toasted country bread.

Pounding My Pestle (and Mortar)

WHEN SETTING UP MY FIRST KITCHEN IN Paris, I went looking for a mortar and pestle. In friends' kitchens, I had seen beautifully aged ones from Provence made of heavy marble with massive wooden pestles lolling inside—and I wanted one. Yet during my shopping quests I kept forgetting the two words in French for them. So, as I usually did, I would resort to making gestures with my hands, which led a lot of people to initially think I was Italian. It wasn't until one saleswoman looked at me in horror as I stood in front of her pumping an imaginary cylindrical object up and down in a rapid motion, that I realized *mortier* and *pilon* were two words that should become a priority in expanding my French vocabulary.

It seems I was not the only one interested in finding a mortar and pestle in France. Whenever I happened to chance across one at a flea market, my initial excitement was tempered by the staggering €250 (about $325 at present) price tag. So as a stopgap measure, and to prevent me from terrifying any more saleswomen, I bought a massive Thai mortar and pestle in Chinatown for less than €20. (When I lugged it home on the métro, which almost made my arm drop off, my neighbor said, "Why didn't you get me one, too?")

I most frequently use my *mortier* and *pilon* to grind spices. And there are certainly wonderful spice markets in Paris. The first time I went into Goumanyat, an *épicerie* that specializes in first-rate spices as well as saffron, I thought my head was going to explode from all the scents. There are the Arab markets in Belleville and the Indian and Sri Lankan shops behind the Gare du Nord; I could spend days poking around their shelves, invariably coming home with some odd vegetable that I bought for no other reason than I'd never seen a four-foot, green leafy root. (Which did help me get a spot on the crowded bus, so it's probably a good idea to learn the word for that, too, as I will be buying those more often.) I also buy my nuts in those shops because in the supermarkets, nuts are usually sold in packages of twelve (as in twelve whole hazelnuts), and I would quickly go to the *maison des pauvres* if I had to buy all the pounds of nuts I use in those tiny packets.

I use some of those nuts to make dukkah, a deliriously spicy mixture that is Egyptian in origin. The name *dukkah* (or *duqqa*) derives from the Arabic "to pound," which is another word that's probably good to know so I can avoid any more misunderstandings in case I move to Egypt.

You can easily vary the blend by replacing the hazelnuts with almonds or peanuts, or dialing the spices up or down. Many recipes have an overload of cumin seeds and so forth, which to me, completely obliterates the nuts. So mine is a bit nuttier than others.

Now that I'm armed with a mortar and pestle, and a few jars of nuts and spices, I can reliably keep myself stocked with dukkah, which is a great base for the world's fastest-to-make dip. You can instantly create a paste by mixing some dukkah with olive oil. I serve it with slices of seeded baguette or fresh pita bread, or a variety of raw vegetables cut into sticks for dipping.

Egyptian spiced nut mix

DUKKAH

Makes 1¹/₂ cups (150g)

Toasting the spices brings out their aromas, and nothing will fill your kitchen with the aromas of the Middle East more than pounding out a batch of dukkah. Each spice needs to be toasted separately because the coriander seeds will take longer than the others and you don't want to burn the spices, which can make them bitter. But it's very easy to do them, one right after the other, in a hot skillet.

The ingredients for dukkah can be ground in a mortar and pestle, in a spice grinder, or a mini food processor. Don't overdo it because you don't want the ingredients too fine; they should not be a powder, but rather stubbly, like the consistency of very coarse cornmeal. You should be able to see little nubbins of nuts in the finished dukkah.

¹/₂ cup (50g) hazelnuts

¹/₃ cup (50g) sesame seeds

¹/₄ cup (35g) hulled pumpkin seeds

2 tablespoons whole coriander seeds

1 teaspoon cumin seeds

1 teaspoon fennel seeds

1¹/₂ teaspoons black peppercorns

1 teaspoon sea salt or kosher salt

1   Preheat the oven to 350°F (180°C).

2   Spread the hazelnuts on a baking sheet and toast them for 8 to 10 minutes, until the nuts are lightly browned and most of the skins are loosened. Remove from the oven. When the nuts are cool enough to handle, rub them briskly in a kitchen towel to remove as much of the skins as possible. Put the nuts into a bowl.

3   Heat a skillet on the stovetop over medium heat. Start with the sesame seeds, spreading them in an even layer in the pan and shaking or stirring them frequently, until they crackle and become lightly browned. Scrape them into the bowl with the hazelnuts. Then toast the pumpkin seeds, then the coriander, the cumin, and finally the fennel seeds in the same way, adding each to the bowl as it is done. Finally, toast the peppercorns. Most will take less than a minute. Add the salt.

4   Grind the nuts, seeds, and spices in a mortar and pestle, with a spice grinder, or in the bowl of a mini food processor, working in batches if necessary, until the mixture is well ground together, but not too fine. Dukkah will keep for about a month stored in an airtight jar at room temperature.

VARIATIONS: Use toasted almonds, peanuts, or cashews in place of the hazelnuts. Make a quick dip by stirring together ³/₄ cup (75g) of dukkah with 6 tablespoons (90ml) of olive oil in a small bowl.

81

CE SOIR

DORADE ROYALE 16€
ET SES TROIS RIZ.

- Os A MOELLE. 9€
- CEVICHE DE HADDOK 16€
  ET DE SAUMON.
- CUISSES DE GRENOUILLES. 12€

- TRAVERS DE PORC. 15,5€
- CARPACCIO DE BOEUF. 14€
- CÔTE DE BOEUF. 4,9€/100g

First courses

ENTRÉES

IN SPITE OF THE VARIOUS CHANGES THAT HAVE TAKEN PLACE IN French cuisine over the last few decades, the French still eat meals in courses. Pass even the most casual café or corner restaurant and invariably, there's a multicourse *formule* or *menu* posted outside.

(On a side note, once inside, many visitors get blank looks from waiters by asking if they can see the *menu*, which is another word for the *formule* written on a chalkboard; *la carte* is the actual menu the waiter hands diners at the table.)

Unlike the little bites served at *l'heure de l'apéro*, which are meant to be enjoyed gathered around the coffee table or nibbled on while standing, first courses are always served *à table*. They can range from a *salade composé* (composed salad) to whatever might be the *soup du jour* to a *salade de crudités* (raw vegetable salad) or even a slab of meaty terrine with a crock of cornichons alongside to cut the richness. But there is rarely a leafy salad served at the beginning of a meal. In France, *les salades vertes* are reserved for the end of the meal, either by themselves or served with the cheese course.

Heartier fare is still warmly welcomed on menus, and such enduring French classics as *œufs mayo* (page 103) and *poireaux vinaigrette* (page 88) resolutely refuse to budge from the tables of traditional cafés and bistros. The only concession to modern tastes seems to be *tartare de saumon* (raw cubed salmon), which has been grudgingly given a spot on menus for diners worried about *la ligne* (their shape).

The first course, called the *entrée* in French, is meant to provide an "entrance" to the meal. I'm not sure why Americans have adopted it as the word we use for our main course; perhaps because we're known for our generous eating habits, and we want to leave room open for the possibility of another course after that?

When faced with a multicourse menu in a restaurant, or at home, the main consideration is that you make balanced choices. You wouldn't present someone with a slice of meaty terrine, then follow that with a hearty bowl of beef stew. And only the most dedicated fish-lover would be able to follow a warm herring and potato salad with *brandade de morue* (page 144). Or someone not worried about his—or her—image. (There was discussion in the media when a woman running for president of France ordered fish in a restaurant rather than the meat, which seemed to cast some suspicion on her abilities. A few months later, a magazine published photos of her in a two-piece swimsuit with a pretty svelte *ligne*. She lost the election; however, in the next round, her ex—whose shape prompted comparisons to a jiggly French custard—went on to become president.)

When I worked in restaurants, one thing I never understood was diners finding fault with a place because they left not feeling completely stuffed. When I leave the table in France, even after a meal that's gone on for more than three courses, I never feel like I've overeaten. Meals are moderated; by the end you should feel like you've had just the right quantity of food.

Multicourse meals aren't about overdoing it. They allow you to choose what to serve for each course to create balance—of texture as well as different flavors—and to prolong one of life's great pleasures: sitting together at the table with friends or family, sharing a bottle of wine, and partaking in good food, whether it's in a café, a restaurant, or at home.

Raw vegetable slaw with creamy garlic dressing 96
SALADE DE CRUDITÉS RAPÉES, SAUCE CRÉMEUSE À L'AIL

Winter salad 98
SALADE D'HIVER

Frisée salad with bacon, egg, and garlic toasts 99
SALADE LYONNAISE

Hard-cooked eggs with chervil mayonnaise 103
ŒUFS MAYO

Celery root salad with mustard sauce 105
CÉLERI RÉMOULADE

Celery root soup with horseradish cream and ham chips 106
SOUPE DE CÉLERI-RAVE À LA CRÈME DE RAIFORT ET CHIPS DE JAMBON

Cherry tomato crostini with homemade herbed goat cheese 110
TARTINES DE TOMATES CERISES, CHÈVRE FRAIS MAISON AUX HERBES

Duck terrine with figs 113
TERRINE DE CANARD AUX FIGUES

Fattoush 116
FATTOUCHE

French onion soup 118
SOUPE À L'OIGNON

Gazpacho with herbed goat cheese toasts 121
GASPACHO, CROÛTONS AU CHÈVRE AUX HERBES

Grated carrot salad 123
CAROTTES RAPÉES

My Leek Lesson

ONE THING THE FRENCH ARE PRETTY FIRM about is not messing with classics. Part of it is their deep attachment to their history and culture. Another is that "thinking outside the box" isn't encouraged. When I met my partner, Romain, one of the things that struck me was how different he was from other Parisians; he smiled and laughed easily and was optimistic and engaged with people around him. He was also uncharacteristically open to new ideas, although I later found out that that didn't necessarily extend to leeks.

One day he decided to make leeks vinaigrette for me and while he prepared the leeks, I got to work on the sauce—under his guidance. As he cleaned and steamed, I chopped and stirred. All was going fine, until I started to cut up some bacon, which I thought would be good with the mustardy dressing I was mixing up.

His brow furrowed. *"C'est pourquoi, Daveed?"* ("What's that for?") he asked, sternly. And when I explained how good the bacon would be with the leeks and the chopped eggs, *"Ah—bon?"* he replied, with that special French way that they can convey two contradictory thoughts in a short phrase, meaning that he was willing to try it, but he actually didn't want to.

He softened his position when he tasted it. But when I suggested a dusting of crunchy bread crumbs to finish the dish, he knew he had to draw the line somewhere. A scattering of bread over the top was . . . well, just a little too much over the top, of both the salad and of his patience with my messing with a classic.

Leeks with mustard-bacon vinaigrette

POIREAUX VINAIGRETTE À LA MOUTARDE ET AUX LARDONS

Serves 4 to 6

Traditionally the leeks were cooked in a big pot of boiling water. However, it's better to steam them, which prevents them from getting waterlogged. Smaller leeks, which appear in the springtime in Paris markets, are preferable for this dish because they're quite tender, although larger leeks are just fine, too. Just make sure that you clean the leeks very well (see page 30), and cook them until they're completely soft all the way through.

When Romain and I made this together and we plated up the leeks, I got an unexpected lesson in the art of arranging the *poireaux*: I learned that it's imperative you lay them with the *queue* (tail) alternating with the *tête* (head). So I recommend you follow those instructions, if you want don't want to raise any Parisian eyebrows.

1 To make the vinaigrette, cook the bacon over medium heat in a skillet until nearly crisp. Transfer the bacon to a paper towel to drain. When cool, chop the bacon into pieces about the size of tiny peas.

2 Whisk together the vinegar, mustard, and salt. Whisk in the oils, 1 tablespoon at a time (the sauce may emulsify, which is fine), then stir in 1 tablespoon of the parsley and two-thirds of the bacon. Set aside.

3 To prepare the leeks, fill a large pot fitted with a steamer with a couple of inches of water. Bring it to a boil over high heat and add the leeks. Cook the leeks until tender; when you poke them with a sharp paring knife, it should meet no resistance at the root ends. (Smaller leeks will take about 15 minutes, and larger ones will take about 30 minutes.)

4 Remove the leeks and let drain and cool on a plate lined with paper towels. Cut the leeks in half crosswise, and arrange on a serving platter, alternating them head to tail.

5 Peel and dice the hard-cooked eggs and scatter them over the leeks. Pour the vinaigrette over the leeks and toss them and the pieces of egg in the dressing so they're thoroughly coated, then scatter over the remaining bacon pieces and parsley.

BACON VINAIGRETTE

2 cups (200g) thick-cut smoked bacon cut into lardons (see page 15)

1 tablespoon sherry vinegar or red wine vinegar

1 tablespoon Dijon mustard

1/2 teaspoon sea salt or kosher salt

3 tablespoons neutral-tasting vegetable oil

2 tablespoons olive oil

2 tablespoons chopped fresh flat-leaf parsley

5 large or 10 small leeks, cleaned (see headnote)

2 hard-cooked eggs (page 328)

D'où?

THE INITIAL QUESTION ASKED WHEN YOU meet a French person is always, *"Vous-êtes d'où?"* or "Where are you from?" In America, the first question is, "What do you do?" This is considered impolite in France, partly because it's associated with something as distasteful as earning money.

Because the French are deeply attached to their particular regions, and people tend to get categorized by the traits (or foods) their *département* is known for, there's a certain amount of stereotyping that goes on. (I once saw an Australian passing through customs at the airport, and when he handed over his passport, the strict-looking guard immediately switched his expression to a goofy grin and started hopping up-and-down in his chair with his hands flopped up in front of his chest, like a kangaroo.) I've met my fair share of people letting me know how much they know about America and Americans, including details about our eating habits, even though they don't actually know any Americans nor have they ever been there.

Just like people are defined by their provenance in France, so is citrus, which takes on extra importance in Paris. Lemons with their leaves attached might be from Sicily or Menton, in the south of France. Oranges arrive from Malta or Morocco, and there is palpable excitement at the market when shiny little clementines from Corsica start tumbling into the stands. Giant billboards in the métro station promote Florida grapefruits, which I had always taken for granted until I saw them holding their own among the ads for luxury Swiss watches and designer suits from the Galeries Lafayette.

When I worked in California, way back in the early 1980s, I remember feeling that each piece of citrus deserved special status, especially when I was slicing open blood oranges flown in from Italy (well before the term "locavore" was coined), each one was more beautiful than the one I had cut open before. When I served them on salads, astonished guests would come over to ask how I got the orange segments to have that deep, ruby red color. Blood oranges are so common in France now that *jus d'orange sanguine* is available alongside the cartons of regular *jus d'orange* in supermarkets, but they're being grown in America now as well, so you can use your carbon credits for something else.

Using blood oranges in salads, especially in the winter, livens things up with their tart flavors, which hold their own next to bolder elements like fennel, crabmeat, and radishes. Instead of giving each person his own individual salad, I've been know to make a large *salade composée* on a big platter and let guests help themselves, because that's what we Americans tend to do. Or so I'm told.

Fennel, radish, orange, and crab salad

SALADE DE FENOUIL, RADIS, ORANGE, ET CRABE

Serves 4

This salad makes good use of such sturdy winter leaves as radicchio, Belgian endive, and watercress. If you wish, you can substitute peeled cooked shrimp or crayfish for the crabmeat. You can make this as four individual salads or arrange it on a large platter.

1 Mix together the vinegar, lemon juice, and salt in a bowl. Stir in the olive oil until well combined. Toss the crabmeat and parsley in the dressing, season with a few generous grinds of the peppermill, and set aside.

2 Trim the fronds off the fennel bulb and remove any tough outer layers. Cut the fennel bulb in half lengthwise and cut out the core. Slice the fennel as thinly as you possibly can, or shave it with a mandoline.

3 Cut the stem and opposite ends off the oranges. Place each orange, cut-side down, on a cutting board. With a sharp paring or serrated knife, cut away the peel, using downward motions that match the curvature of the fruit. Slice out *suprêmes* (sections) of the oranges, leaving the membranes behind.

4 Arrange the salad leaves on four large plates (or a large serving platter). Scatter the shaved fennel over the salad leaves and tuck the orange segments and radishes in between the fennel and the salad leaves.

5 Distribute the crabmeat and parsley over the salads, spoon the remaining dressing over the tops, sprinkle with flaky sea salt, and serve.

2 teaspoons white wine vinegar

4 teaspoons freshly squeezed lemon juice

3/4 teaspoon sea salt or kosher salt

6 tablespoons (90ml) mild-tasting olive oil

8 ounces (230g) lump crabmeat

1 cup (10g) fresh flat-leaf parsley leaves

Freshly ground black pepper

1 fennel bulb

2 navel or blood oranges

6 cups (230g) torn or sliced radicchio or Belgian endive, or picked watercress sprigs (100g)

10 radishes, thinly sliced

Flaky sea salt, to finish

Vegetable soup with basil puree

SOUPE AU PISTOU

Serves 6 to 8

As neighbors, Italy and France have had an uneasy relationship. It wasn't until 1860 that Nice became part of France. But the Italians are probably still miffed, which is the only explanation for why they continue to punish us by not bringing their great Italian coffee across the border. Perhaps in retribution, some unfortunate culinary atrocities against Italian cuisine can be found in France, such as pizza baked with canned corn on top and bland risotto that would make an Italian grandmother shove the cook aside to show 'em how it's done. And all year round, there is the continuous presence of *salade Caprese* on café menus, a dish that absolutely depends on having perfect, dead-ripe summer tomatoes to make it work.

Nowadays, aside from my own grudge against some of the unapologetically harsh coffee served in Parisian cafés, the wounds have mostly healed. One remnant that survives, and prospers, is *pistou.* This is the French version of pesto without the nuts, though sometimes melded with tomatoes, which are added to loosen it up and make it easier to disperse into *soupe au pistou.*

Fresh basil is a precious commodity in Paris, even in the summer. My suspicion is that the *Provençaux* don't want to share! Making *pistou* to stir into soup helps extend the limited bounty. People in Provence like to briskly mix the *pistou* into the soup, but I prefer to add a dollop to the center and give it a gentle stir so that you can taste the contrast between the warm soup and the summery flavor of the fresh basil.

To peel the tomato, drop it into a hot pot of water and let it sit for a minute. Remove it with a slotted spoon and run it under cold water, then pull the skin off. If you don't have a mortar and pestle, you can pulse all the ingredients in a blender or food processor. Just be careful not to overdo it because you don't want to make the *pistou* creamy or overly smooth. It should still retain the texture of the basil leaves so that when you stir it into the soup, little bits of leaves are still discernable.

This is a quintessential "recipes are guidelines" soup. There's some dispute, as with many dishes from Provence, about what vegetables go into *soupe au pistou*, but you should use what is available in your area and what's in season. I've made versions with everything from sliced green beans and diced tomatoes to cubes of pumpkin and (fresh) corn kernels. The only nonvariable? Plenty of *pistou* to pass around.

BEANS

1 cup (200g) dried beans, such as Great Northern or Borlotti

2 bay leaves

3 quarts (3l) water, plus more if needed

PISTOU

1 large clove garlic, peeled

1/2 teaspoon sea salt or kosher salt

4 cups packed (100g) fresh basil leaves

3 tablespoons (45ml) olive oil

1 small tomato, peeled, seeded, and finely diced

1 cup (3 ounces/90g) freshly grated Parmesan cheese

SOUP

1 onion, peeled and diced

6 cloves garlic, peeled and minced

1 tablespoon sea salt or kosher salt, plus more if needed

2 carrots, peeled and diced

2 zucchini, diced

1 cup (130g) fresh or frozen peas

3/4 cup (80g) very small dried pasta, such as elbows or ditalini

Freshly ground black pepper

Finely grated Emmenthal (or another Swiss-style) cheese, or Parmesan, for garnishing (optional)

1 Rinse the beans and sort for debris. Soak them overnight covered in cold water.

2 To make the *pistou*, pound the garlic to a paste in a mortar and pestle with the salt. Coarsely chop the basil leaves and pound them into the garlic until the mixture is relatively smooth. Drizzle in the olive oil slowly, pounding all the while, then pound in the tomato and Parmesan. If it needs thinning, add a bit more olive oil. The *pistou* can be stored for up to 4 days; pressing a sheet of plastic wrap over the surface will prevent it from discoloring. (The *pistou* can also be made by pulsing the ingredients in a food processor.)

3 Drain the beans and put them in a large pot or Dutch oven with the bay leaves; add the water. Cook the beans for about 1 hour, or until tender, adding more water if necessary to keep them immersed.

4 To make the soup, add the onion, garlic, and salt to the pot of beans and simmer for 10 minutes. Add the carrots and zucchini and continue to simmer for another 10 minutes. Then add the peas and pasta and simmer for another 10 minutes, or until the pasta is tender. Add a generous amount of black pepper and season with additional salt, if necessary.

5 To serve the soup, remove the bay leaves and ladle the hot soup into bowls. Add a generous spoonful of *pistou* to each bowl or pass the bowl for guests to add their own. Keep extra *pistou* within reach, because you'll likely want to add more to the soup as you go. In Provence, people will often have a bowl of finely grated Emmenthal or Parmesan cheese handy, which can also be sprinkled over bowls of the soup. The soup can be stored for up to 5 days in the refrigerator. It will thicken up and can be thinned with additional water.

VARIATION: Instead of *pistou*, add a dab of harissa (page 330) to make a spicy vegetable soup.

Parsley Paradise in Paris

WHAT IS COMMONLY SERVED ELSEWHERE IN the world as tabbouleh bears little resemblance to the tabbouleh that I was served in Lebanon, which was a revelation. Lebanese tabbouleh is *not* a giant heap of soggy bulgur wheat, wet with too much dressing and a few chopped herbs mixed in here and there. It *is* a lively, fresh, verdant salad made with heaps and heaps of fresh parsley and mint leaves, dotted with a few tomatoes and a scattering of cracked wheat to give it a little crunch and texture. In fact, some versions leave the bulgur out completely. Fortunately, at the markets in Paris, flat-leaf parsley and fresh mint are always cheap and abundant and I never go home without at least one bunch of each, but usually more, in my basket.

This tabbouleh was adapted from a recipe by my friend Anissa Helou, a cookbook author who lived in Paris for many years. It has a little bit of allspice and cinnamon in it, meant to replicate a commonly used blend of Lebanese spices whose identity I haven't been able to discern since the only words of English amongst the tangle of words in Arabic on the package she gave me were "mixed spices."

I was making this tabbouleh one day when a Lebanese contractor came over to correct some of the kitchen construction goofs from a less-than-exemplary remodeling experience (which everyone seems to have a story about in Paris, making me feel like I've passed some sort of initiation in becoming Parisian). Mohammed took a break from closing off the pipe that was leaking toxic fumes into my kitchen, looked into the big bowl of chopped herbs and tomatoes I was tossing, and insisted I try adding a little pomegranate molasses to it. So aside from being an ace electrician, carpenter, and my all-around hero for saving my sanity (and probably my life), I have to say he had pretty good instincts about tabbouleh seasoning as well.

Tabbouleh

TABOULÉ

Serves 4 to 6

2 tablespoons fine bulgur wheat

2½ tablespoons warm water

2 tomatoes

10 cups (250g) well-packed fresh flat-leaf parsley leaves and small, upper stems

2 cups (20g) lightly packed fresh mint leaves (no stems)

3 scallions, white and tender green parts, thinly sliced

6 tablespoons (90ml) olive oil

¼ cup (60ml) freshly squeezed lemon juice

1 teaspoon sea salt or kosher salt

¼ teaspoon ground allspice

¼ teaspoon ground cinnamon

Freshly ground black pepper

1 to 2 teaspoons pomegranate molasses (optional)

Romaine lettuce or cabbage leaves, to serve

This tabbouleh takes a lot of chopping, no doubt about it. But let me tell you, the first time I made it I couldn't stop "taste testing" it as I mixed it all up, and had to restrain myself so I'd have enough for my guests.

This tabbouleh is best made within a few hours of serving. There's a lot of parsley here. And although on a recent visit to Lebanon everyone insisted that I should use only the leaves of the parsley, in reality, most everyone that I saw making tabbouleh just chopped up the bunch by holding it down and finely slicing with a chef's knife, leaving only the tough lower stems behind.

If you want to prepare the tabbouleh ingredients in advance, chill the slivered parsley and mint, but don't dress the tabbouleh until just before serving. In Lebanon, tabbouleh is eaten by scooping up the salad using leaves of romaine lettuce—or cabbage, which sounded odd until I tried it.

1   Mix the bulgur and the water in a large salad bowl and set aside to plump.

2   Halve the tomatoes horizontally and squeeze out the liquid and seeds. Dice the tomatoes and set aside to drain in a colander.

3   Chiffonade the parsley and mint leaves by gathering bunches of the herbs in a tight cluster with one hand, and slicing the herbs into thin ribbons with a chef's knife. (Don't run your knife over them repeatedly, which will bruise them and make them bitter.) Add them to the bowl of bulgur along with the scallions and the drained tomatoes.

4   Drizzle the olive oil over the herbs with the lemon juice. Sprinkle with salt, allspice, and cinnamon, along with a few grinds of pepper. Add the pomegranate molasses. Toss well and serve with crisp leaves of romaine lettuce to scoop it up.

Raw vegetable slaw with creamy garlic dressing

SALADE DE CRUDITÉS RAPÉES, SAUCE CRÉMEUSE À L'AIL

Serves 4 as a side salad, or 2 as a (generous) main course

There's no word for "slaw" in French so it's unlikely that this would turn up on a French menu. But the dressing is inspired by aïoli (page 145), and it's one of my go-to lunches. I'll admit that I sometimes cheat and use store-bought mayonnaise—and don't tell, but sometimes I buy the *allegé*, or light, variety. I don't know what they do to their mayonnaise, but French store-bought mayonnaise tastes much, much better than the stuff sold in jars elsewhere. I think it's the sizable dollop of Dijon mustard they add to it—although for the timid, they offer unspiced mayonnaise, which promises a *goût delicat*. Mild Dijon mustard is available as well, but I haven't tried that, because I don't want to encourage that kind of adulteration. (And that's coming from someone who buys low-fat mayonnaise.)

The best way to cut vegetables into matchstick slices is to peel them and use a chef's knife to slice them thinly. Then stack up the slices and julienne them.

For herbs, I keep it simple, though if I have tarragon on hand, I'll chop up some leaves and add those for a sharp note. And I often slip some pumpkin seeds or maybe some toasted sliced almonds into the salad for a little extra crunch, as well as any leftover rotisserie chicken.

I've given two options for dressing: one is mayonnaise based, which results in a coleslaw-like salad, and is very garlicky—just the way I like it. (I avoid eating it if I'm planning on taking a crowded métro later that day.) The other is a garlic vinaigrette (see Variation) that makes a more lightly dressed salad, and is more suitable if future travels take you close to others.

1   To make the dressing, mix the mayonnaise, vinegar, garlic, mustard, and pepper in a small bowl until smooth. Cover and chill for several hours (if possible).

2   To assemble the salad, toss the raw vegetables in a large bowl. Add the parsley and chives, toss with the dressing, and mix well. Garnish with additional chopped parsley and chives.

VARIATION: Make a garlic vinaigrette instead of the dressing. Combine 1 1/2 teaspoons of minced garlic, 1 teaspoon of Dijon mustard, 3/4 teaspoon of sea salt or kosher salt, and 1 tablespoon of red wine or sherry vinegar with a fork. Add 1/4 cup (60ml) of olive oil and stir well.

DRESSING

1 cup (240g) mayonnaise, homemade (page 331) or store-bought

4 teaspoons red wine vinegar

2 tablespoons minced garlic

1 1/2 teaspoons Dijon mustard

1 teaspoon freshly ground black pepper

6 cups (460g) sliced and hand-shredded raw vegetables, any mix of:

- cabbage, red or green, thinly shredded
- radicchio or Belgian endive, shredded
- carrots, peeled and cut into thin matchsticks
- beets, peeled and cut into thin matchsticks
- apples (firm, crisp), peeled and cut into matchsticks
- broccoli or cauliflower florets, thinly sliced
- radishes, thinly sliced or quartered
- fennel, thinly sliced
- kohlrabi, peeled and cut into thin matchsticks
- avocados, peeled and sliced or cubed
- hard-cooked eggs (page 328), peeled and cubed
- flat-leaf parsley or chervil leaves

2 tablespoons chopped fresh flat-leaf parsley, plus more for garnish

2 tablespoons chopped fresh chives, plus more for garnish

Les Endives

I ALWAYS LAUGH WHEN I SEE BELGIAN ENDIVE at the markets in Paris because it's so ridiculously inexpensive compared to elsewhere. I jokingly refer to it as the "trash" lettuce of France, though I have no idea why I've anointed it with such an inelegant and, frankly, incorrect name. I guess I'm just amused because I can pick up more than a dozen spears of Belgian endive in Paris for the same price as a head of iceberg in America, which we joke about as low-class salad fare. But the contrast is amusing because elsewhere, Belgian endive is presented in elegant boxes, lined up like precious jewels, and priced as such!

I like Belgian endive very much, as well as iceberg lettuce; both have an affinity for strong-tasting blue cheese. And both are especially appreciated in the winter, when heartier foods are needed to fortify us against the persistant chill in the air. Yet we still crave, and need, salads.

There are many articles and books written about how French women cook, but until this story that you're now reading (and this book), there was very little mention of how men cook in France at home. One particularly great cook is my partner's late father, who never measured anything, was rarely clear about what he'd done, and whose knife skills would not be featured in any culinary school handbooks. But it was easy to forgive him because he continued to cook into his nineties, and whatever he made was always excellent.

He brought a winter salad (page 98) to the table once, and I took one bite and couldn't believe how good it was. When I asked what made it so good, he shuffled into the kitchen and showed me a crumbly, damp wedge of Roquefort and said that was pretty much it. Of course, I had to know more, and made the salad with him another time—measuring the ingredients—so it's easy for anyone, man or woman, to recreate.

97

Winter salad

SALADE D'HIVER

Serves 4

Roquefort is a special blue cheese, made of sheeps' milk and inoculated with rye bread mold, which gives it a particular flavor—milky-sweet, with a piquant muskiness that distinguishes it from other blue cheeses. It was the first cheese given AOC (quality- and name-control status), in 1926, and the quality is still well controlled. Roquefort is made in the southwest of France and aged in vast Roquefort caves. You'll never see a whole Roquefort because each one is cut in half before leaving the caves to ensure the greenish mold has reached all the way through. Do try to find and use it if you can because the flavor is more pronounced than in other blue cheeses.

This salad is best tossed shortly before serving, but it can be assembled up to an hour ahead. The dressing can be made up to 3 days in advance and refrigerated.

1 In a large bowl, use a fork to mash the Roquefort with the yogurt, chives, lemon juice, and salt.

2 Remove any wilted exterior leaves from the endive spears, trim off the root ends, and cut the spears lengthwise into 1/4-inch (.75cm) slices. Lay them flat and cut them lengthwise again so the endive is sliced into batons.

3 Toss the endive thoroughly with the dressing, adding a liberal amount of pepper, and additional lemon juice and salt, if necessary. Sprinkle with additional minced chives before serving.

VARIATION: Peel, core, and quarter 2 firm, ripe pears or tart apples. Slice them, cut the slices lengthwise into thick matchsticks the same size as the endive, and toss them into the salad right before serving. Garnish with toasted walnuts or pecans, if desired.

1 cup (5 ounces/130g) crumbled Roquefort cheese

1 cup (240g) Greek yogurt

2 tablespoons minced fresh chives, plus more for garnish

1 tablespoon freshly squeezed lemon juice, plus more if needed

1 teaspoon sea salt or kosher salt, plus more if needed

1 pound (450g) Belgian endive (6 to 8 spears)

Freshly ground black pepper

Frisée salad with bacon, egg, and garlic toasts

SALADE LYONNAISE

Serves 4 to 6

Salade lyonnaise was the first dish that made me fall in love with French cuisine. Even though the French can be rather territorial about their food ("You want bouillabaisse? Go to Marseille!" "Aïoli? Too much garlic. That's for *les Provençaux* . . . "), *salade lyonnaise* is universally beloved across France, and beyond. But I have to say, if you want the best version, you should go to Lyon.

As much as people love to travel to Paris, few make the trip to Lyon, which can be reached in two hours on the high-speed TGV train. Dotted around the city are gut-busting restaurants called *bouchons*, where the food is brought to the table in big earthenware bowls and rustic terrines, and diners are encouraged to help themselves—repeatedly, if you wish. (Which is the first reminder that you're not in Paris anymore.) At the end of a meal, most places will not let you leave unless you have at least one glass of eau-de-vie, a spirited shot of high-test distilled brandy that will help you digest whatever came before. (And can make you forget it, the day after.)

If that isn't enough to put you on a train, Lyon is also home to Bernachon. This is the only location of the world-famous chocolate shop that imports its own cocoa beans, which they blend, grind, and melt to make their chocolates and confections. But what makes me crazy are their Kalouga bars, which are the gold standard of salted caramel–filled chocolate bars, and I've been known to buy out their entire inventory, and stockpile them in my apartment back in Paris.

Like good chocolates, *salade lyonnaise* is a confluence of good, yet humble, ingredients coming together to become something more important than each one could be on its own. The frisée should be crisp and fresh, to stand up to the warm ingredients that would turn other salad greens into a mushy pile. The pieces of bacon should be lightly browned, not too crunchy, so they have a bit of juicy chewiness still left in them. And the fingerling potatoes should be warm when the salad is tossed, which helps them soak up the mustardy flavor of the dressing. Poached eggs are added, and the runny yolks get stirred into the salad to enrich the vinaigrette. There are other versions that use hard-cooked eggs, if you'd rather keep things simple.

continued

Although this salad is hearty enough to feed a normal person as a meal, it's considered a first course where it originated. Drink this with a fruity red wine, such as a Brouilly or Beaujolais, slightly chilled, as they do in Lyon. And if you ever have this salad in the city where it originated, get yourself to Bernachon for a salted butter caramel-filled chocolate bar afterwards. You can thank me later, preferably with a chocolate bar filled with salted butter caramel.

1   To make the croutons, heat the oil in a skillet over medium heat. Add the garlic and cook until it's deeply golden brown; be careful not to burn it. Remove and reserve the garlic, then add the bread, stirring the cubes in the oil, turning them frequently. Add a sprinkle of salt and a dribble more oil if necessary, until the bread is brown on all sides, about 5 minutes. Set aside until ready to serve.

2   To make the salad, put the potatoes in a saucepan with enough cold water to cover. Add some salt and bring to a boil over high heat. Decrease the heat to a low boil and cook for 15 minutes, until the potatoes are tender when pierced with a sharp knife. (If done in advance, cook them slightly less, and let them rest in the warm water for up to 45 minutes.)

3   While the potatoes are cooking, fry the bacon in a skillet over medium heat until just starting to crisp. Drain the pieces on a plate lined with paper towels.

4   In a large salad bowl, whisk together the vinegar, mustard, 1/4 teaspoon of salt, the oil, water, and garlic. (If you like garlic a lot, you can chop up the fried garlic clove from making the croutons and add that as well.)

5   To assemble the salad, slice the potatoes and add them to the bowl along with the bacon and toss gently. Add the frisée, parsley, and some black pepper. Add the croutons and hard-cooked eggs (if using) and toss very well. Divide among four salad bowls. If using poached eggs, slide one on top of each salad and serve.

VARIATION: Although it's not traditional, I sometimes add 2 cups (260g) of crumbled blue cheese to the salad at the last minute, omitting the eggs.

GARLIC CROUTONS

2 1/2 tablespoons olive oil, plus more if needed

1 clove garlic, peeled and slightly crushed

1 1/2 cups (65g) cubes or torn pieces of bread, about 3/4 inch (2cm) in size

Sea salt or kosher salt

SALAD

8 to 12 new potatoes (12 ounces/ 360g)

Sea salt or kosher salt

2 cups (300g) diced, thick-cut bacon, smoked or unsmoked

4 teaspoons red wine vinegar

1 1/2 tablespoons Dijon mustard

5 tablespoons olive oil or neutral-tasting vegetable oil

1 tablespoon water

2 teaspoons peeled and minced garlic

8 cups (150g) loosely packed frisée or escarole leaves

2 tablespoons finely chopped fresh flat-leaf parsley or fresh chives

Freshly ground black pepper

4 poached eggs (page 329) or 4 hard-cooked eggs (page 328), peeled and quartered

An Organization of Œufs

THERE IS ONLY ONE THING THE FRENCH engage in more than eating—and that's organizing. I'm not sure if they enjoy it quite as much, but it's essential to ensure that you systematize and keep a paper trail of every transaction, bill, payment, agreement, document, and the all-important *attestation* (which attests that the document you are presenting is actually the right document), because you will most certainly be called on to produce it at a later date, no matter how trivial you think it is.

Organizing has become my part-time job in France, as I can certainly say from the row of *dossiers* of official paperwork—copied in triplicate, then signed, stamped, and officially attested to—in my apartment, which is surely responsible for the decimation of several forests' worth of trees.

Equally as challenging as keeping all that paperwork in order are the names of all those organizations we need to file them for, which have multiword names that confound even the French. So much so that they get abbreviated to acronyms such as URSAFF, AGESSA, CLEISS, RNCPS, CPAM, AMELIE, ONDAM, and UCANSS, which are just a few we need to keep up with for our *sécurité sociale* (health care), which naturally gets shortened to *le sécu*. Otherwise we'd be so busy saying all those names that we'd never have time to eat!

Speaking of eating, even the defenders of one of the most unassuming dishes of French bistro cuisine have their own acronym, the ASOM, or *Association de sauvegarde de l'œuf mayonnaise*, formed to preserve the heritage and culture of the classic bistro starter of hard-cooked eggs doused with mayonnaise. As you probably can assume by now, this also gets shortened, to *œufs mayo*. While I should probably get moving on a *dossier* of places in Paris that serve this dish, for the time being, I head to A la Biche au Bois, whose version is a bit fancified, with the mayo piped in decorative rosettes over the eggs.

I haven't checked in with the ASOM to see what they think of my version of *œufs mayo*, and I'm not sure I have the time to go through all the paperwork that's probably required to get on their list. But I can personally attest to the fact that I enjoy them very much, and leave it at that.

Hard-cooked eggs with chervil mayonnaise

ŒUFS MAYO

Serves 6

A Parisian cook once told me, "I never used olive oil until about fifteen years ago. It was unthinkable—it was always butter!" Now there are olive oil shops all over Paris, and it's not considered an exotic ingredient at all. However, a neutral-tasting oil is still what I prefer for this mayonnaise because the flavor of olive oil overwhelms the eggs and the delicate, anise-like bite of chervil. If you can't find chervil, substitute fresh tarragon, basil, or chives, or a combination of them.

I use a whole egg in this mayonnaise, rather than just the yolk, which works only if you use a blender or food processor to make it (which you should). The egg white also gives the mayonnaise a certain *légèreté* (lightness).

1 To make the mayonnaise, crack the egg into the bowl of a blender or food processor and add the salt, lemon juice, and 1/4 teaspoon of the mustard.

2 Pour the oil into a measuring cup with a spout and, with the motor running, drizzle the oil in slowly. Around the halfway point, the mayonnaise will start to thicken. Continue to add the oil with the motor running until you've added it all. Add the shallots, chervil, and a tiny pinch of sugar and pulse the blender or food processor a few times until everything is well incorporated. Taste, and add the remaining 1/4 teaspoon of the mustard, if you wish. (The mayonnaise can be served immediately, although holding it overnight in the refrigerator nicely melds the shallot flavor into the sauce. Fresh mayonnaise will keep for 2 or 3 days in the refrigerator. It may get a little stiff when refrigerated; stirring briskly will smooth it out.)

3 Put a few leaves of lettuce on each of six plates, along with a wedge or two of tomato. Peel the eggs and cut them in half lengthwise. Put three halves on top of the lettuce on each plate. Spoon mayonnaise liberally over the eggs and scatter a few chervil leaves over the top.

CHERVIL MAYONNAISE

1 large egg, at room temperature

1/2 teaspoon sea salt or kosher salt

2 teaspoons freshly squeezed lemon juice

1/4 to 1/2 teaspoon Dijon mustard

3/4 cup (180ml) neutral-tasting vegetable oil

1 tablespoon minced shallots

1 tablespoon minced chervil leaves, plus a few reserved for garnish

Pinch of granulated sugar

Butter lettuce

Tomato wedges

9 hard-cooked eggs (see page 328)

Sizing Up Celery Root

I ANNUALLY LEAD A TOUR OF PARIS. THE TOUR used to focus exclusively on chocolate, but then I realized that even the most hard-core chocophiles start begging for mercy around the third day. So I've learned to mix things up, adding stops for cheese and charcuterie, and to include a few wine tastings along the way to help wash everything down. (And calm the guide down, too.)

I've also learned to include some vegetable-centric meals because Americans invariably begin to crave fresh fruits and vegetables, which aren't well-represented on Parisian restaurant menus. Even when there are salads on offer, they're heavy on the meat and cheese, and scant on anything crispy and crunchy. At Le Nemrod, a classic café on the Left Bank, a *salade Auvergnate* consists of a heap of bacon surrounded by cubes of bread sautéed in bacon fat, with a warm poached egg perched on top, its golden-rich yolk ready to ooze out everywhere as the dressing. Admittedly, underneath are a few leaves of lettuce, but those are basically just there for—well, I haven't quite figured out why.

Still, when visitors see anything indicating that it might have the possibility of vegetables in it, they jump on it. Especially appealing is the *salade des crudités*, which literally translates as "raw vegetable salad." But then I have to break it to them that it isn't going to be a platter of garden vegetables served *au naturel*, but a plate of little salads, some bathed in creamy dressing. The trio of salads is portioned as a first-course, and they're going to have to order something else after that— whether they want to or not. One Left Bank brasserie got so fed up with people opting for just a salad, they posted a note in English at the top of the menu in big red letters: "No salad is a meal."

Yet once people taste their first forkful of *céleri rémoulade*, they quickly forget about the plain, undressed vegetables they were craving and wipe their plates clean. Celery root is one of those underappreciated vegetables in America, and folks are often reluctant to toss one in their shopping basket, wondering what the heck they're going to do with the crazy-looking ball with dirty, tangled roots dangling from the end. I buy them all the time, and because the celery roots in France are huge (some are almost the size of bowling balls!), vendors will gladly cut them in half and sell them as such at the market.

And I know exactly what I'm going to do with it; I'll take it home, peel it and slice it up into matchstick-sized pieces, then toss it in a creamy dressing with two kinds of mustard, which gives it a lively kick. Then I sometimes eat the salad just as it is—as a meal, at home. Where no one can tell me to do otherwise.

Celery root salad with mustard sauce

CÉLERI RÉMOULADE

Serves 6

½ cup (120g) mayonnaise, homemade (page 331) or store-bought

¼ cup (60g) crème fraîche or sour cream

2 tablespoons grainy mustard

2 tablespoons freshly squeezed lemon juice

1 tablespoon Dijon mustard

1 teaspoon sea salt or kosher salt

2 pounds (1kg) celery root

2 tablespoons finely chopped fresh flat-leaf parsley

You can use a coarse grater to prepare the celery root, although I like the salad better when the pieces are hand-cut into matchsticks. They're a bit thicker and tend to stay crunchier in the creamy dressing when cut that way.

Even though I'll sometimes have a big plate of this for lunch (as a meal), I also serve it alongside Grated carrot salad (page 123) with perhaps a few radishes, and some salted butter to smear on them, to make a *salade des crudités*. Celery root salad is also a good accompaniment to Duck terrine with figs (page 113).

1   In a large bowl, mix together the mayonnaise, crème fraîche, grainy mustard, lemon juice, Dijon mustard, and salt.

2   Using a chef's knife, lop off the top and bottom ends of the celery root and set it on a cutting board with one of the flat sides down. Cut away the coarse skin, slicing it with a curved motion to match the curvature of the root, conserving as much of the flesh as possible. Cut the peeled celery root in half or in quarters (whatever size makes it more manageable for you). Cut the flesh into thin slices. Working in batches, lay several slices on top of each other, then julienne the celery root, or cut the celery root into small strips. Because celery root has a tendency to discolor when exposed to air, toss the pieces in the dressing as you go.

3   Add the chopped parsley and stir well to incorporate it into the salad. Once dressed, this salad will keep for up to 2 days in the refrigerator. It will lose some of its crispness the longer it sits.

105

Celery root soup with horseradish cream and ham chips

SOUPE DE CÉLERI-RAVE À LA CRÈME DE RAIFORT
ET CHIPS DE JAMBON

Serves 6

In addition to the pack of cigarettes and the now-ubiquitous cell phones that are ceremoniously plopped down on every café table before a group of Parisians even sits down—a tableau that isn't quite as painterly as those in days past—Parisians also carry little packets of tissues around with them. It is *nécessaire* to have them with you always, especially in the winter, when the temperatures drop and noses start doing something else that's not so picturesque.

To breathe easier, my favorite head-clearer is horseradish. I grew up eating horseradish so I always keep it on hand. Whenever I have a head cold, I unscrew the jar and inhale deeply, which works like a charm. Not so pleasant was the time I did the same when someone was grating fresh horseradish in a food processor in a restaurant kitchen. I took a big sniff and nearly burned away the linings of my sinuses. So now I take it easy because I'm not sure horseradish burns are covered by the French health care system.

The recipe calls for crème fraîche because its sturdy richness stands up well to the soup, but you can use heavy cream instead. If you do use heavy cream, whip it very stiff, to the point where it just about turns to butter.

1 To make the horseradish cream, whip the crème fraîche in a metal bowl with a whisk until it thickens and holds its shape when you lift the whisk. Whisk in the salt and lemon juice, then stir in the horseradish. Let chill for at least 1 hour, to allow the flavors to develop. (The horseradish cream is best made at least 3 to 4 hours in advance.)

2 To make the ham chips, preheat the oven to 350°F (180°C). Line a baking sheet with parchment paper and lay the slices of ham evenly spaced on it. Bake for 7 to 10 minutes, turning over the slices midway through. The actual time will vary depending on how thin the ham is sliced, so after 5 minutes, watch carefully. When they feel firm and dry, remove them from the oven and let cool until crisp. Store the chips in an airtight container until ready to use.

HORSERADISH CREAM

1½ cups (360g) crème fraîche (page 327), or 1 cup (250ml) heavy cream, stiffly whipped

Generous pinch of sea salt or kosher salt

2 teaspoons freshly squeezed lemon juice

2 tablespoons prepared horseradish

HAM CHIPS

6 very thin slices country ham or prosciutto

SOUP

4 large leeks, cleaned (see page 30)

6 tablespoons (3 ounces/85g) salted or unsalted butter

2½ teaspoons sea salt or kosher salt, plus more if needed

1½ pounds (680g) celery root

1 bay leaf

6 sprigs thyme

6 cups (1.5l) water

½ teaspoon freshly ground white pepper

Minced fresh chives, for garnish

3   To make the soup, slice the leeks into $^1/_4$-inch (1cm) pieces. Melt the butter in a large pot or Dutch oven over medium heat. Add the sliced leeks and cook for 10 minutes, or until the leeks are completely soft, adding the salt midway through cooking.

4   While the leeks are cooking, peel the celery root. Using a chef's knife, lop off the top and bottom ends of the celery root and set it on a cutting board with one of the flat sides down. Cut away the coarse skin, slicing it with a curved motion to match the curvature of the root, conserving as much of the flesh as possible. Slice the celery root about $^3/_4$ inch (2cm) thick, then cut the slices into cubes. Add the cubes to the pot along with the bay leaf, thyme, and water. Bring to a boil, decrease the heat to a simmer, and cover, keeping the lid askew. Cook for 30 to 40 minutes, until the celery root is tender; a sharp paring knife should easily pierce one of the cubes and meet no resistance.

5   Pluck out the bay leaf and thyme, and let the soup cool to tepid. Add the white pepper. Blend the soup (if the soup is still hot, do not fill the blender more than halfway full, or use a hand blender or food processor) until completely smooth. Taste, and add additional salt, if desired. (At this point, the soup can be stored, covered, in the refrigerator for up to 4 days.)

6   To serve the soup, reheat the soup and ladle into serving bowls. Add a generous dollop of the horseradish cream, then crumble the ham chips over the top, finishing each bowl with a sprinkling of chives.

107

Les Tomates Cerises

I HAVE YET TO ATTEND A PARTY IN PARIS WHERE a bowl of cherry tomatoes wasn't offered. Yes, there's usually wine and some other snacks, but cherry tomatoes have become *obligatoire* when entertaining. No matter what the season, you can count on there being a bowl of the little red orbs, shiny and perfectly smooth, ready for popping in your mouth.

To see how seriously Parisians take their cherry tomatoes, stroll through the produce aisle at La Grande Épicerie, the chicest supermarket in Paris, and you'll pass shelves and shelves of cherry tomatoes. The produce person at La Grand Épicerie once took great care when I inspected the many varieties on offer (at moderate to staggering prices) to tell me which particular cherry tomatoes are the best, and why. (Naturally the ones that were the most expensive, he explained, were the only ones worthy of such a man of great taste, namely, myself.)

Some cherry tomatoes have fanciful names like Pigeon Heart; I don't know if this is an accurate name because I've never actually seen a real pigeon heart (and if you live in Paris, it's hard to imagine pigeons having hearts). Other cherry tomatoes come attached to the vines in neat rows, each one so perfect that it feels like it would be an act of savagery to break off even one tomato and ruin the whole look.

Cherry tomatoes signify so many things to Parisians. They're expensive, and they're good for the *régime* (diet), but I think my friend Olivier Magny, a sommelier in Paris, put it best when he said in his book *Stuff Parisians Like* that cherry tomatoes appeal to Parisians because they have "all the qualities of a tomato, minus the defects."

But even more important is that those little tomatoes provide an opportunity for Parisians to make good use of the word *petite*, which seems to precede every noun in Paris. When someone mentioned to me that I spoke French with just a *petit accent*, my head was in the clouds for a few days beacause I thought I had finally broken the hurdle of being burdened with my American accent . . . until I heard everyone referring to everything as *petit*: *un petit dessert, un petit verre de vin, un petit voyage, une petite problème,* and *les petits vacances*, even when the French vacation is five weeks long, and not exactly *p'tit* by anyone else's standards. (And because even *petit* is too long for Parisians to say, the actual word itself gets *petit*-sized into *p'tit*.)

I try to buy cherry tomatoes in the summer, when they're practically tumbling off the stands at the outdoor market. But the beauty of the recipe that follows is that it can be made any time of year since it's usually possible to find nice-tasting cherry tomatoes, no matter where you live or what the season. I'm a little embarrassed to admit this, but the cheese spread is inspired by Boursin, that popular French herbed cheese that was cocktail party fare in 1970s America. I hadn't had it in decades, but when a Parisian friend showed up at a dinner party with a *p'tit* Boursin, we were astonished, when we pulled back the foil and dug into the creamy herbed cheese spread, by how much we kind of loved it all over again.

Living in a country with the best cheese in the world, I'm not ready to fully switch my allegiance to foil-wrapped supermarket cheese. So I make my own version, mixing in freshly chopped garlic, herbs, and shallots. I used to bring back reams of cheesecloth from the states for projects such as this, until I found *étamine* at the huge fabric store, the Marché Saint-Pierre, in Montmartre. I buy a good length of the soft, ivory-colored cotton gauze that is also used for jelly-making, and is so inexpensive that I can buy a year's supply for just a *p'tit* euro or two. And I can save my money for fancy, Left Bank cherry tomatoes, just in case I ever decide to upgrade my tastes to the next level.

Cherry tomato crostini with homemade herbed goat cheese

TARTINES DE TOMATES CERISES, CHÈVRE FRAIS MAISON AUX HERBES

Serves 4

I like to roast the tomatoes ahead of time—up to 8 hours in advance—so they have time to marinate in their own savory juices, which caramelize slightly, making a nice bit of sauce to drizzle over the top.

1 To make the herbed goat cheese, line a mesh strainer with a few layers of cheesecloth or muslin and set it over a bowl. Scrape the yogurt into the lined strainer, fold the cloth over the yogurt, and refrigerate for 24 hours.

2 Put the strained yogurt into a bowl and mix in the herbs, shallots, garlic, salt, and cayenne pepper. Refrigerate until ready to use.

3 To roast the tomatoes, preheat the oven to 350°F (180°C). Combine the cherry tomatoes, olive oil, garlic, and herbs in a baking dish or pan that will hold them all in a snug single layer. Season with salt and pepper, mix well, and spread them out on the baking dish.

4 Roast the tomatoes for about 45 minutes, stirring once or perhaps twice during baking, until they're wilted and their juices are start-ing to concentrate—and perhaps brown a bit—in the bottom of the baking dish. Scrape the tomatoes and any juices into a bowl and let cool to room temperature. They can sit up to 8 hours, and they improve the longer they sit.

5 When ready to serve, make the toasts. Preheat the oven to 350°F (180°C). Evenly brush the bread slices with olive oil. Place them on a baking sheet and toast for about 5 minutes, until light golden brown. Remove from the oven and when just cool enough to handle, rub the slices generously with the garlic clove. Let cool to room temperature.

6 To serve, thickly smear each piece of toast with the fresh herbed cheese. Pluck out the herbs and spoon the tomatoes and their juices over the toasts. Coarsely chop the herbs for the garnish, and scatter them over the top of each portion.

HERBED FRESH GOAT CHEESE

2 cups (480g) whole goats' (or cows') milk yogurt

1 generous tablespoon very finely minced mixed fresh herbs (be sure to include chives, as well as an assortment that could include thyme, sage, basil, or flat-leaf parsley)

1 tablespoon minced shallots

1 teaspoon minced garlic

3/4 teaspoon sea salt or kosher salt

Generous pinch of cayenne pepper

ROASTED CHERRY TOMATOES

1 1/2 pounds (680g) cherry tomatoes, stemmed and halved

3 tablespoons olive oil

2 cloves garlic, peeled and thinly sliced

Handful of fresh herbs (any combination of rosemary or thyme sprigs, bay leaf, and basil or sage leaves)

Sea salt or kosher salt and freshly ground black pepper

TOASTS

4 thick slices bread, such as ciabatta, a country bread, or a sourdough that's not too dense

Olive oil

1 clove garlic, peeled

A few leaves of fresh basil, sage, or flat-leaf parsley, for garnish

Les Terrines

WHEN PEOPLE WANT TO INVOKE CULTURAL snobbery, words like *arugula* and *pâté-eaters* often come up, conjuring visions of the European elite sipping Champagne and nibbling fancy canapés. In fact, terrines and pâtés are among the most rustic foods in France, something peasants would put on a slice of crusty sourdough bread with local red wine poured from a jug for lunch. And judging by the ordinary folks lined up at the charcuterie at my market, I wouldn't say they are any more or less chic than the people who aren't buying pâtés or terrines. (Except for the woman who shows up in purple silk tights, velvet boots, and matching purple make-up with a cigarette always fired up, whom I try not to get behind in line because I prefer to come home with my sausages smoked, not me.)

If you go to an outdoor market in Paris, you will invariably come across charcuterie stands—as well as a few interesting characters—with a shelf lined with heavy earthenware terrines holding all sorts of terrines and pâtés. Oddly, the word *pâté* is derived from "paste" or "dough" (*pâte*), and sometimes you'll find *pâté en croûte*, which literally means "paste in dough."

Terrines aren't wrapped in dough, but are named for the dish they are baked in, and can range from coarse and fatty to silky-smooth and refined, so there's something to appeal to all palates. I usually bring home a slice of my favorite, which is a blend of pork and duck with bits of dried figs, whose seeds provide a crackly contrast to the unabashedly rich slab of meat.

There's no need to be bashful about tackling a terrine at home; it's actually quite simple. I'll make one to serve as an appetizer with toast and a dab of shallot marmalade (page 335) if I have guests, and the leftovers get eaten during the rest of the week for lunch at home. But even in France, where terrines and pâtés are commonplace, guests are always wowed when they find out the terrine they're slicing and putting on crusts of bread was actually made in my own kitchen. And although I don't think of myself as a cultural elitist, I do take a little bit of pride when I—an American—successfully make something that is squarely in the French domain.

Most terrines are made with a combination of meats, though it's common to name them after the most luxurious pieces of meat used. In the recipe that follows, I use pork and bacon as a base but it's the duck and dried fruits that give the terrine its fine flavor. One of my very favorite lunches is a freshly baked *baguette tradition*, split in half and smeared with lots of grainy mustard, with cornichons and slices of terrine inside. I press it firmly together before I eat it, which melds all the flavors, and is highly recommended.

Duck terrine with figs

TERRINE DE CANARD AUX FIGUES

Makes 1 (9-inch/23cm) loaf

For the duck meat, buy a duck breast or the tenders (which they sell in France and are considered a delicacy), or a couple of thighs and remove the bone. Cut the duck into cubes and freeze them partially, along with the bacon, to firm them up for easier cutting. Since duck isn't as available elsewhere as it is in France, you can use the meat from boneless, skinless chicken thighs in place of the duck. You can also vary the dried fruit, using apricots or prunes in place of the figs. It's nice to serve a little Celery root salad (page 105) alongside, as a first course.

3/4 cup (100g) diced dried figs

1/2 cup (125ml) Cognac or brandy

12 ounces (340g) boneless, skinless duck meat or chicken thighs, cubed

1³/4 cups (170g) unsmoked cubed thick-cut bacon or pancetta

8 ounces (225g) chicken livers

1³/4 pounds (800g) boneless pork shoulder or pork butt, ground

4 small shallots, or 1 small onion, peeled and minced

2 cloves garlic, peeled and minced

2 tablespoons Dijon mustard

2 teaspoons sea salt or kosher salt

1 teaspoon chopped fresh thyme, or 1/2 teaspoon dried

3/4 teaspoon ground allspice

1/4 teaspoon ground cloves

1/4 teaspoon dried ground ginger

Freshly ground black pepper

2 large eggs

1/3 cup (40g) coarsely chopped cornichons or pickles

1/4 cup (60ml) juice from the cornichon jar

Shallot marmalade (page 335)

1 In a small saucepan, heat the dried fruits with the Cognac until the liquid just begins to simmer. Remove from the heat, cover, and set aside.

2 Scatter the duck meat and bacon on a dinner plate and place the plate in the freezer until the edges of the meats are frozen.

3 Preheat the oven to 350°F (180°C).

4 Puree the livers in a food processor, add the partially frozen duck meat and bacon, and process until the mixture is almost a smooth paste, but still slightly chunky.

5 Scrape the mixture into a large bowl and add the pork, shallots, garlic, mustard, salt, thyme, allspice, cloves, ginger, and a few grinds of a peppermill. Add the eggs, cornichons, pickle juice, and the plumped dried fruits and their liquid; mix very well.

6 Pack the terrine mixture into a deep 9 by 5-inch (23 by 13cm) loaf pan (see Note on page 114). Cut a piece of parchment paper large enough to fit over the top, then seal the top of the pan with aluminum foil. Set the loaf pan in a larger baking dish and add enough very hot water to reach a little over halfway up the outside of the loaf pan.

7 Bake for about 1¹/2 hours, or until an instant-read thermometer stuck in the center registers 160°F (71°C). Remove from the oven. Lift the terrine out of the water bath and carefully pour out the hot water. Place the terrine back in the larger dish and put a brick (or another flat, heavy object) on the foil on top of

continued

the terrine and let cool to room temperature. During the cooling, any juice that overflows should be collected and chilled; a
dab of the jelly makes an excellent accompaniment when serving, along with the shallot marmalade.

**Duck terrine with figs,
continued**

8   Once cool, refrigerate the terrine for 2 days before serving, to
allow the terrine to season. Slice it directly from the pan. It may
crumble a bit, as it's a country-style (chunky) terrine. It can be
kept in the refrigerator for up to 10 days. I don't recommend
freezing because it changes the texture of the terrine.

NOTE: This terrine mixture will fit into a loaf pan that has a
2¹/₂-quart (2.5l) capacity, or you can bake it in any kind of deep
mold that you wish; those made of metal, glass, earthenware, or
ceramic will work well. If you have a little terrine mixture left
over, it can be baked in a smaller vessel alongside the larger one;
cook it until the internal temperature reaches 160°F (71°C).

Honesty, My Best Policy

WHEN I WAS APPLYING TO WORK AT CHEZ Panisse back in the early 1980s, I was told that I would need to have an interview with the owner, Alice Waters. At the time, Chez Panisse was getting an enormous amount of attention, and it was A Big Deal to work there. And I really, really wanted that job.

During my trial shift, I happened to hit it off with a few of the staff members, who coached me on what to say. "She's going to ask you what cookbooks you own," they said, "so make sure to say *Simple French Cooking* by Richard Olney, or anything by Elizabeth David." I assured them that they were, indeed, favorites of mine, and that I certainly would.

And when I left, I went down the street to the local bookstore to find out who Richard Olney and Elizabeth David were.

I'll admit that I didn't get too far because the books had a lot of words and not a lot of pretty pictures of food, as cookbooks nowadays do. Plus I was so tired from being on my feet all day, racing around the incredibly busy restaurant, and I just wanted to go home, lie down, and watch reruns of *The Love Boat*. So when the interview came, I sat in the famed downstairs dining room at Chez Panisse, surrounded by the iconic hand-crafted copper lamps and sconces, and Craftsman-style woodwork, face-to-face with Alice. And lo and behold, the first question out of her mouth was "So, what cookbooks do you own?"

I sat there for a moment, frozen, quickly having a discussion with my conscience, deciding if I should lie and get the job, or tell the truth and go home and see if the cruise director and the purser would at long last consummate their love.

"I have *The Joy of Cooking*... and, uhhh ...."

There was an uncomfortable moment of silence, until she went on to the next question, which was, "What do you eat at home?" That one, I could answer easily: "I eat mostly salads. I make them in big bowls, mixing everything together and eating them right out of the bowl." And that, my friends, was the jackpot, as I'd hit on exactly the same thing that we both loved to eat. In fact, she told me her favorite job at the restaurant was washing the lettuce that arrived every morning from local farms. Honesty pays off: I spent the next couple of years working in the café, making hundreds of salads every night, until moving on to the pastry department.

Fattoush

FATTOUCHE

Serves 6

I love nothing more than a big bowl heaped with salads of all kinds, especially one dressed with a pungent lemony garlic dressing and a jumble of ingredients, including sturdy hearts of romaine or Little Gem lettuces. And one of the most interesting salads is fattoush, a Middle Eastern dish that's sprinkled with ground sumac, a powder that's both a little fruity and a little tart, and tossed with *fatteh*, the Arabic word for shards of toasted pita bread, which gives the salad its name.

Sumac is probably a spice you don't have in your pantry, but you should, if only to use in this recipe. You'll find it's also good sprinkled over Hummus (page 60) or *moutabal* (page 64). Most markets that specialize in Arabic ingredients have it, or you can mail order it from Kalustyan's or Penzeys (see Sources, page 339).

1   Preheat the oven to 350°F (180°C). Put the pita breads on a baking sheet, brush them evenly with olive oil, and toast in the oven for 5 to 8 minutes, or until crisp. Remove from the oven and let cool completely.

2   In a large salad bowl, whisk together the lemon juice, salt, garlic, and mustard. Whisk in the 1/2 cup (125ml) of olive oil.

3   Add the lettuce, scallions, cucumber, tomatoes, parsley, mint, and radishes. Toss the salad with 1 teaspoon of the sumac and a few generous grinds of the peppermill. Crumble the pita into irregular pieces that are slightly larger than bite-size and gently toss until coated with the dressing. Sprinkle the salad with the remaining 1/2 teaspoon of sumac and serve.

2 large or 4 small rounds of pita bread

1/2 cup (125ml) olive oil, plus additional for brushing the pita breads

1/3 cup (80ml) freshly squeezed lemon juice

1 teaspoon sea salt or kosher salt

2 cloves garlic, peeled and minced

1 teaspoon Dijon mustard

8 cups (300g) torn or wide-cut ribbons hearts of romaine or Little Gem lettuce

4 scallions, white and tender green parts, thinly sliced

1 cucumber, peeled, seeded, and cut into large dice

20 cherry tomatoes, halved

1/2 cup (30g) coarsely chopped fresh flat-leaf parsley

1/2 cup (30g) coarsely chopped fresh mint

1/2 bunch of radishes, thinly sliced

1 1/2 teaspoons ground sumac

Freshly ground black pepper

La Soupe for Dinner

THERE IS AN INDESCRIBABLE LURE TO FRENCH onion soup for visitors to Paris. Perhaps they are nostalgic for the days when it was served at 4 a.m. to nocturnal revelers who rubbed elbows with the blood-stained, aproned butchers from Les Halles, the central food market that stood in the center of Paris for centuries. Or else they just can't resist a steaming bowl of caramelized onions in hearty broth, topped with a crust of bread and lots of browned cheese, even if the market is gone and few places still replicate this classic as well as they used to.

Speaking of nostalgia, the French word for soup also refers to supper in parts of France. Which is why you'll pass old Parisian bistros with fading words somewhere on the outside that include "Bouillon." Or people might invite you over for *la soupe*, which is a proposition for dinner, not necessarily just a bowl of soup. (In French, *souper* means "to have supper"—no matter what's on the menu.)

But the main reason that French onion soup may have fallen out of favor in restaurants is that it's impossible to look even remotely dignified when eating it. Trying to spoon up croutons whose every nook is filled with steaming-hot bouillon, topped with lava-like cheese that forms a saliva-like string when you pull the spoon away from your mouth after each bite doesn't make for graceful eating in public. So I enjoy it at home, for lunch or *soupe*.

French onion soup

SOUPE À L'OIGNON

Serves 6

Beef stock is thought to be traditional in this soup, but it's heavier, and I rarely have beef stock on hand, so I use chicken stock (page 326). For a heartier stock, you can roast the chicken bones in a 400°F (200°C) oven on a baking sheet for 30 to 45 minutes, until well browned, then use those bones to make the stock.

1   Melt the butter in a large pot or Dutch oven over medium heat. Add the onions and sugar and cook for 20 minutes, stirring occasionally, until soft and transluscent.

2   Add the garlic, salt, and pepper and continue to cook for $1^{1}/_{2}$ hours, stirring less frequently and decreasing the heat to avoid burning as the onions continue to cook down. (You may wish to use a flame diffuser if your cooktop doesn't allow low enough heat.) As the onions cook, if they brown on the bottom of the pan in places, use a spatula to scrape those appetizing brown bits into the onions because they'll add flavor. The onions are done when they have collapsed into a thick amber-brown paste.

3   Stir in the flour and cook, stirring constantly, for 1 minute. Add the wine and use a flat utensil to loosen any remaining brown bits from the bottom and sides of the pan, stirring them into the onions. Add the stock, bring to a boil, then decrease the heat and simmer slowly for 45 minutes. Turn off the heat and add the vinegar, tasting it to get the balance right, adding a touch more vinegar, salt, and pepper, if desired.

4   Preheat the oven to 400°F (200°C). Set six ovenproof bowls on a baking sheet lined with parchment paper or aluminum foil.

5   Divide the hot soup among the bowls. Rub both sides of the toasted bread with the garlic. Put the toasts on the soup, then sprinkle the tops with the cheese. Bake the soup on the upper rack of the oven until the cheese is deeply browned, about 20 minutes. Alternatively, if your bowls can withstand the heat, you can set the cheese-topped soups under a hot broiler, cooking them until the cheese is melted and starting to brown. Serve immediately.

4 tablespoons (2 ounces/55g) unsalted butter

$2^{1}/_{2}$ pounds (1.2kg) yellow or white onions, peeled and very thinly sliced

1 teaspoon granulated sugar

2 cloves garlic, peeled and minced

2 teaspoons sea salt or kosher salt, plus more if needed

1 teaspoon freshly ground black pepper, plus more if needed

2 teaspoons all-purpose flour

$3/_{4}$ cup (180ml) white wine or sherry

2 quarts (2l) chicken stock (page 326)

1 to 2 teaspoons sherry vinegar or balsamic vinegar, plus more if needed

6 thick slices hearty white bread, or about 18 thick-sliced pieces of baguette, well toasted

1 to 2 cloves garlic, peeled and left whole, for rubbing the toast

3 cups (255g) grated Emmenthal, Comté, or Gruyère cheese

La Canicule

COMING TO PARIS FROM SAN FRANCISCO, where summers meant that there might be a day here and there where you could go out and maybe not bring a sweater (and jacket) with you, Paris weather was a shock. Right after I arrived in 2003, we had a week-long heat wave that sent temperatures through the roof—in my place, literally.

I lived in a rooftop *chambre de bonne*, and the temperature in my apartment reached an extremely unpleasant 104°F (40°C). Not only was my beloved chocolate stash suffering a serious meltdown, so was I. It got to the point where even wearing clothes became impossible, which was the case for my neighbors of all ages (and weights and sizes) as I learned whenever I leaned out my window in hopes of catching the faintest breeze of fresh air.

The infamous *canicule* (heat wave) changed a few things in France. It didn't change how people view the government, which somehow got blamed for the heat wave. But the following year, air conditioners were prominently for sale in stores, even though most people in France view being in an air-conditioned room as akin to a death sentence. And the government stepped up their responsibility, not by changing the weather, but by issuing guidelines that advised that, in case of another heat wave, we should all go to an air-conditioned place for "2 to 3 hours" a day. (The only places that are air-conditioned in Paris are the supermarkets. And as much time as I spend shopping for food, 2 to 3 hours is a little too much, even for me.)

We were also told to drink at least 2 liters of water a day, which basically meant you had to stay at home, because as anyone who's tried to find a restroom in Paris can attest, there are very few places to get rid of that water. But those were only minor objections compared to what I thought about the rule that said to stop drinking alcohol, as icy rosé was the only thing keeping me going.

I've discovered the strategy that works best for coping with the heat is making lots of gazpacho, a favorite soup among Parisians. I use the juiciest, pulpiest summer tomatoes I can find, searching out ones that are almost ready to explode and nearing the end of their prime. The vendors are always happy to have someone take these tomatoes off their hands, and they give them to me for a good price. In exchange, I promise them the tomatoes will have a bright future, whirled up in a bowl of refreshing summer soup.

Gazpacho with herbed goat cheese toasts

GASPACHO, CROÛTONS AU CHÈVRE AUX HERBES

Serves 6

121

I like to think of gazpacho as more of an icy-cold liquid salad than a slurry, similar to tomato juice. Juicy, ripe tomatoes have the best flavor, and I like the other vegetables to be finely diced. So if you can wipe some of the sweat off your brow, this is a good place to practice your knife skills. But for those who like their gazpacho smooth, feel free to simply puree everything together.

I add a bit of piment d'Espelette, a Basque pepper powder, and a shot of vodka, which makes the soup taste even colder. And because it's hard to imagine a meal in France without cheese, no matter what time of the year it is, I make garlicky croutons and smear them with fresh goat cheese mixed with fresh herbs.

The gazpacho and the goat cheese spread can be made up to 3 days in advance and refrigerated.

GAZPACHO

3 pounds (1.5kg) ripe tomatoes

1 slice firm, white country-style bread, crusts removed

1 cucumber, peeled, seeded, and finely diced

1 red onion, peeled and finely diced

1/2 red, green, or yellow bell pepper, seeded and finely diced

2 cloves garlic, peeled and minced

1/4 cup (60ml) olive oil

1 1/2 tablespoons red wine vinegar

2 1/2 teaspoons sea salt or kosher salt, plus more if needed

1/2 teaspoon piment d'Espelette (or smoked paprika or chile powder)

Freshly ground black pepper

1 tablespoon vodka

HERBED GOAT CHEESE TOASTS

16 baguette slices, about 1/3 inch (1cm) thick

Olive oil

2 cloves garlic, peeled

2 cups (8 ounces/225g) crumbled fresh goat cheese (see Note on page 122)

1 tablespoon chopped fresh basil, dill, chervil, or mint

Sea salt or kosher salt

1 To make the gazpacho, fill a large pot half full with water and bring it to a boil. Remove the cores of the tomatoes and cut an X in the bottom of each.

2 Plunge the tomatoes into the boiling water (work in batches if your pot won't hold them all), and let the tomatoes blanch for 30 seconds, or until the skins loosen. Transfer them to a strainer and rinse under cold water. Peel the tomatoes, discarding the skins.

3 Cut the tomatoes in half horizontally. Set a coarse-mesh strainer over a bowl and squeeze the liquid and seeds out of the tomatoes; press the pulp through the strainer. (Discard the seeds, but save the tomatoes and tomato liquid.)

4 In a small bowl, soak the bread in cold water for 1 minute, drain, and squeeze the excess water out of the bread.

5 Working in batches, pulse the tomatoes and tomato liquid in the bowl of a food processor or blender with the bread, until they're almost liquefied, yet still have bits of tomato visible.

6 Mix the nearly pureed tomatoes in a large bowl with the cucumber, onion, pepper, and garlic. Stir in the olive oil, vinegar, salt, and piment d'Espelette; season with pepper and add the vodka. Taste, and add additional salt if necessary. Chill thoroughly.

continued

7 To make the toasts, preheat the oven to 350°F (180°C). Place the baguette slices on a baking sheet and brush the tops lightly with olive oil. Bake for 5 to 8 minutes, until the toasts are light golden brown. Remove from the oven, and as soon as they're cool enough to handle, rub each very generously with the garlic.

8 With a fork, mash the goat cheese in a small bowl with the herbs and 1 teaspoon of olive oil, and season with salt. Smear each toast with a tablespoon of the cheese mixture.

9 Divide the soup among six chilled bowls and serve the toasts alongside or floating on top.

NOTE: If you don't have fresh goat cheese, substitute queso fresco or feta cheese creamed with a bit of milk to smooth it out.

Gazpacho with herbed goat cheese toasts, continued

Grated carrot salad

CAROTTES RAPÉES

Serves 6

It's impossible to write a book about French cuisine without including grated carrot salad. There is no one in this country who doesn't like this salad, and it's so commonplace that I don't think you'll find it mentioned in any of the books on traditional French cuisine. It's just a given that if you're French, it's in your DNA to know how to make this salad, although if you ask 60 million Frenchmen, or French women, how to make this salad, you will likely end up with 60 million recipes.

Since my recipe files are stuffed, I asked a certain Frenchman, the one who makes my favorite version of this salad and a pretty fine version of leeks vinaigrette (page 88), for his tips. He pulled out a Moulinex grater called a *mouli-julienne*, which is available only in France. This handy device makes the slender, long, and slightly curly strands of carrots that are the signature of the salad. (I've been thinking of working a co-branding arrangement, because everyone I know who's had this salad in France goes home and then writes back to me that they have searched high and low to find one of these French graters.)

Although I'm not one to mess too much with something that's a hallowed French tradition, this salad is good with avocado or with grated raw beets to augment the carrots. To make it a more complete salad-as-lunch, you can toss in some quartered hard-cooked eggs (page 328), sliced roasted chicken breast, or large crumbles of blue cheese or feta.

- 2 pounds (900g) carrots
- ¼ cup (60ml) olive oil
- 2 tablespoons freshly squeezed lemon juice
- 1 teaspoon sea salt or kosher salt
- 1 teaspoon Dijon mustard
- ½ teaspoon granulated sugar or honey
- 3 tablespoons minced fresh flat-leaf parsley, chervil, or chives, plus additional chopped herbs for sprinkling on top

1 Using the large holes of a box grater or a stand mixer or food processor fitted with the shredding disk attachment, grate the carrots.

2 In a large bowl, mix together the olive oil, lemon juice, salt, mustard, and sugar. Toss the grated carrots in the dressing along with the chopped herbs. Serve on plates and sprinkle with additional fresh herbs.

VARIATION: To make a carrot-beet salad, substitute 1 pound of raw beets, peeled and shredded, for 1 pound of the carrots. Or add 2 ripe, peeled, and diced avocados to make a carrot-avocado salad.

4me ARR^t
PLACE
DE LA
BASTILLE

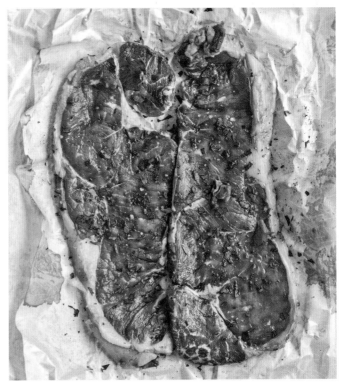

Main courses

PLATS

The owner of a fancy three-star restaurant in Paris was quoted as saying, "The first time you come to our restaurant, you're a stranger. The second time, you're a guest. The third time, you're part of our family." And that's pretty indicative of the Parisian attitude about strangers, guests, and friends and family. Much has to do with becoming a regular customer, and as the staff gets to know you, you become a member of the extended family. Some old bistros in Paris still have the cubbyhole-like drawers where regulars would leave their cloth napkins, to use on their next visit.

But no matter if it's your first—or fiftieth—visit, instead of the usual "the customer is always right" attitude when you go to a restaurant in France, the relationship is more fifty-fifty (or *feefty-feefty*, as they say). The cooks and servers are there to prepare and bring you the food, and your task is just to relax and enjoy it. True, some Parisian waiters live up to their cranky reputations. But if you look around the dining room, you won't see an army of hosts, busboys, waiters, and runners. Instead there are usually no more than just a couple of waiters in the dining room, skirting around in long black aprons, uncorking wine, taking orders, bringing out food, bantering with the kitchen, setting (and resetting) tables, and yes, in some cases, taking great care to avoid the diners' gaze.

I find the whole thing fascinating, and each restaurant in Paris has its own personality. The main thing that I impress upon visitors is to go back to the same place and become a regular guest rather than remain a stranger. Or better yet, become a friend.

Entertaining at home in Paris is reserved for friends and family; invitations are limited to people you already know. If you're meeting someone you don't know well, cafés are popular neutral spaces to socialize, which is why I often refer to cafés as the "living rooms" of Paris.

Nevertheless, many of the unspoken rules about entertaining at home elude me in Paris. I love having people over, either for an *apéro*, or for dinner. When people come to visit, they arrive armed with a spreadsheet of "must go to" restaurants. But I wave them away and invite them to my place instead, preferring to hit the market and gather ingredients for dinner, including rifling through the bottles of wine randomly stashed in every available opening around my apartment, making sure I have a well-chilled bottle of Champagne or crémant so I can greet people with a *flûte* of something bubbly and festive right after they step inside. And after cooking all day, I can generally use a drink right about then, too!

Preparing for a dinner party begins with shopping, and I visit my favorite vendors and shops in my neighborhood where they know me, so I get the best peaches, oranges, or pears (and don't end up paying a premium for the vendor's thumb that's also resting on the scale). The women at my *fromagerie* will label certain cheeses as *"Génial!"* or *"C'est super!"* noting what's the best or most interesting that day. The butcher will take the time to eviscerate a chicken for me, so I just unwrap the stiff paper when I get home and find a perfectly prepared *poulet* inside, waiting to be cooked. I stop at the bakery for a *baguette tradition*, and while the pastries tempt—and I might buy myself a little snack (lately I've been partial to éclairs and can't seem to get enough . . .)—I invariably make the dessert myself, often accompanied with a scoop of homemade ice cream or sorbet, using ripe fruits I picked up at the market.

I don't have a dining room in my apartment. Instead I have a *cuisine américaine*, or an "open kitchen." This style of eating bucks the tradition of having the cooking done by *la domestique*, in a closed room far away from the diners. But with the size of Parisian apartments, many have taken a nod from *les américains* and have opened up their kitchens, and now they pull stools to the kitchen counter and eat *au comptoir*. When folks come for dinner, they sit at my kitchen counter as well. I like being able to talk to them while I whisk up dressing for the salad or tend to a braise that is simmering away in the oven. Since people in France know that it's special to get invited to someone's home for dinner, they are always appreciative. You don't come across picky eaters, and I've seen people who are normally reserved and well behaved at dinner in restaurants, take seconds (or thirds) when having dinner in my kitchen. I like that people feel relaxed enough to pick up a chicken leg to get every last bit of meat off the bone. Or grab a knife to slice more bread so we can polish off the last of the Camembert. (I once even had someone lift up a plate and lick it clean, but I'll chalk that up to a one-time indiscretion.) Or take the initiative to open another bottle of wine when they see glasses running low.

When eating alone or *à deux*, I'll crack a few eggs for a quick Fresh herb omelet (page 133) or *galette complète* (page 135). When entertaining, I'm a fan of long-simmered dishes, like *carbonade flamande* (page 198), *coq au vin* (page 177), and *cassoulet* (page 195), which can be made in advance and usually provide me with tasty leftovers for the next day, when the party's over. My quick version of duck confit (page 179) doesn't require constant tending, and you can make your own sausages and form them into *caillettes* (page 185), meaty, single-servings that come with an accompaniment of greens tucked right inside.

While I don't advocate plate-licking, my main objective is to have a good time dining together in my kitchen. Just like I do when cooking the food. And, of course, doing the shopping, too.

Differences, or Disagreements?

FRENCH PEOPLE MAKE A SPORT OF BANTERING and complaining. But lest you think I'm being critical, you should know that in France, complaining is not considered a fault, but just something everyone does. Because really, everyone has something to complain or disagree about, right?

No matter how beautifully blue the sky might be, if you say it's blue, *non*, they will certainly tell you—it's not blue, it's *marine*. And add that it's probably going to rain. And it's not uncommon to overhear people complain about how dirty the streets are (as they flick their cigarette butt onto the sidewalk). I came to understand that the French bicker to assert a sense of authority; complaining about something shows you have information that someone else doesn't. (But, of course, a solution rarely figures into the discussion.)

I'm no stranger to engaging in a little complaining and trading barbs and have learned to hold my own against the best of them. When I first met Paule Caillat, a cooking teacher, we had a fairly contentious discussion about the state of tomatoes in Paris, something I *râle* about every summer. I grumbled about how there were amazing tomatoes in Provence, but somehow they rarely made it to Paris, and she insisted that I didn't understand. I wasn't sure what I didn't understand—especially since she speaks perfect English—but that conversation was one of my first moments of *c'est comme ça*, or "that's just how it is," an irrefutable French way to win any argument.

One night, while sharing dinner in Paule's kitchen, I was blown away by her family specialty, *gnocchis à la parisienne*, which had me scraping (but not licking) my dish clean. Since Paule and I had become friends, and she's quite good-natured, it has become my own sport to give her a hard time. So when she showed up in my

kitchen a few days later to teach me how to make the dish and asked me if I had "one of those hard, flat, plastic American things," I returned with, "You mean one of these *French* pastry scrapers?" while holding up one of the scrapers I got when I was at *French* pastry school in *France*.

As we prepared the recipe, I asked her what kind of cheese we'd be using and she replied, *"le Gruyère."* "*Gruyère!?*" I wondered aloud. "No wonder it's so good." "Well, it's not really Gruyère, *Daveed*," she said. "In France, we just call any grated cheese *Gruyère*, because, well, *c'est comme ça*." Since I know how protective the French are about their own cheeses and appellations, I remarked that that was similar to my grabbing any old rubbery wedge of cheese at the supermarket and saying, "Well, let's just call this

Brie de Meaux." But I got waved away, and we kept cooking. (And then I realized a few minutes later that in America, we call any cheese with holes in it *Swiss cheese*, no matter where it's from. And that *Gruyère* also refers to a type of cheese. But I decided to withhold this information because, like the good Frenchman I've become, I didn't want to insert logic into an argument.)

Next she remarked on the bag of all-purpose French flour I had, bought from a different grocery store than where she got hers, which raised an eyebrow. And when I gave her a fork for stirring the eggs, she looked at my modern three-tined fork and said, "*Daveed*, don't you have a real fork?"

Yet all was forgiven when I managed to drum up some four-tined models and we sat down with the baking dish of cheese-crusted gnocchi bubbling away between us. I didn't bother asking how this dish got the name *gnocchi*, because these are not what comes to mind when most people think of gnocchi. Nor did I argue about how inferior I felt having a kitchen stocked with flour from the wrong supermarket. And I let it go that my "American" pastry scraper was actually made and purchased in France. But perhaps attesting to the power of an agreeably rich casserole topped with cheese called by whatever name you want to call it, no matter what our disagreements are or where we're from, Paule and I cast our differences aside and dug into this communal dish, calling each other *des vrais amis*, or true friends, in the common language of cooks.

129

Parisian gnocchi

GNOCCHIS À LA PARISIENNE

Serves 6

This dish is considered humble fare, and one you would never see in a restaurant. Hence it's largely unknown to folks outside of France. Paule Caillat (see page 128) gave me her family recipe, to which I made a few changes (authorized, of course). The dumplings are made of pâte à choux dough, similar to that used for profiteroles. The gnocchi are partially cooked by poaching, then baking, where they'll puff up gloriously before settling down, waiting to be scooped up from under a blanket of browned cheese. This is a pretty rich dish; serve it with a simple green salad.

1   To make the pâte à choux, heat the water, butter, and $^1/_2$ teaspoon of salt in a saucepan over medium heat just until the butter is melted. Dump in all the flour at once and stir the mixture briskly for about 2 minutes, until the dough forms a smooth ball. Remove from the heat and scrape the dough into the bowl of a stand mixer fitted with the paddle attachment. (If you don't have a stand mixer, simply leave it in the saucepan.) Let the dough sit for 3 minutes, stirring it every so often to release some of the heat.

2   With the mixer on medium-high speed, or by hand, add the eggs one at a time, making sure each one is fully incorporated before adding the next. Add the dry mustard and beat until the dough is completely smooth. Cover with a kitchen towel and set aside.

3   To make the Mornay sauce, melt the butter in the saucepan over medium heat. Add the flour and cook, letting the mixture bubble and stirring constantly, for 2 minutes, until the paste is thickened. (Don't let it brown.) Gradually whisk in the milk, beginning slowly and stirring constantly to avoid lumps.

4   Decrease the heat to low and cook the Mornay for 6 minutes, stirring frequently, or until the sauce is about as thick as a milkshake. Remove from heat and add the salt, cayenne, and $^1/_2$ cup (40g) of the Swiss-style cheese; stir until the cheese is melted.

5   Butter a shallow $2^1/_2$- to 3-quart (2.5 to 3l) baking dish. (A wide dish is preferable to a deep one for browning the cheese topping.) Sprinkle half of the Parmesan over the bottom and sides. Spread 1 cup (250ml) of the Mornay sauce over the bottom of the baking dish.

PÂTE À CHOUX

$1^1/_4$ cups (310ml) water

7 tablespoons ($3^1/_2$ ounces/100g) unsalted butter, room temperature, cubed

$^1/_2$ teaspoon sea salt or kosher salt

$1^1/_4$ cups (175g) all-purpose flour

4 large eggs, at room temperature

2 teaspoons dry mustard or mustard powder

MORNAY SAUCE

5 tablespoons ($2^1/_2$ ounces/70g) salted or unsalted butter

$^1/_3$ cup (45g) all-purpose flour

3 cups (750ml) whole or low-fat milk, warmed

1 teaspoon sea salt or kosher salt

Generous pinch of cayenne pepper

$1^3/_4$ cups (140g) grated Swiss-style cheese, such as Emmenthal, Gruyère, or Comté

$^1/_3$ cup (1 ounce/30g) freshly grated Parmesan cheese

6   Line a large dinner plate with a few layers of paper towels. Bring a pot of salted water to a low boil. Either using two soupspoons—one to scoop up some of the dough and the other to scrape it into the boiling water—or a spring-loaded ice cream scoop, scoop up about 1 generous tablespoon of dough and drop it into the water. (The ice cream scoop was a little newfangled for Paule, although she did agree—reluctantly—that it was more expedient and made nicer gnocchi.) Working in batches, poach 8 to 10 gnocchi at a time. Let them poach for 2 minutes, then retrieve them from the water and drain them on the paper towels. (They won't be fully cooked inside.) Repeat, poaching the rest of the gnocchi the same way.

7   Preheat the oven to 350°F (180°C) with the oven rack in the top third of the oven.

8   Once the gnocchi are parcooked, place them in a single layer on top of the Mornay in the baking dish, and then spoon the rest of the Mornay over the gnocchi in a fairly even layer. Sprinkle the remaining 1¼ cups (100g) of Swiss-style cheese over the top, along with the remaining Parmesan. Put the baking dish on a foil-covered baking sheet and bake for 15 minutes. Increase the oven temperature to 400°F (200°C) and bake for another 15 to 20 minutes, until the cheese on top is well browned. Let cool a few minutes, and then serve in the baking dish, family style.

VARIATIONS: Add 1 cup (130g) diced ham or cooked bacon to the dish, distributing them over the bottom layer of Mornay before placing the gnocchi in the baking dish. Or put some coarsely chopped, sautéed arugula, kale, mustard greens, or radicchio under the gnocchi.

Omelet Overtures

MY FIRST "AHA!" MOMENT IN PARIS, WHEN I really felt the magic of the city, was when I had just met my partner, Romain. We didn't know each other very well; he barely spoke English, and my French was pretty nonexistent. It was late in the evening, and we were wandering around his *quartier*. Deciding we were hungry, we pulled up seats in a busy café near Montmartre to have a bite.

As we sat down on rickety café chairs surrounded by tables of lively young Parisians drinking and chattering away, suddenly the whole scene came alive for me: the worn tables with the raised, sharp metal rims that encircle them; the glass window with the menu scribbled on it in cursive French handwriting; the stained, battered ashtrays; the little caddy of mustard, salt, and pepper that the waiter swiftly plunked down after delivering our omelets; the basket holding thick slices of baguette cut sharply on the bias. And there I was, sitting with an honest-to-goodness Parisian, looking at Sacré Cœur glowing just up the hill. It was truly magical, and was the second time in my life that my dreams had came true over an *omelette aux fines herbes*, courtesy of a handsome Frenchman.

When I worked in the pastry department at Chez Panisse with my pal Mary Jo Thoresen, we loved working together and we laughed a lot. In fact, one night we were laughing so hard at something that was probably ridiculously silly that the kitchen manager sternly asked us to step out of the kitchen until we had pulled ourselves together. Despite the laughter, we worked very hard. As pastry folks, we rarely had time to eat because just when the kitchen crew was sitting down for their staff meal after serving the guests, we had to shift into high gear to serve the desserts.

During one of our bouts of silliness, for some reason Mary Jo and I got the phrase *omelette aux fines herbes*, stuck in our heads. In French, this is pronounced as one word: *omletohfinszerb*, and to us it sounded fancy, funny, and quintessentially French. So we begged the chef, Jean-Pierre Moullé, another honest-to-goodness Frenchman, to make us an *omeletohfinszerb*, giggling every time we said it. I don't know if he was flattered, or just trying to shut us up, but he finally fired up his omelet pan, and made one.

In France, an omelet isn't fancy or funny—it's a meal, and sometimes a romantic one, at that. The herbs are up to you. For a true French *omeletohfinzerb*, add some chervil and tarragon to the mix. Since these herbs have strong flavors, temper them with some parsley or chives. Just make sure they are very finely chopped. Don't use rosemary and sage, as these can both be overpowering, a feeling better left for those times when sharing an omelet with someone you care about.

Fresh herb omelet

OMELETTE AUX FINES HERBES

Serves 1 to 2

2 or 3 large eggs

1 to 2 teaspoons heavy cream or milk

2 to 3 teaspoons finely chopped fresh herbs, plus a little extra for garnish

Sea salt or kosher salt and freshly ground black pepper

1½ teaspoons salted or unsalted butter

2 tablespoons finely grated Gruyère or Comté cheese (optional)

I've read multipage manifestos from chefs about how to make a good omelet, but they rarely mention the most important factor: using good eggs. People wince at the price of farm eggs, but unless you live in an unreasonably exorbitant area, I can't imagine a few good eggs breaking the bank.

Omelets in France are served *baveuse* (drooling), but I like mine a bit more cooked. Cafés serve them with a green salad or *frites* (page 219), although Duck fat–fried potatoes (page 220) are an excellent accompaniment. If anyone gives you a hard time about that combo, explain the French paradox—and pour them a healthy glass of red wine while you do.

I use a large 12-inch (30cm) nonstick skillet since a large surface area gives a bit more crispness to the outside of the omelet, which I like. A smaller pan will make a taller, softer omelet.

I find that a two-egg omelet is sufficient for one person—namely, me. That gives me extra leeway to enjoy some of those potatoes fried in duck fat. But I'll often turn out a three- or even four-egg omelet to make a nice dinner *à deux*.

1   In a bowl, stir the eggs and the cream together briskly with a fork (use 1 teaspoon of cream for 2 eggs and 2 teaspoons of cream for 3 eggs). Reserve some herbs for a garnish and add the rest (2 teaspoons for a 2-egg omelet), using the fork to blend in the herbs, a big pinch of salt, and a few grinds of the peppermill.

2   Heat the butter in a large, nonstick skillet (or a small skillet if you like a thicker omelet) over moderately high heat. When the butter starts to sizzle and foam a bit, spread it all over the pan with a spatula so the bottom and part of the sides of the pan are coated.

3   Pour the eggs into the hot pan and let them cook until the edges start to set, which will happen before a minute is up. Lift the pan, tilt it toward you, and use a heatproof spatula to lift up the lip of the omelet closest to you, allowing the liquidy, uncooked eggs from the center to flow underneath. Put the pan back on the burner and sprinkle the cheese in a line down the center.

4   Before the omelet is completely set (depending on how you like your eggs), fold it in half and slide it onto a warm plate. Garnish with the reserved chopped herbs.

Standing Up for French Street Food

MANY PEOPLE HAVE HAPPY MEMORIES of eating a warm crêpe on a street in Paris—except for me. A while back, I was minding my own business, enjoying a warm, cheese-filled crêpe wrapped up in a piece of waxed paper while standing on the sidewalk next to a crêpe stand, when a horrified tourist barked at me, "How can you eat that?!" I froze, too astonished to respond. And to this day I have no idea why she was so alarmed. But nowadays whether I buy a crêpe from a stand or a *crêperie* or make one at home, if someone were to ask me how I could eat one, my answer would be, "It's easy."

Each *crêperie* has its own distinct way of making crêpes (which are made with white flour) and *galettes* (made with buckwheat flour). Some fold them into a sharp square with four right angles that would make an architect envious. Others might double them over into loose quarters, slip them into pieces of waxed paper, and hand you a warm packet that you can eat on the run. Still other places might form them into squares, flip the whole shebang over, and fry it on both sides.

The French prefer serving the classic *crêpe complète* with a sunny-side up egg, and the diner breaks the yolk, which creates its own sauce. You can use a fancy cheese, like Comté or Gruyère, but Emmenthal (Swiss cheese) is the cheese preferred by most *crêperies* in France. It's customary to use *jambon de Paris*—regular boiled ham—although I've been known to slip pieces of top-quality dry-cured ham or prosciutto in mine at home.

Normally I'm not a fan of preground pepper, but it does provide the authentic Paris "street stand" flavor. If you have it, use that instead of freshly ground black pepper. Come to think of it, maybe that's what the woman was referring to when I got my scolding?

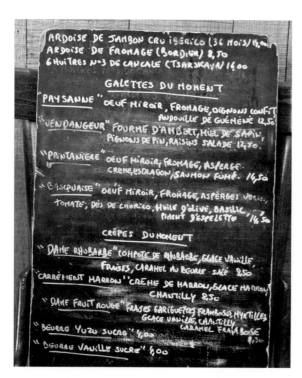

Buckwheat crêpes with ham, cheese, and egg

GALETTES COMPLÈTES

Makes 2

Normally, *galettes* are made one at a time, but you could prepare two simultaneously if you want to have two pans going. Since they cook quickly, I just have everything ready to go for the second one, and do them one right after the other.

Salted or unsalted butter, for reheating the galette

2 Buckwheat galettes (page 47)

4 slices prosciutto or thinly sliced dry-cured or boiled ham

1 cup (3 ounces/85g) grated Emmenthal cheese

2 eggs, at room temperature

Sea salt or kosher salt and black pepper

1 Melt a bit of butter in a skillet with a lid over medium heat. When the butter is foamy, place one buckwheat *galette* in the pan, the underside (with the larger bubbles) facing up.

2 Arrange 2 slices of the prosciutto side by side in the center of the *galette*. Sprinkle with half of the Emmenthal. Crack an egg into the center and move the whites around a little with the back of a fork to spread them so the egg will cook evenly. (Be careful not to disturb or break the yolk.) Cover the skillet with the lid and cook until the egg white is set but the yolk is still quite liquid, or it's cooked to your liking.

3 Remove the lid and use a spatula to fold over about 1 inch (3cm) of the top edge of the *galette*. Do the same with the other three edges, creating a square. Slide the *galette complète* onto a warm dinner plate and follow the steps above to make the second *galette*. Serve with salt and black pepper.

Fried ham and cheese sandwich

CROQUE-MONSIEUR

Serves 2

Croque-monsieur is one of those "I gotta have it" things. I don't crave one every day, but on those days that I do, I just gotta have one. A well-made croque-monsieur can be elusive—gone are the days when any corner café made a good one. If you are unlucky, you might get one served on Harrys bread, which is similar to American white bread and is wildly popular in France. Harrys was started in 1970 by a Frenchman who was fascinated by the bread he saw Americans eating on the local army base. According to the *New York Times*, Harrys now makes 130 million loaves of bread a year, and I have friends who tell me their French partners or spouses won't eat anything else for their morning toast.

Fortunately, many cafés offer *le croque-monsieur* on your choice of white bread or *pain levain*, which, if you're lucky, is *pain* Poilâne, the marvelously crusty sourdough loaf baked every morning in a wood-fired oven located beneath its shop on the rue Cherche-Midi. To me, it's not even a decision; I'll take the *pain* Poilâne any day.

You can easily turn this sandwich into a croque-madame, which is a croque-monsieur sporting a sunny-side up egg resting on top. Since the French don't eat sandwiches with their hands when sitting at a table, their first gesture is to slash open the egg yolk with a knife, letting it flow all over the sandwich and making rivulets of sauce to dip forkfuls of the sandwich into.

continued

If you want to get your croque-monsieur fix at home, dry-cured ham is best for a *monsieur* (or *madame*). Comté and Gruyère make a premium treat, although Emmenthal is used most often in Paris. For bread, try to find a hearty sourdough loaf, and make sure the slices aren't too thick; no more than 1/4 inch (.75cm) is optimal.

To temper the unrestrained amount of cheese, *le croque-monsieur* is always served with a green salad dressed with a very mustardy vinaigrette (page 335). If I order this at a café, I usually accompany it with a cold Orangina or a carafe of chilled rosé in the summer, or a mellow Côte du Rhone in the winter. And I don't see any reason why you shouldn't do the same at home.

1 To make the béchamel, melt the butter in a saucepan over medium heat and stir in the flour. When the mixture starts to bubble, cook for 1 minute more. Whisk in 1/4 cup (60ml) of the milk, stirring to discourage lumps, then whisk in the remaining 1/2 cup (120ml) of milk. Cook for about 1 minute more, until the sauce is thick and creamy, like runny mayonnaise. Remove from the heat and stir in the salt and cayenne; set aside to cool a bit and thicken.

2 To make the croque-monsieur, spread the béchamel evenly over the four slices of bread. Lay a slice of ham over two of the bread slices, top them with slices of cheese, and then top with the remaining ham slices. Finish with the two remaining slices of bread, béchamel side down (on the inside), and brush the outsides of the sandwiches without restraint with the melted butter.

3 Turn on the broiler and heat a large ovenproof frying pan or grill pan over medium-high heat on the stove top. (Make sure to use a pan with a heatproof handle, for broiling later.) Place the sandwiches in the frying pan, drape with a sheet of aluminum foil, and then rest a cast-iron skillet or other heavy pan or flat object on top. Cook until the bottoms of the sandwiches are well browned. Remove the skillet and foil, flip the sandwiches over, replace the foil and skillet, and continue cooking until the other side is browned.

4 Remove the cast-iron skillet and foil and strew the grated cheese on top of the sandwiches. Put the pan under the broiler and broil the sandwiches until the cheese melts. Serve immediately.

VARIATION: To make a croque-madame, while the sandwiches are broiling, cook a sunny-side up egg for each sandwich. Slide the eggs on top of the sandwiches after you plate them.

Fried ham and cheese sandwich, continued

BÉCHAMEL

1 tablespoon salted or unsalted butter

1 tablespoon all-purpose flour

3/4 cup (180ml) whole milk

Pinch of sea salt or kosher salt

Pinch of cayenne pepper

CROQUE-MONSIEUR

4 slices sourdough or country-style bread

4 slices prosciutto or thinly sliced dry-cured ham, or 2 thick slices boiled ham

2 thin slices Comté or Gruyère cheese

4 tablespoons (2 ounces/55g) salted or unsalted butter, melted

3/4 cup (60g) grated Comté or Gruyère cheese

Cheese, bacon, and arugula soufflé

SOUFFLÉ À LA ROQUETTE, LARDONS, ET FROMAGE

Serves 8

I've read plenty about the demise of France and French cuisine, including one article that simply summed up the entire situation by saying, "They are no longer at the forefront of, well, anything really."

Yes, it's true, *les trente glorieuses*, the thirty-year period after World War II when France experienced an upsurge in innovation and prosperity, is far behind it. What many people love about France, however, is the reluctance to modernize that sometimes means falling behind. While this is frustrating for those of us who live here (and who believe that online banking should mean that you can do something with your bank account other than gaze longingly at your balance on a computer screen), the one thing no one has been able to surpass is French cheese.

Walk into any *fromagerie* and take a whiff, and you'll know exactly what I'm talking about. The cheese shops are among the sturdiest bastions of French culinary culture, and as much as others have tried, French raw milk cheeses have not been successfully replicated anywhere. Smear a bit of Langes, with its brilliant orange rind and tangy, creamy center on a slice of baguette, or lop off a wedge of Camembert de Normandie that's just at that point of ripeness where it's both gooey and sticky and fills your mouth with the flavor of aged butterfat, butterscotch, and well-used barnyards, and you might agree that modernization can be overrated.

Along with cheese, another thing that hasn't been improved upon is the soufflé. When I was a pastry chef, I made over a hundred soufflés a night, whipping each one by hand, then baking each until it was just perfect. Then, while the waiter stood patiently by the hot oven, I'd remove the trembling dessert and slide it onto an awaiting plate, and it would be whisked out to a diner.

I always make individual soufflés, which are more fun to eat because everyone gets their own crusted soufflé (and because they are easier to bake exactly right). Even easier to make are twice-baked soufflés like this one. They are less fussy and get baked once in their molds, then released and rebaked, where they puff a little further, giving them a chance to develop an all-over golden brown exterior.

continued

1 In a wide saucepan or skillet with a lid, cook the bacon over medium heat until nearly crisp. Transfer the bacon to a paper towel to drain.

2 Wipe any excess bacon fat from the skillet and add the arugula to the pan with a pinch of salt. Cover and cook over medium heat for a few minutes, turning the arugula a couple of times, until completely wilted. Remove the pan from the heat, uncover, and let the arugula cool completely. Squeeze the arugula with your hands as hard as possible to extract as much water as you can, then finely chop the arugula.

3 Preheat the oven to 400°F (200°C). Generously butter eight individual 4-ounce (125ml) soufflé molds. Coat the inside of each soufflé mold with some of the grated Parmesan. Set the molds in a deep-sided baking dish. Line a baking sheet with parchment paper, lightly grease the paper, and set it aside.

4 Heat the milk with 1/4 teaspoon of salt in a small saucepan over low heat until warm. Set aside.

5 Melt the butter in a saucepan over medium heat. Add the flour and cook for about 2 minutes, stirring constantly with a whisk, until the mixture is smooth.

6 Gradually add the warm milk, whisking to remove any lumps, and cook until all the lumps are gone and the sauce is smooth, 1 to 2 minutes. Remove from the heat and add most of the remaining Parmesan (reserve a bit for sprinkling over the tops of the soufflés before baking). Add half of the Comté. Briskly stir in the egg yolks, the remaining Comté, cayenne pepper, and chives. Stir in the chopped arugula and bacon.

7 In a separate bowl, whip the egg whites until stiff. Fold one-quarter of the egg whites into the soufflé base, then fold in the remaining egg whites until just a few streaks of white are visible. Don't overmix. Divide the soufflé mixture among the prepared soufflé molds, and sprinkle the tops with the remaining Parmesan.

8 Add hot water to the baking pan to reach halfway up the sides of the molds. Bake the soufflés for 20 to 25 minutes, or until they feel just set; they should feel slightly soft and jiggly when you touch the centers. Remove the soufflés from the water bath and cool on a wire rack. (The tops will fall a little.) Once cool enough to handle, run a knife around the outside of each soufflé to loosen it. Tip each soufflé into your hand. One by one, place them on the prepared baking sheet, right side up.

Cheese, bacon, and arugula soufflé, continued

1 1/2 cups (150g) diced thick-cut smoked bacon

8 ounces (250g) arugula

Sea salt or kosher salt

1 cup (3 ounces/90g) freshly grated Parmesan cheese

1 cup (250ml) whole or low-fat milk

3 tablespoons salted or unsalted butter

3 tablespoons all-purpose flour

1 1/2 cups (4 1/2 ounces/125g) grated Comté or Gruyère cheese

4 large egg yolks

1/4 teaspoon cayenne pepper

1/4 cup (15g) minced fresh chives

5 large egg whites, at room temperature

Freshly ground black pepper

9 Increase the oven temperature to 425°F (220°C) and return the soufflés to the oven for 10 minutes, until they puff up a bit. Sprinkle with pepper and serve.

VARIATION: Substitute small spinach leaves or watercress for the arugula, blanching them in the same fashion and squeezing out all the excess moisture.

NOTES: If you want to make these soufflés in advance, once you've done the first baking (step 8), you can let them sit at room temperature for about 1 hour and do the second baking (step 9) just before serving. Feel free to substitute another cheese for the Comté, such as a Swiss-style cheese. Sharp Cheddar is a good option, too.

Fishing for Ingredients

Shopping for food in Paris can be a long, leisurely affair, requiring you to set aside a wide berth of time in your schedule. Fortunately it's one of my favorite things to do. Though between waiting in line at the market (while *madame* in front of you inspects and approves every grape in the bunch to make sure each meets her exacting standards) and crossing town in search of a much-needed ingredient (and invariably finding the inevitable *rupture de stock*—I've concluded that the distance I have to go directly correlates to how likely something will be out of stock), I've learned to slow down and not let it drive me nuts when I need a few oranges, and *monsieur* in front of me is negotiating the price of a lone tangerine, or someone at the *fromagerie* has to ask a question about each of the 246 kinds of cheeses in France. (Charles de Gaulle is said to have come up with that number, but he was wrong, there are actually more—perhaps the day he counted, he experienced a *rupture de stock*, too?)

Consequently I spend (a lot) more time buying food than I do preparing it. Yet thankfully, one of the joys of France is the availability of so many wonderful, time-saving prepared foods: butcher shops offer premade duck confit; beef *roulades* are stuffed, tied up, and ready to roast; and spit-roasted chickens are sold ready-to-eat at the *volailler*.

There isn't as much of the DIY spirit in Paris because the combination of tiny kitchens, locals not taking kindly to neighbors setting up chicken coops and smokehouses behind their apartments (and people who can afford backyards in Paris aren't likely the types to get their hands dirty), and the excellent charcuterie already available doesn't provide much incentive or turn a closet into a curing shed, à la Brooklyn. That said, I do make my own brandade, the hearty spread made of salt cod, quite a bit of garlic, and olive oil mashed up with potatoes and cream, because the brandade you buy is often heavy on the potatoes and less so on the cod (and garlic!).

Outside of France, you can usually find salt cod in fish markets and shops specializing in Italian or Portuguese foodstuffs; it's also available online. (Cod is a fish in decline, so some fish sold as "salt cod" is actually made from similar varieties. You can also find salt cod made from fish that was line-caught in the North Atlantic, Scandinavia, or Iceland. Ask your fishmonger for guidance.)

Salt cod can vary in quality and firmness, and it's sold in various grades (and prices) in Parisian fish markets, and even at supermarkets. Some is rock-hard with bits of skin and bones; some is soft, pliable, and pristine. I've learned to go with the best quality because the more choice fillets have less skin and bones, which are a chore to pick through. And after an exhilarating day gathering ingredients, I'm happy to have one less thing to do when I get home. The soaking usually takes about 24 hours, and while I've read about folks in Provence who soak dried fish in the tank of the toilet since the water is constantly being changed and refreshed, well, that's past my limit as to how far I'll go as a do-it yourselfer, and will stick to preparing mine in the refrigerator.

Salt cod and potato puree

BRANDADE DE MORUE

Serves 4

In Paris, restaurants serve *brandade de morue* in individual serving dishes, and it comes to the table very hot and browned on top, accompanied with toasted bread and a bowl of salad greens. It's not traditionally topped with bread crumbs, but I've given the option here because I like the extra crunch on top.

If you're using this brandade for the Salt cod fritters (page 73), you will make more than you need, but you can freeze the other half of the brandade to use later, or bake it in a small baking dish for a nice lunch *à deux*. Serve with plenty of toasted bread for spreading the brandade and a simple green salad.

1   Rinse the excess salt off the pieces of salt cod and submerge them in a bowl of cold water in the refrigerator for 24 hours, changing the water three times.

2   Combine the olive oil, garlic, and thyme in a small saucepan and heat until the oil just starts to bubble. Turn off the heat, cover, and set aside.

3   Drain the salt cod and put it and the potatoes in a large pot and cover with cold water. Bring the water to a boil, decrease to a simmer, and cook for 25 to 30 minutes, until the fish and the potatoes are both very tender.

4   Drain the salt cod and potatoes. When cool enough to handle, remove any bones, fins, and tough pieces of skin. Be sure to go through the fish carefully as any trace of skin or bones will be unpleasant to come across in the final dish.

5   Transfer the fish and potatoes to the bowl of a stand mixer fitted with the paddle attachment. (You can also mash it by hand with a potato masher or pass it through a food mill fitted with the disk with the largest holes—do not use a food processor because it will make the brandade gluey.) Remove the thyme from the garlic-infused oil and scrape the oil into the mixer bowl; add the cream and black pepper. Mix on medium speed until smooth. It shouldn't need any salt, but you may want to taste it and add some, if necessary.

144

1 pound (450g) salt cod

2/3 cups (160ml) olive oil

6 cloves garlic, peeled and minced

2 sprigs thyme

2 large potatoes (1 1/2 pounds/700g), peeled and cut into 1-inch (3cm) cubes

3/4 cup (180ml) heavy cream

1/2 teaspoon freshly ground black pepper

Sea salt or kosher salt (optional)

Toasted or grilled bread, to serve

TOPPING (OPTIONAL)

2 tablespoons dried bread crumbs

2 tablespoons freshly grated Parmesan

Olive oil

6 Preheat the oven to 400°F (200°C) with a rack in the top third of the oven. Butter a baking dish that will hold all the brandade in a layer at least 1¹/₂ inches (4cm) thick, and spread the brandade in it. Set the pan on a foil-lined baking sheet.

7 To make the topping, toss the bread crumbs and grated Parmesan together in a small bowl with a small pour of olive oil—just enough to moisten the crumbs—then sprinkle the mixture evenly over the top. Bake for 20 minutes, until bubbling hot and nicely browned on top. Serve with toasted bread.

Garlic mayonnaise with accompaniments

LE GRAND AÏOLI

Serves 6 to 8

Vegetables have yet to take center stage in Parisian restaurants—except for one very posh restaurant where I was served a lone roasted shallot half in the center of a very large plate as a first course. French restaurants prefer to go heavy on the meats and starches and light on the *légumes*. So when I have a vegetable craving, I take a cue from *les Provençaux* and prepare *le grand aïoli*—a seasonal selection of fresh vegetables, either raw or barely cooked—along with some salt cod or roast chicken and a bowl of garlicky mayonnaise. (The chicken isn't traditional, but no one seems to mind because it goes so well with the garlic-heavy dip.)

It's not fair to write a strict recipe for *le grand aïoli* because much depends on personal preferences and seasonal availability. Most raw vegetables will work: sliced fennel, celery sticks, carrots, and cauliflower florets. Parisians aren't so fond of vegetables that have too much crunch, including green beans, and I've come to appreciate them more cooked than I used to as well. Now I give most a quick blanching for a few minutes in salted water, which also brings out the flavor. I've given some guidelines below for serving 6 to 8 people, figuring about 12 ounces (340g) of vegetables per person, but it's up to you to decide which ones you prefer, or to choose what's in season. Garlic can vary in strength of flavor, depending on the season; so if you're a bit timid, you may want

continued

to start with the smaller amount and add the rest to taste, when making the garlic mayonnaise.

The perfect dessert after the garlic overload is Tangerine-Champagne sorbet (page 317).

Garlic mayonnaise with accompaniments, continued

1   To make the aïoli, mash the garlic with the salt in a mortar and pestle, then stir in the egg yolks. (The aïoli can also be made in a blender or food processor.) Mix the oils in a measuring cup with a spout.

2   Drop by drop, add the oil to the garlic while continuously pounding the pestle to incorporate the oil. (If using a machine, dribble the oil in slowly, in a continuous stream, while the machine is running.) Continue to stir and as the mixture begins to thicken, increase the flow of oil, stirring until all the oil is added. If the aïoli is too thick, add the warm water, until it reaches the desired consistency. Cover and let sit at room temperature if you're planning to serve it shortly. Otherwise refrigerate it. (The aioli will keep for up to 24 hours.)

3   To make the accompaniments, bring a pot of salted water to a low boil. Blanch the carrots for 1 minute. Remove them with a slotted spoon to a baking sheet lined with a kitchen towel. Blanch the green beans in the same water for 3 minutes and remove them to drain next to the carrots. Add the potatoes to the pot and cook for 10 to 15 minutes (depending on size), just until tender—they are done when they can be pierced easily with the tip of a sharp paring knife. Drain in a colander.

4   To cook the salt cod, put the soaked and drained fish in a pot of cold water and bring to a low boil. Let simmer for 15 to 20 minutes, or until soft. Drain and let cool to room temperature.

5   Arrange the remaining accompaniments decoratively on a large serving platter along with the bowl of aïoli and let guests help themselves.

VARIATION: Though this isn't traditional, you can substitute a whole, roasted chicken—cut into pieces and served cold—for the salt cod.

AÏOLI

6 to 8 cloves garlic, peeled and minced

1/4 teaspoon sea salt or kosher salt

2 large egg yolks

1 cup (250 ml) olive oil

1 cup (250 ml) neutral-tasting vegetable oil

1 to 2 tablespoons warm water (optional)

ACCOMPANIMENTS

2 large or 3 medium (28g) carrots, peeled, halved crosswise, and cut into 1/2-inch-wide (1.5cm) sticks

12 ounces (320g) green beans, ends removed

2 pounds (900g) small new potatoes

1 1/2 to 2 pounds (700 to 900g) salt cod, soaked for 24 hours in the refrigerator, changing the water three times

6 hard-cooked eggs (page 328), peeled and halved lengthwise, each topped with an anchovy fillet and a few grinds of black pepper

1 pound (450g) cherry tomatoes

1 large or 2 small (230g) beet(s), peeled and thinly sliced

1 large or 2 small (230 to 280g) kohlrabi, peeled and thinly sliced

2 bunches radishes, trimmed

Toasted or grilled bread

Potato, feta, and basil tortilla

TORTILLA DE POMMES DE TERRE À LA FETA ET AU BASILIC

Serves 6 to 8

When I was packing up everything I owned for the big move to Paris, I shipped two cases of my most treasured cookbooks, which were famously lost in transit. (I've railed about this once or twice, which you'll have to excuse me for because I'm still upset about it.) What made the pain particularly acute was that most of them were signed for me by their authors—Julia Child, Richard Olney, Marion Cunningham, and James Beard—all of whom were my heroes and are now deceased. And I'll never be able to replace those books.

While it took me a while to get over the loss (nine years, seven months, and sixteen days, to be exact), I decided to treasure the cookbooks that did manage to make the journey across the Atlantic. One such cookbook is *The Basque Kitchen* by San Francisco chef Gerald Hirigoyen, who hails from the Basque region, straddling the borders of France and Spain.

Unlike my lost cookbooks, one thing that you will find in Paris are tortillas, Spanish omelets served in slices at room temperature. I was inspired by a tortilla in Gerald's book, which features a light dusting of piment d'Espelette, a red chile powder from the Basque region that is both spicy and sweet. It's not as overwhelming as other red chile powders, but it has a bit of heat that sneaks up on you after a few bites.

Fortunately, another thing that didn't get lost in the mail is my cast-iron skillet, one that I personally lugged from the United States back when luggage allowances were a little more generous. It works perfectly for making Spanish tortillas, and the next time I move, I'm hand-carrying it with me.

2 tablespoons olive oil

1 pound (450g) potatoes, peeled and cut into ¾-inch (2cm) cubes

1¼ teaspoons sea salt or kosher salt

6 scallions, white and tender green parts, thinly sliced

9 large eggs

¼ teaspoon piment d'Espelette or sweet or smoked paprika

2 cups (40g) loosely packed fresh basil leaves, coarsely chopped

1 cup (120g) very coarsely crumbled feta cheese

1 Heat the oil in a 10-inch (25cm) cast-iron or nonstick skillet over medium heat. (Make sure your pan has an oven-safe handle.) Add the potato cubes and 1 teaspoon of the salt. Cook, stirring frequently, until the potatoes are tender and cooked through, 12 to 15 minutes.

2 A few minutes before the potatoes are done, add the scallions and cook until they're wilted.

3 Preheat the oven to 450°F (230°C), or, if using a nonstick skillet, the highest temperature recommended for your particular pan, which is usually 375°F (190°C).

4   Mix the eggs in a bowl with the remaining $1/4$ teaspoon of salt and the piment d'Espelette. Stir the basil into the eggs and pour the mixture over the potatoes in the skillet.

5   Crumble the feta, not too finely, over the potatoes and press the pieces down gently with a spoon. Cook the tortilla until the bottom is golden brown and well set, rotating the pan from time to time as it cooks. It will take 15 to 20 minutes; don't check it too soon or you'll break the crust.

6   When the crust is browned, slide the skillet into the oven and let it cook until the eggs are set, about 5 minutes.

7   Remove the skillet from the oven. Set a baking sheet or serving plate on top of the skillet, then flip both the baking sheet and the skillet simultaneously, releasing the tortilla from the skillet. Serve slightly warm or at room temperature. You can store the tortilla in the refrigerator for up to 2 days.

VARIATION: To spice things up, add 1 cup (120g) cubed Spanish chorizo or another cooked spiced sausage along with the feta cheese. Chorizo from Spain is a cured or smoked sausage and different from Mexican chorizo, which is a loose sausage sold uncooked. If you wish to use that or another spicy sausage (sold cooked or uncooked), heat it until cooked through, then slice it or cut it into cubes.

Project: Kale

B EFORE I LIVED IN PARIS, WHENEVER I VISITED, I stayed at various inexpensive hotels around the city. But instead of paying twenty bucks for a cup of coffee and a warmed-over croissant at the hotel, I'd hit a local café, which had a lot more personality (and personalities). Standing at the counter were invariably a few weathered gents enjoying an early morning glass of wine while I nursed my steamy café au lait and baguette, which the waiter put down in front of me along with a ramekin of softened butter and a dab of raspberry jam. And that was it.

You'll never see French people eating eggs in the morning, as is the custom in America and other countries. But it's fine to drink white wine, accompanied by cigarettes smoldering in over-flowing ashtrays (when smoking was still allowed in cafés), enveloping them—and the rest of us—in a gauzy cloud of smoke.

I asked my first French language teacher whether this was considered common in France. She seemed surprised by my question, responding with, "The cigarettes, or the wine?" Eventually I realized that the folks imbibing at the bar in the predawn hours of the morning had likely been working the night shift and were celebrating *les happy hours.*

Although the French enjoy other things in the morning, they don't eat eggs with their morning coffee—or wine. However, when the temperature drops in the winter, I often crack an egg or two in the morning. It might be soft-boiled or fried and served on buttered toast, or sometimes baked, but French eggs are so good that I'll often have them for lunch or dinner, as the French do.

Another thing the French don't eat is kale. Or I should say "didn't," because for years kale wasn't available in Paris. I never really paid that much attention to kale back in the States because I took it for granted: it was just always available,

in tight, curly bunches in the produce section. But after a few years of living in France, I started to miss kale, and so did other Americans in Paris. Whenever people moved here, the inevitable question was no longer, "Does everyone here smoke?" but rather "Where can I find kale?" I speculated that perhaps kale is too rough, even when cooked, and it's somewhat aggressive and bitter tasting, qualities that don't appeal to the French palate. After a few kale-less years, I got a hot tip that there was a natural foods store in the 5th *arrondissement* that had kale. So I ran over there and swept the whole shelf of kale into a big bag. At the cash register, the astonished young man looked at the heap in front of him and asked me (in English), "Where are you from?"

Eventually another American transplant, Kristen Beddard, launched The Kale Project, and cajoled local farmers into growing the leafy greens, which became available at selected markets. But first, the farmers had to come up with a French name for it. It seemed to be uni-versally agreed that it would be called *chou frisé,* or feathered cabbage. However I've also seen it referred to as *chou plume, chou vert demi-nain, chou borécole,* or *chou hollandais,* although I lobbied for *chou américain* because we seem to be its number one fans. When I first saw kale at my *ruche* (a collective for buying local products), I ordered two bunches, which were so huge they filled up my enormous double-wide sink. I had so much kale that I sautéed a lot of it with garlic and red chile flakes and stored it in the freezer in small portions so I could use it when I pleased. It was definitely an illustration of "be careful what you wish for" because I had a freezer full of kale that seemed to last forever. And consequently, it took me a while before I could share the excitement of finally having kale again—or whatever you call it—in Paris.

Baked eggs with kale and smoked salmon

ŒUFS AU FOUR AVEC CHOU FRISÉ ET SAUMON FUMÉ

Serves 2

1½ tablespoons salted or unsalted butter

2 cloves garlic, peeled and minced

⅓ cup (40g) dried or fresh bread crumbs

1 teaspoon minced fresh thyme leaves

⅛ teaspoon sea salt or kosher salt

KALE

1 tablespoon salted or unsalted butter

1 clove garlic, peeled and minced

3 ounces (85g) kale, rinsed, not too well dried, and coarsely chopped

Sea salt or kosher salt

Freshly ground black pepper or red pepper flakes

BAKED EGGS

2 slices (55g) smoked salmon, preferably wild

4 to 6 large eggs

2½ ounces (70g) fresh goat cheese or feta

2 tablespoons heavy cream or crème fraîche (page 327)

I probably shouldn't admit this, but I collect small enameled gratin dishes. At flea markets in France they are practically giving them away. (Or at least they were, until I opened my big mouth.) Most have a couple of dings, but I can't resist the vintage ones that come in sunny orange or 1950s red colors. And I put them to good use with our newfound supply of kale.

I top these eggs, baked on a bed of kale, with crisp bread crumbs made from *pain* Poilâine, though any sturdy bread will do. Pan-toasting the crumbs first ensures that they will be crisp, a nice contrast to the softly cooked eggs and a few strips of smoky salmon underneath.

People say that you can't pair wine with eggs, although I find that baked eggs go well with mild white wines like Muscadet or Sancerre, which I'll sometimes enjoy with lunch. I guess that's the best reason to eat eggs for lunch, French-style, instead of breakfast.

1 To make the bread crumbs, melt the butter in a skillet with a cover over medium heat. Stir in the garlic, then mix in the bread crumbs, thyme, and salt. Cook, stirring frequently, until the bread crumbs are nicely toasted, 3 to 5 minutes. (But don't overdo it; burning the garlic can turn it bitter.) When the bread crumbs are done, scrape them into a small bowl.

2 To prepare the kale, wipe the pan clean and melt the butter in the same pan over medium heat. Add the garlic and wet kale and season with salt and pepper. Cover the pan and let the kale steam until wilted and soft, about 5 minutes, lifting the lid and turning the kale a few times while it's cooking.

3 To assemble the baked eggs, preheat the oven to 350°F (180°C). Coat two small baking dishes (such as 8-ounce gratin dishes) with nonstick spray or a liberal amount of butter. Divide the kale between the dishes. Tear the smoked salmon into large, bite-size pieces, and lay them over the kale. Crack two or three eggs into each dish and crumble the cheese over the eggs. Dribble a tablespoon of heavy cream over each of the dishes and sprinkle each with 2 to 3 tablespoons of bread crumbs.

continued

4 Bake the eggs for 10 to 12 minutes, or until the eggs are cooked to your liking. Serve immediately.

VARIATIONS: Substitute a slice of ham torn into pieces, crumbled crisp-fried bacon, crumbled cooked sausage, or sautéed mushrooms for the smoked salmon. Use smoked trout instead of the smoked salmon. Use other greens, such as sautéed spinach, collards, or Swiss chard in place of the kale; allow about 1/3 cup packed (40g) cooked greens per serving.

NOTE: I keep garlic bread crumbs on hand, since they're pretty delicious over a warm bowl of polenta with wilted greens or pasta with cherry tomatoes. So feel free to double or triple the recipe and use the leftovers later in the week. You can store them in an airtight container in the refrigerator for about a week.

152

Mixing and Matching Food Cultures

CALL ME NAÏVE, BUT I DIDN'T REALIZE WHAT a controversial trip my visit to Israel would be. I was invited to come and sample the diverse cuisines, which, being a nation of immigrants, included dishes from Lebanon, Syria, Iran, Tunisia, France, Algeria, and even the United States. The food was more fresh and exciting than I could have imagined, and I was excited to share everything I had eaten on my blog. Within minutes of posting, messages came flooding in accusing me of everything from being an international spy to attempting to redefine geographical borders, which I was apparently doing while sitting in front of my laptop in my pajamas, uploading pictures of chickpea dip.

I didn't realize that a dish of pickled vegetables or a bowl of chickpeas were such charged subjects. Every time I wrote about a dish, I was informed that, no—that dish isn't Israeli—it's Lebanese or Syrian or Iranian. Israel is a very young country and has a culinary *mélange* of immigrants, so most dishes are, indeed, from elsewhere—just like the foods we eat in the United States, such as hamburgers and hot dogs (Germany), doughnuts (probably Holland), pizza (Italy), ice cream (Arabia or China, depending on whom you talk to), cole slaw (Holland), pie (Great Britain), and bagels and cheesecake (Eastern Europe), which aren't technically American at all. But like croissants (Austria) and macarons (Italy) in Paris, dishes like pie and ice cream have become so iconic to our culture that they're associated with the United States.

Once you taste shakshuka, you'll understand why a number of cultures want to claim it as their own. (Most consider it to be a dish that originated in Tunisia.) *Shakshuka* means "mixture," in Arabic and always contains tomatoes, chile peppers, and eggs. But other ingredients can be added, including greens, potatoes, beans, artichokes, sausages, and cheese.

Someday, I hope to visit each and every country that makes a version and try them all. But in the meantime, being a multicultural mix myself, I came up with my own recipe, which melds a few other versions.

My shakshuka (page 154) has its own history, which crisscrosses a few cultural boundaries: It's inspired by versions from Adam Roberts of amateurgourmet.com (who got the recipe from Chef Einat Admony of Taïm and Balaboosta restaurants in New York City) and Yotam Ottolenghi and Sami Tamimi (who own Ottolenghi and Nopi restaurants in London, where I first had shakshuka). Feel free to vary the greens, adjust the spices, or use a different cheese. Just be sure to add me to the lists of credits, to avoid any controversy about where it came from.

Shakshuka

CHAKCHOUKA

Serves 3 or 4

I don't peel the tomatoes for this dish because the skins don't bother me. But if you wish to peel the tomatoes, first remove the cores, score an X on the other end of the tomato, and drop them—a few at a time—into a pot of boiling water. After a minute, transfer the tomatoes to a bowl of ice water and slip the skins off. You can also use canned tomatoes.

I find spicy chiles at the shops on the rue de Faubourg du Temple, a hub of storefronts that cater to people from Africa and Arabia and, nowadays, to one American in particular. They sell all sorts of spices, roots, vegetables, and chiles, which spill out on tables cluttering the sidewalks. Use whatever chile meets your comfort level of heat and spiciness.

The sauce can be made up to 3 days in advance and refrigerated. Rewarm it in a skillet before serving, adding a little more water, if necessary, to thin it out.

1   Heat the olive oil in a large skillet with a lid over medium-high heat. Add the onion and garlic and cook for 8 to 10 minutes, until soft and translucent. Add the chile pepper, salt, pepper, and spices. Cook for another minute, stirring constantly to release their fragrance.

2   Add the tomatoes, tomato paste, honey, and vinegar. Decrease the heat to medium and cook for 12 to 15 minutes, until the sauce has thickened somewhat but is still loose enough so that when you shake the pan it freely sloshes around. (Fresh tomatoes may take a little longer to cook than canned.) Stir in the chopped greens.

3   Turn off the heat and press the cubes of feta into the tomato sauce. With the back of a spoon, make six indentations in the sauce. Crack an egg into each indentation, and then drag a spatula gently through the egg whites so they mingle a bit with the tomato sauce, being careful not to disturb the yolks.

4   Turn the heat back on so the sauce is at a gentle simmer, and cook for 10 minutes, taking some of the tomato sauce and basting the egg whites from time to time. Cover and cook for 3 to 5 minutes, until the eggs are done to your liking. When ready, the yolks of the eggs should still be runny. Serve hot with lots of crusty bread.

2 tablespoons olive oil

1 onion, peeled and diced

3 cloves garlic, peeled and thinly sliced

1/2 to 1 chile pepper (depending on the chile, and your taste), stemmed, halved, seeded, and finely diced

1 1/2 teaspoons sea salt or kosher salt

1 teaspoon freshly ground black pepper

1 teaspoon sweet or smoked paprika

1 teaspoon caraway seeds, crushed

1 teaspoon cumin seeds, crushed, or 3/4 teaspoon ground cumin

1/2 teaspoon ground turmeric

2 pounds (900g) ripe tomatoes, cored and diced, or two (14-ounce/400g) cans diced or crushed tomatoes, with their liquid

2 tablespoons tomato paste

2 teaspoons honey

1 teaspoon red wine or cider vinegar

1 cup (20g) loosely packed greens, such as radish greens, watercress, kale, Swiss chard, or spinach, coarsely chopped

1 cup (5 ounces/130g) feta cheese, cut in generous, bite-sized rectangles

4 to 6 eggs

Crusty bread, to serve

Ham, blue cheese, and pear quiche

TARTE SALÉE AU JAMBON, AU BLEU, ET AUX POIRES

Serves 8

CRUST

1 cup (140g) all-purpose flour

¹/₃ cup (55g) cornmeal

¹/₂ teaspoon sea salt or kosher salt

8 tablespoons (4 ounces/115g) unsalted butter, cubed and chilled

1 large egg

FILLING

1 tablespoon olive oil

6 shallots, peeled and thinly sliced

Sea salt and freshly ground black pepper

1 large, firm, ripe pear, peeled and diced into ¹/₂-inch (1.5cm) cubes

1 cup (130g) diced cooked (boiled) ham

1¹/₂ cups (375ml) heavy cream or half-and-half

8 ounces (225g) cream cheese

Freshly grated nutmeg

4 large eggs

2 egg yolks

1¹/₂ cups (150g) crumbled blue cheese or Roquefort

2 tablespoons minced fresh flat-leaf parsley

In the 1980s, quiche was all the rage in America. It was especially popular in vegetarian restaurants, like the one where I worked, not only because it was infinitely adaptable to all sorts of vegetables and herbs, but also because of its creamy richness and overload of cheese, making it easily tolerated by uncomfortable meat-eaters dragged to dinner by their friends. Fortunately we served wine as well, which kept everyone happy.

Unfortunately, some people had a hard time pronouncing the word *quiche*, and more than a few of the waitresses in our restaurant were inadvertently propositioned by customers asking their server for a "quickie."

What we call *quiche* (politely pronounced as "keesh," by the way), comes in a loftier version, known as *tarte salée* in France. *Salée* can mean "dirty," but it also means "salty" or "savory." The tarts are usually tall and don't resemble the pie-like quiches you can find in America. (If you are looking for a *quickie* in Paris, there are some tall, salty tarts in Pigalle that can help you out, but I would avoid propositioning waitresses unless you are prepared for the consequences.)

Tarte salée is generally quite rich; there's just no getting around it. But if it's any consolation, I've seen quite a few svelte women digging into one for lunch, with a healthy green salad alongside, of course. The pear in this quiche is not a dominant flavor, but I find it lightens the texture and gives it a *soupçon* of sweetness to offset the cheese and ham. Use a firm pear, such as Bosc or Anjou, rather than a very juicy one.

1 To make the crust, in the bowl of a stand mixer fitted with the paddle attachment (or in a bowl, by hand with a pastry blender), combine the flour, cornmeal, and salt. Add the butter and beat on low speed until the butter is broken up and the mixture is sandy. Add the egg and mix until the dough begins to clump and come together. Use your hands to gather the dough and shape it into a disk. Wrap it in plastic and chill for at least 30 minutes. (The dough can be made up to 2 days in advance.)

continued

2 Roll out the chilled dough on a lightly floured surface until it's 14 inches (35cm) across. Wrap aluminum foil around the outside of a 9- to 10-inch (23 to 25cm) springform pan to catch any leaks, and then transfer the dough to the pan. Press the dough against the side, allowing it to come a bit more than halfway up the sides of the pan. If there are any cracks, patch them with a bit of dough from the edges—you don't want the filling to leak out during baking. Chill the dough in the pan while you make the filling.

3 Preheat the oven to 375°F (190°C).

4 To make the filling, heat the oil in a skillet over medium heat and cook the shallots with some salt and pepper until soft and translucent, 3 to 5 minutes. Remove from the heat and stir in the diced pear and ham.

5 In a large bowl, blend together the cream, cream cheese, a few gratings of nutmeg, the eggs, and the yolks until smooth. Stir in the blue cheese, the pear and ham mixture, and the parsley.

6 Set the springform pan on a rimmed baking sheet and pour in the filling, using a spoon to make sure the ingredients in the filling are evenly distributed. Bake the tart for 45 to 50 minutes, until the top is lightly browned, the filling still jiggles, and a toothpick inserted into the center comes out clean. Let cool until firm enough to slice, then serve warm or at room temperature.

VARIATIONS: For bacon-lovers, substitute 1 cup (125g) cooked diced bacon for the ham. For a vegetarian version, leave out the ham. You can also add to taste whatever fresh herbs appeal to you, such as chervil, thyme, tarragon, dill, or marjoram.

Buckwheat polenta with braised greens, sausage, and poached eggs

POLENTA AU SARRASIN, LÉGUMES BRAISÉES, SAUCISSE, ET ŒUFS POCHÉS

Serves 2

There's no equivalent to the moniker "comfort food" in France. Perhaps *cuisine maison* (home cooking), or more colloquially, *cuisine de grand-mére* (grandmother's cooking) are the closest. But I have a little trouble with that term because I don't like anyone telling me what to eat to make me feel better or more comfortable. I can figure that one out for myself, thanks. And in my case, polenta is it.

I didn't think I could find polenta to be any more comforting. Er . . . I mean, I didn't think I could like polenta any more, until I went to Milan and my friend, blogger Sara Rosso (www .msadventuresinitaly.com), and I drove up to the mountains over Lake Como, where we had a robust country-style lunch of wild boar served on a thick bed of polenta with dark flecks of buckwheat. It's called *polenta taragna*, and now I make it in the comfort of *ma maison* in Paris by pulsing bits of whole buckwheat (called groats or kasha) in a blender or mini food chopper until it's broken up into pieces the size of birdseed, and cooking it with the polenta.

The polenta can be prepared in advance and kept warm in a double boiler, or just reheated in the same pot, stirring in a bit more liquid if it gets too thick. This recipe makes a little more polenta than you'll need because I like to rewarm an extra bowl the next day for breakfast, along with a pat of salted butter and a drizzle of *sirop d'érable* (maple syrup).

1 To make the polenta, bring the water to a boil in a saucepan. Stir in the polenta, buckwheat, and salt. Decrease the heat to low and simmer for 30 to 45 minutes, stirring frequently, until soft and creamy. Remove the polenta from the heat and stir in the butter and Parmesan. Cover and keep warm until ready to serve.

2 To make the greens, in a large skillet with a lid, heat the olive oil over medium heat. Add the onion and cook for 8 to 10 minutes, until soft and translucent. Add the garlic and thyme and cook another minute or so, then add the greens. Season with salt and pepper, stir a few times, cover, and cook, stirring every once in a while until the greens are wilted, about 5 minutes.

3 Remove the lid and add the stock along with the vinegar, sausage, and sun-dried tomatoes; stir to heat through. Cover to keep warm.

POLENTA

3 cups (750ml) water

²/₃ cup (90g) polenta (not instant)

2 tablespoons (18g) cracked buckwheat

Scant ¹/₂ teaspoon sea salt or kosher salt

2 tablespoons salted or unsalted butter

³/₄ cup (2 ounces/70g) freshly grated Parmesan, pecorino, or asiago cheese

GREENS

1 tablespoon olive oil

1 red onion, peeled and thinly sliced

1 clove garlic, peeled and thinly sliced

1 teaspoon finely chopped fresh thyme or sage

6 cups packed (8 ounces/225g) bite-size pieces radicchio, escarole, or other bitter greens

Sea salt or kosher salt and freshly ground black pepper

³/₄ cup (180ml) chicken stock (page 326) or water

1 tablespoon balsamic vinegar

8 ounces (230g) herbed sausage, pan-fried, and sliced

3 tablespoons slivered oil-packed sun-dried tomatoes, or 3 tablespoons slivered (pitted) black or green olives

¹/₂ cup (2¹/₂ ounces/65g) ricotta salata or feta cheese

2 poached eggs (page 329; see Note)

Freshly ground black pepper

4   Divide the polenta between two bowls and spoon the braised greens and sauce over the top; crumble the ricotta salata over the greens and top each with a poached egg. Season with a few grinds of the peppermill and serve.

NOTE: Because there are a couple of things going on—the polenta, the greens, and the poached eggs—I bring a pot of water to a simmer on the stovetop while cooking the greens and poach the eggs right before serving.

159

CHAMPIONING
LES CHAMPIGNONS

One thing many people don't know is that all pharmacists in France are trained to identify wild mushrooms. If you pick your own, you can count on your local pharmacist to let you know whether or not they're edible. I'm not a mushroom hunter, but a friend who does go hunting told me that the pharmacists always tell you that your mushrooms aren't edible because they don't want to be responsible for anyone getting sick.

I often top bowls of polenta with chanterelles (wild mushrooms) instead of sautéed greens and sausage, which I'll (safely) buy at the market from the professionals. Brush the mushrooms clean of any grit and slice them not too thinly. Melt 2 tablespoons of salted or unsalted butter in a large, nonstick skillet over high heat (you don't want to crowd them in a small skillet, which will cause them to steam, rather than brown). When the butter is sizzling hot and foamy, add 8 ounces (230g) of sliced chanterelles, seasoning them with salt and pepper. Add 2 teaspoons of minced garlic and 2 teaspoons of minced fresh thyme. Sauté until the mushrooms are slightly browned, 3 to 5 minutes, and then add another tablespoon of butter and 1/2 cup (125 ml) of dry white wine. Let the mushrooms cook for another minute or so, until the sauce has thickened. Remove from the heat and stir in a generous sprinkling of minced fresh flat-leaf parsley. Spoon the mushroom and sauce over the buckwheat polenta and top with long, thin shavings of Parmesan cheese.

Stuffed vegetables

LÉGUMES FARCIS

Serves 6

I love getting an invitation to dinner at my friend Marion Lévy's apartment. After her husband, Jean-Baptiste, greets me at the door and offers me a glass of wine, I find Marion in the kitchen wearing colorful, comfy slip-ons, chopping up vegetables and bundles of fresh herbs from the market. On the coffee table, in between the piles of art books, there's always a cutting board with country ham and slices of cured chorizo, olives jumbled in a bowl, and some sort of spiced dip that she quickly mashed together in the short time between the moment I walked in and the time I sat down.

The only thing Marion has in common with those impossibly chic Parisian hostesses who totter around on high heels and finish their dinner parties with an impressive strawberry charlotte is that she makes everything look effortless. (And unlike many of those fancy Parisian dinner parties, you won't find any empty frozen food dessert boxes hidden away in Marion's trash.)

Hers isn't the kind of glamorous dinner party you read about taking place in the swankier *quartiers* of Paris, but I find it to be much more fun when someone is comfortable enough to plunk down rustic bowls of food in the middle of the table and let everyone help themselves.

I've had a lot of dishes at Marion's, and one of my favorites is her stuffed vegetables. When Marion came over to make it with me one day, I pulled out an earthenware dish to bake the vegetables in, and she said, "Oh? I just bake them on the oven shelf directly." (French ovens come with a shallow shelf that people use instead of baking sheets.) Imagining myself on all fours the next day scraping the oven clean, I pulled out a rimmed baking sheet, and she was happy to use that.

During the preparations, she cut up just one clove of garlic. I told her that Americans really like garlic—a lot—so she said, "Okay, I will add another—for *les Américains*!" Then as she stirred and stirred, and tasted, she said, "Okay, I will add another one—for me!"

This is a dish that comes together *au pif* (see page 11), and you can use whatever kind of ground meat you wish and I usually serve it with rice. To vary the heat, use any variety of chile you want. A bell pepper or two can be swapped in for one of the other vegetables. And during the summer, I'll chop up a bunch of basil for the *farce*, instead of the parsley. And like Marion, feel free to add more garlic, *au pif*.

4 firm, ripe tomatoes

2 eggplants

2 zucchini

Olive oil

1 onion, peeled and diced

3 to 4 cloves garlic, peeled and minced

2 1/2 teaspoons sea salt or kosher salt

1 tablespoon finely chopped
fresh sage

1 tablespoon finely chopped fresh
thyme leaves

1 pound (450g) ground meat (beef,
lamb, pork, or turkey)

1 small chile pepper, seeded and
finely chopped

Freshly ground black pepper

1 tablespoon freshly squeezed
lemon juice

1/2 cup (30g) chopped fresh flat-leaf
parsley or basil

1 large egg

1/2 to 2/3 cup (1 1/2 to 2 ounces/45 to
60g) freshly grated Parmesan cheese

1 Brush a large baking sheet with olive oil.

2 Remove the stems from the tomatoes, and slice the tomatoes
in half horizontally. Gently squeeze out the juices and seeds
(discard them), then cut and dig out some of the pulp (not too
deeply) using a paring knife or soup spoon. Chop the pulp into
small pieces and put into a bowl. Arrange the tomato halves,
cut-side up, on the baking sheet.

3 Trim both ends off the eggplants and the zucchini and slice
them in half lengthwise. Cut each half crosswise in half again.
With a paring knife, carve out a gulley in the centers, leaving
the sides about 1/2 inch (2cm) thick to make a "boat" to hold the
filling. Chop the inside pieces you removed and add them to
the chopped tomatoes. Arrange the zucchini and eggplant "boats"
on the baking sheet, cut-side up.

4 Heat 2 tablespoons of olive oil in a large skillet over medium heat.
Add the onion and cook until it begins to soften, stirring occasionally, 8 to 10 minutes. Add the garlic, the chopped vegetables,
and 1 teaspoon of the salt, and continue to cook until the vegetables are completely softened and most of the liquid is cooked off.

5 Stir in the herbs and cook for another minute, then add the meat
and chopped chile. Season with the remaining 1 1/2 teaspoons of
salt and black pepper. Cook the meat, stirring frequently, until
it's just cooked through, 8 to 10 minutes. Remove from the heat,
add the lemon juice, and let cool to room temperature.

6 Preheat the oven to 350°F (180°C).

7 Scrape the cooled meat mixture into the bowl of a food processor along with the parsley and egg. Pulse the mixture a few
times until it is just mixed together, but still chunky. (If you
don't have a food processor, you can do this by hand.)

8 Fill the hollowed-out vegetables with the meat mixture and
drizzle a bit of olive oil over the top.

9 Bake the vegetables for 1 hour, until fully cooked through,
sprinkling the grated cheese over the top about 15 minutes
before they are done. Serve warm.

Butternut squash bread soup

PANADE DE BUTTERNUT

Serves 8

I get a kick out of telling French friends about all the French-style products that one sees in America, ranging from French-cut green beans (when I've asked, no one in France has any idea what "French-cut" means) to a French-style refrigerator, a behemoth that looks nothing like the modest-size refrigerators you see in France.

When I first served this *panade* at a dinner party, none of my Parisian friends had ever heard of the dish either. In fact, they told me that *panade* refers to someone who finds himself in a bad situation; they weren't aware of the baked casserole that's served like soup but is hearty enough to be a full meal.

This *panade* is one of the few dishes I've eaten in my life that I've never forgotten. I was baking one night in the kitchen at Chez Panisse and was so busy that I barely had time to enjoy all the wonderful food that I watched the cooks send out to the guests. Seeing my rapt interest, cook Seen Lippert offered me a warm bowl of *panade*: slices of toasted sourdough bread soaked in flavorful broth with lots of fresh herbs and layers of hearty butternut squash holding everything together. I took one spoonful and had to stop what I was doing and sit down to savor it. (Belated apologies to the customers who had to wait a little longer for their dessert that night.)

Seen has since left the restaurant business, which is unfortunate for the diners, but very good for her husband. Yet she was happy to share her recipe for *panade*, which is one of those dishes that gets better as it sits, and is even better rewarmed the next day.

For baking the dish, a 4-quart (4l) baking dish is preferred, because the greater the width, the more crusty cheese topping you'll have when the *panade* is finished. Whatever size baking dish you use, it should have sides that are at least 3 inches (8cm) high.

For the bread, find a sturdy, tangy sourdough loaf that's quite dense. Depending on the size of your dish, you may need a little more or a little less bread, so you might want to have extra bread on hand. (Never a problem in France!) Sturdy rye bread will also work well, if sourdough loaves aren't available.

This is one of those dishes where the quality of the chicken stock is very important, so I urge you to use homemade. Although this is called a "soup," it's more like a very moist casserole. As you serve, ladle additional warm broth over each bowl, if you wish.

continued

1 Melt the butter with the olive oil in a wide skillet or Dutch oven over medium heat. Add the onions, the 2 cloves of sliced garlic, and 1 teaspoon of the herbs. Cook for about 35 minutes, stirring occasionally, until the onions are completely wilted and beginning to brown on the bottom and edges.

2 While the onions are cooking, preheat the oven to 375°F (190°C). Put the slices of bread on baking sheets in a single layer and toast in the oven, turning the slices over midway, until both sides are dry, 10 to 12 minutes. Remove from the oven and when cool enough to handle, rub both sides of the bread with the whole garlic cloves.

3 When the onions are done, pour in the wine, scraping the bottom of the pan to loosen up any of the flavorful brown bits. Cook for a minute or two, so the wine is absorbed. Add 2 cups of the stock to the onions and cook until the stock is mostly absorbed, 10 to 15 minutes, and then add the rest of the stock and heat until the stock is hot. Remove from the heat.

4 To assemble the *panade*, cover the bottom of a 3- to 4-quart (3 to 4l) baking dish with a layer of bread, breaking any pieces so they fit in a single layer, but keeping them as large as possible. Ladle about half of the onions and some of the stock over the bread, and then cover with half of the squash slices. Season lightly with salt, pepper, and half of the remaining herbs. Sprinkle with 1/2 cup (40g) of the Comté. Add a second layer of bread and ladle the rest of the onions and more stock over the bread. Cover with the remaining squash slices. Season the squash with salt and pepper, and then add the remaining herbs. Sprinkle another 1/2 cup (40g) of the Comté over the squash layer. Cover the squash with a final layer of bread and then ladle the rest of the stock over the bread and press down on the ingredients to encourage them to meld together. Top with the remaining 1 cup (90g) of Comté, and the Parmesan.

5 Cover the baking dish with aluminum foil and tighten it around the edges, but don't press it down on the surface or some of the cheese may stick to it during baking. Set the baking dish on a foil-lined baking sheet to catch any spills. Bake for 45 minutes, uncover the *panade*, and bake for another 30 minutes, or until the *panade* is very well browned and crisp on top. Let cool for about 15 minutes and then spoon portions of the *panade* into soup bowls, making sure everyone gets a highly prized layer of the crusty topping, and serve.

164

Butternut squash bread soup, continued

3 tablespoons unsalted butter

3 tablespoons olive oil

4 onions, peeled and sliced

4 cloves garlic, peeled (2 thinly sliced and 2 whole)

2 tablespoons mixed chopped fresh thyme and sage

2-pound (900g) loaf firm-textured sourdough bread, sliced

1/2 cup (125ml) white wine

2 quarts (2l) warm chicken stock (page 326), plus additional stock for serving

2-pound (900g) butternut squash or similar winter squash (such as Kabocha), peeled and sliced into 1/8-inch (.5cm) slices

Sea salt or kosher salt and freshly ground black pepper

2 cups (170g) grated Comté, Gruyère, Jarlsberg, or Fontina cheese

1/2 cup (11/2 ounces/45g) freshly grated Parmesan cheese

The Déception of Monsieur Parmentier

*B*ISCUIT IS ONE OF THOSE WORDS, LIKE *déception* (which means "disappointment" in French), that doesn't mean the same thing in French as it does in English. A *biscuit* in the French baking lexicon refers to sponge cake that is used for layering. If you told someone that we baked *un biscuit* on top of pie, it would probably confirm some of the worst suspicions French people have about over-the-top American food.

Because the French often Frenchify other foods, I Frenchify chicken potpie. In lieu of the biscuits that American often top our potpies with, I top the filling with pureed potatoes, taking a cue from *hachis Parmentier*, a potato-topped meat pie named after Antoine-Augustin Parmentier, who is credited with staving off a famine in the late eighteenth century in France when he promoted potatoes as a source of nutrition at a time when people wouldn't go near the dirty tubers. Understanding the contrarian nature of the French, he set up a "private" garden that was, deceptively, off-limits to all. *Quelle déception!* Shrewdly knowing that people would want whatever they couldn't have, he arranged to have the armed guards who watched over the potatoes take nights off. And soon enough, people began slipping into the garden at night, and potatoes started appearing in local kitchens. Nowadays Parmentier is so beloved that there is a métro station in Paris named after him, with a mini-museum of his achievements, including a colorful panorama of potato recipes that you can peruse while waiting for your train to come.

Chicken pot Parmentier

HACHIS PARMENTIER AU POULET

Serves 6 to 8

Parmentier (see page 165) would definitely be surprised to see that I've used a chicken filling as a variation on the classic meaty *hachis Parmentier* (after he got over the shock of seeing a train that runs underground!). Still, I think he'd be happy that I'm carrying on his mission to this day of getting people to eat their potatoes, although I frequently enjoy making this American-style with biscuits for French guests as well.

I use a rotisserie chicken from the market, which has become popular with time-pressed cooks in other countries, as it is in France. You can also make it from poached boneless chicken breasts: Heat a pot of salted water until boiling. Drop 4 large chicken breast halves in the water, turn off the heat, and cover. The breasts will be done in about 10 minutes.

Tarragon and chervil add a decidedly French touch to this dish, tarragon being the bolder of the two options.

1   To make the filling, heat the stock in a saucepan over medium-high heat with the carrots, celery, and onions. Let simmer until the vegetables are almost tender, about 15 minutes. Turn off the heat and set aside.

2   Melt the butter in a large pot or Dutch oven over medium heat. Stir in the flour and cook, stirring constantly, for 2 minutes. Whisk a few ladlefuls of the warm stock into the flour mixture, which will appear lumpy at first but will smooth out as you go. Gradually add all the stock, including the vegetables, stirring as you go. Cook for about 10 minutes, until thickened. During the last minute of cooking, add the garlic and white wine. Remove the pot from the heat and stir in the chicken, peas, tarragon, parsley, salt, and pepper. Taste and add a bit more salt, if desired. Transfer the mixture to a 2¹/₂- to 3-quart (2.5 to 3l) shallow baking dish set on an aluminum foil–lined baking sheet (to catch any spills).

3   Preheat the oven to 400°F (200°C).

4   To make the potato topping, bring a large pot of lightly salted water to a boil. Add the cubed potatoes and cook until fork-tender, about 25 minutes. Drain well. Return the potatoes to the pot and cook over medium heat for 1 minute, stirring constantly, to remove some of the moisture.

CHICKEN FILLING

4 cups (1l) chicken stock (page 326)

3 carrots, peeled and diced

2 ribs celery, diced

16 pearl onions, peeled (see Note on page 178)

6 tablespoons (3 ounces/85g) salted or unsalted butter

6 tablespoons (60g) all-purpose flour

1 clove garlic, peeled and minced

2 tablespoons dry white wine

4 cups (500g) diced or shredded cooked chicken

1 cup (130g) fresh or frozen peas or shelled fava beans

2 tablespoons finely chopped fresh tarragon or 3 tablespoons chopped chervil leaves

2 tablespoons finely chopped fresh flat-leaf parsley

1 teaspoon sea salt or kosher salt, plus more if needed

¹/₂ teaspoon freshly ground black pepper

POTATO TOPPING

2¹/₂ pounds (1.2kg) russet potatoes, peeled and cubed

6 tablespoons (3 ounces/85g) unsalted butter, cubed and at room temperature, and 2 tablespoons melted

1 teaspoon sea salt or kosher salt

3 large egg yolks

¹/₃ cup (80ml) heavy cream

Freshly ground black pepper

Pinch of freshly grated nutmeg

5 Pass the potatoes through a food mill or potato ricer (don't use a mixer or food processor because it will make the potatoes gluey). Mix in the cubed butter and salt, let stand 5 minutes, stirring once or twice while they're cooling.

6 Stir the egg yolks into the warm potatoes. Add the cream, a generous amount of pepper, and the nutmeg. Either spread the potato mixture over the chicken filling with a spatula, or transfer the mixture to a pastry bag fitted with a star tip and pipe the potatoes decoratively over the filling. With a pastry brush, gently dribble the melted butter over the potatoes. Bake the potpie for 30 minutes, until the potatoes are golden brown and burnished in places.

VARIATION

Chicken Potpie with Biscuits

Drop biscuits save a lot of time (and fuss), since they don't need to be rolled out. The dough will be rather wet, so I use a spring-loaded ice cream scoop to distribute it over the top of the potpie.

2 cups (280g) all-purpose flour

$\frac{1}{2}$ teaspoon sea salt or kosher salt

$\frac{3}{4}$ teaspoon freshly ground black pepper

$1\frac{1}{2}$ teaspoons baking powder (preferably aluminum-free)

$\frac{1}{2}$ teaspoon baking soda

8 tablespoons (4 ounces/115g) unsalted butter, chilled and cubed

$\frac{1}{2}$ cup packed (50g) finely chopped watercress (optional)

1 cup (250ml) buttermilk

1 In the bowl of a stand mixer fitted with the paddle attachment (or in a large bowl, by hand), combine the flour, salt, pepper, baking powder, and baking soda.

2 Add the butter and mix on low speed until the butter is broken up into pieces the size of peas. (If making by hand, you can use a pastry blender or your fingers.) Add the watercress, then the buttermilk, mixing just until the dough holds together.

3 Distribute the dough over the chicken filling in pieces the size of unshelled walnuts, evenly spaced. You can use two spoons, using one to scoop up some of the dough and the other to scrape it onto the chicken filling, or a spring-loaded ice cream scoop. Bake the chicken potpie for 30 minutes, or until the topping is deep golden brown and the filling is hot.

A Multitude of Mustards

THE CONSUMPTION OF DIJON MUSTARD IN France is through the roof. Which is exactly where I thought the top of my head was going to go when I tasted my way through various French brands. A few are especially spicy, and although folks tend to let mustard linger for a while, Dijon mustard is best when it's freshly opened.

When stocking my first kichen in Paris, I was riding home on the bus from the grocery store, and a woman commented on the giant jar of Amora mustard pressing against the side of the bulging plastic bag I was holding on to for dear life, as we lurched through Paris traffic. Nodding with obvious approval, she noted that it was good, and added that it was *"très, très forte"* (very, *very* strong). Since then, I've switched my mustard allegiances a few times—from artisanal brands like Edmond Fallot to Maille, which you can get drawn from a spigot at their fancy boutique in the Place de la Madeleine. But despite my fickle allegiences, I always keep a jar of Amora on hand, for nostalgic reasons, and for its *fortitude*.

Chicken with mustard

POULET À LA MOUTARDE

Serves 4 to 6

Many years ago, when prices were ridiculously low, I bought an enormous copper pan at E. Dehillerin, the famed cookware shop in Les Halles. This one-pan meal is a perfect fit for your largest, most extravagant pot. This dish requires you to brown the thighs and legs. Unless you have a very large skillet or a Dutch oven, fry the chicken in batches—you want them to have room to brown, not steam, which overcrowding creates. This dish is best served with a tangle of Herbed fresh pasta (page 230), which is exactly the right vehicle for sopping up the delicious sauce, or Celery root puree (page 217).

1/2 cup (135g), plus 3 tablespoons Dijon mustard

1/4 teaspoon sweet or smoked paprika

Freshly ground black pepper

3/4 teaspoon sea salt or kosher salt

4 chicken thighs and 4 legs (8 pieces, total)

1 cup (100g) diced smoked thick-cut bacon

1 small onion, peeled and finely diced

1 teaspoon fresh thyme leaves, or 1/2 teaspoon dried

1 cup (250ml) white wine

1 tablespoon whole mustard seeds or grainy mustard

2 to 3 tablespoons crème fraîche (page 327) or heavy cream

Warm water (optional)

Chopped fresh flat-leaf parsley or chives, for garnish

1 Mix 1/2 cup (135g) of the Dijon mustard in a bowl with the paprika, a few generous grinds of the peppermill, and the salt. Toss the chicken pieces in the mustard mixture, lifting the skin and rubbing some of it underneath.

2 Heat a wide skillet with a cover or a Dutch oven over medium-high heat and add the bacon. Cook the bacon, stirring frequently, until it's cooked through and just starting to brown. Remove the bacon from the pan and drain on paper towels. Leave about 1 tablespoon of bacon fat in the pan, discarding the rest. Add

continued

the onion and cook for about 5 minutes, until soft and transluscent. Stir in the thyme, and let cook for another few minutes, and then scrape the cooked onion into a bowl.

3 Add a little bit of olive oil to the pan, if necessary, and place the chicken pieces in the pan in a single layer. (If they don't all fit, cook them in two batches.) Cook over medium-high heat, browning them well on one side, then flip them over and brown them on the other side. It's important to get the chicken nicely colored as the coloring—as well as the darkened bits on the bottom of the pan, called the *fond*—will give the finished sauce its delicious flavor.

4 Remove the chicken pieces and put them in the bowl with the onions. Add the wine to the hot pan, scraping the darkened bits off the bottom with a sturdy flat utensil. Return the chicken pieces to the pan along with the bacon and onions. Cover and cook over low to medium heat, turning the chicken in the sauce a few times during cooking, until the chicken is cooked through, about 15 minutes. Check doneness by sticking a knife into the meat next to the thigh bone; if it's red, continue cooking for a few more minutes.

5 Remove the pot from the heat and stir in the 3 tablespoons Dijon mustard, the mustard seeds, and the crème fraîche. If the sauce has reduced and is quite thick, you can thin it with a little warm water. Sprinkle chopped parsley over the top and serve.

170

French Food—Fast

THIS MIGHT SOUND FUNNY, BUT ONE OF THE biggest concerns I had before I packed up and left for Paris was whether I would find a go-to "fast food" there. I don't mean in terms of fast-food restaurants, but rather would I be able to find a reasonably healthy, quick, affordable hot meal that I could pick up easily, like the burritos I had become accustomed to wolfing down in San Francisco's Mission District?

My answer came pretty quickly when I went to the Bastille market right next to where I was living, one Sunday morning. Over the din, the high-pitched warble of a Frenchwoman wielding a sharp, two-pronged meat fork (the French don't use tongs because, I've been told, they pierce the meat and you lose all the juices . . . which, somehow, stabbing it with two sharp prongs manages to avoid), beckoned shoppers as she presided over an impressive array of deeply bronzed rotisserie chickens.

People were waiting patiently in line, and not because everyone was huddling near Catherine's hot rotisserie for the warmth, but because of the magnificent birds she splayed out in front of her. I became a client *très (très) fidèle* and learned to get there early on Sunday morning before she sold out, as lunchtime rolled closer. Catherine and I became friendly enough for her to beckon me from across the market, letting me know that she would keep a chicken hot me for while I did the rest of my shopping.

The best of her chickens were *les crapaudines*, a term which means "spatchcocked," because when they are split open and roasted flat, they resemble *crapaudines*, or bullfrogs. In spite of the unsightly moniker, their taste is a thing of beauty and the flat-roasting technique ensures plenty of crispy skin. It's so good that I rip open the paper bag as soon as I get in my front door and yank all the skin off, getting my fingers oily, stuffing pieces of skin into my mouth before I even begin to unpack the rest of my market haul. Catherine's chicken is so good that I had to go through a *demi*-detox, limiting myself to buying a demi-chicken rather than a whole bird, because I can't be responsible if I'm by myself with a whole chicken in the house.

The longer I lived in Paris, however, the rounder I looked. (Anyone who tells you that people in France don't gain weight doesn't live within walking distance of a good rotisserie chicken stand.) So I began going to *le bootcamp* in one of the parks. These workouts drew a lot of stares from the locals, but I persevered, feeling good that someday I'd be able to fit back into my Euro-style jeans. Unfortunately, each workout required me to travel across Paris with two very heavy cast-iron hand weights in a gym bag, which were nearly impossible to maneuver during rush hour on the métro. And that gave me an excuse to quit *le bootcamp.* So I vowed to eat less chicken skin and skip the workouts. So far I've been good at keeping the latter promise to myself, but not quite the other.

Chicken lady chicken

POULET CRAPAUDINE FAÇON CATHERINE

Serves 4

3 cloves garlic, peeled and minced

1½ teaspoons sea salt or kosher salt

2 tablespoons olive oil

2 tablespoons freshly squeezed lemon juice

2 tablespoons white wine

1 tablespoon soy sauce

2½ teaspoons harissa (page 330), Sriracha, or Asian chile paste

2 teaspoons Dijon or yellow mustard

2 teaspoons honey

1 (3-pound/1.5kg) chicken

One thing I learned pretty quickly about the differences between French and American recipes is that in America, one chicken yields two servings, whereas in France, it yields four and sometimes six. However, when it comes to Catherine's *poulet crapaudine* (see page 172), one chicken yields one serving—mine.

Catherine now divides her time between Paris and her rotisserie in Bordeaux, but she gave me a few clues to how she prepares her birds, and this is a very close approximation, which I was able to replicate in my home oven. If you have an outdoor grill, by all means use it, weighing down the chicken with a brick until the skin side is nice and crispy, before flipping it over. For the best flavor, marinate the chicken for one to two days before cooking. Serve with Raw vegetable slaw (page 96) dressed with the garlic vinaigrette variation (page 96) or French fries (page 219).

1 Put the minced garlic and salt in a large, sturdy resealable plastic bag and crush it with the heel of your hand to make a paste. Add the olive oil, lemon juice, white wine, soy sauce, harissa, mustard, and honey to the bag, combining the ingredients well.

2 Remove the backbone of the chicken by snipping down both sides of the spine with poultry shears, or taking a chef's knife and cutting along both sides of it, and pulling it off. With the breast side down on the cutting board, take a knife and crack the bone between the breasts, then push the chicken down with your hands so it spreads out and lies flat. Flip the chicken over so it's skin-side up and press down with the heels of your hands on the chicken very firmly—like you're giving it a shiatsu massage—to flatten it as much as you possibly can. Don't go easy on it.

3 Loosen the skin from the breast and thigh meat and spoon some of the marinade under the skin. Put the chicken in the bag, close it securely, and use your hands to rub the marinade into the chicken. Refrigerate it for 1 to 2 days, flipping the bag over a few times as it marinates.

continued

173

4 Preheat the oven to 400°F (200°C). Heat a cast-iron skillet or grill pan over medium-high heat on the stovetop and place the chicken in it, breast side down. Drape a sheet of heavy-duty aluminum foil over the top and set a heavy weight on top of it. A good option is a brick or a large saucepan filled with water. (I use a leftover weight from the boot camp I quit.)

5 Cook the chicken until the skin is a deep golden brown, which usually takes about 10 minutes or so—check it often. Once it's browned, flip the chicken over, replace the weight, and let it cook for about 5 more minutes.

6 Remove the weight and the foil and place the chicken in the oven for 25 minutes, until it's cooked through. To serve it French-style, cut the chicken into six pieces: two legs, two thighs, and cut each breast in half crosswise, leaving the wings attached.

174

Cooking Offline

A LOT OF PEOPLE ARE SURPRISED—INCLUDING me—when I tell them that I launched my blog in 1999, which was around the time I left the restaurant business and started writing cookbooks. Food blogging began to catch on around 2003, when software was developed that allowed anyone to create and upload content to the Internet with remarkable ease. When I started my site, I would write articles and take photos, and then someone with more technical experience than a cookie-baker would upload them manually to my page for me. It was a little complicated, but the new medium was fun, and I liked having the flexibility to write about whatever I felt like and sharing it instantly.

Before I knew it, what had started as a way to share recipes and stories with friends became a full-time obsession. And soon there was a vast, diverse network of food bloggers, which meant there were lots of other folks from around the world with whom I could cook. The virtual exchange was great, but I missed physically working alongside other cooks, swapping ideas, tasting as we baked, and discussing what ingredients or seasonings we might want to add to a dish. Though we all heartily embraced the online world, there's still no substitute for rolling up your sleeves with a friend, and chopping, mixing, and cooking up a meal while sharing a glass of wine. And then sitting down afterward to enjoy the results of a job well done together.

One of my fellow food bloggers from the early days was another David L. who loved to cook—and eat. David Leite launched his site, Leite's Culinaria, either just before or just after I did (he says I launched first, and I say he did). In addition to specializing in Portuguese cuisine, David has taken on a number of French classics. It took us more than ten years to finally meet, and when we did, it was over an enormous Southern dinner in Atlanta. Sitting around a large table, he ordered everything from the menu, many things twice—or even in triple portions. Of course, I liked him immediately and we made plans to cook something together on his next trip to Paris.

When at long last he came for dinner in Paris, he arrived bearing a bottle of rosé Champagne (which further endeared him to me). Then he tied on an apron and rolled up his sleeves to make *coq au vin* with me, a dish traditionally made with stewing chicken. The first time I attempted to make the dish in Paris, I ordered a *coq entier*. The *volailler* insisted that I wanted only half. But I'm stubborn and didn't take his advice, insisting on the entire bird. And he was right; when I got home and unwrapped the butcher paper package of chicken parts, it contained what must have been at least twenty-two pieces of chicken. I didn't count them all, but I had leftovers for days. And days and days and days.

Chicken in red wine sauce

COQ AU VIN

Serves 4

This recipe, which David Leite brought to Paris, was inspired by one from Anthony Bourdain. It uses a regular chicken, but it does call for chicken blood. I don't know where one finds that in America, but it's not something sold on the shelves of my local supermarket in Paris either, so I skipped it.

I'd always assumed that the rich, dark sauce for *coq au vin* was thickened with chocolate. (Or perhaps that was just wishful thinking.) David made my wish come true, and at my suggestion, we added a slurry of cocoa powder in place of the blood. And since we're both fans of smoked bacon, he was happy with the nice *lardons* of French bacon that I had prepared. Commercial American bacon throws off a lot of fat, so if you can't find bacon from an artisanal source, you may want to carefully blot some of the fat from the pan with paper towels (holding them with tongs) as it cooks.

Note that the chicken needs to marinate for 1 to 2 days in the red wine before cooking. Serve with Mashed potatoes (page 216) or Herbed fresh pasta (page 230).

1 bottle Côte du Rhone, or another fruity red wine

1 onion, peeled and diced

1 carrot, peeled and diced

Sea salt or kosher salt

1 teaspoon freshly ground black pepper

1/8 teaspoon ground cloves

2 bay leaves

10 sprigs thyme

1 large chicken, cut into 8 pieces (2 legs, 2 thighs, 2 breasts cut crosswise with wings attached)

3 tablespoons olive oil

2 tablespoons unsalted butter

1 1/2 cups (150g) diced thick-cut smoked bacon

8 ounces (230g) large mushrooms, sliced in half

1 tablespoon all-purpose flour

16 pearl onions, peeled (see Note on page 178)

3/4 cup (180ml) water

1 tablespoon red wine vinegar

1 1/2 tablespoons unsweetened cocoa powder

1 In a large, wide bowl, mix the wine, onion, carrot, 1 teaspoon of salt, the pepper, cloves, bay leaves, and thyme. Add the chicken pieces and press down to submerge. Marinate in the refrigerator for 1 to 2 days, turning the pieces once or twice during that time.

2 Remove the chicken from the marinade and blot it dry with paper towels. Strain the marinade through a fine-mesh sieve set over a bowl, saving the vegetables and herbs as well as the wine.

3 Heat 2 tablespoons of the olive oil and 1 tablespoon of the butter in a large pot or Dutch oven over medium-high heat. Cook the chicken pieces in a single layer until dark brown on one side, about 5 minutes; turn and cook the other side, about 5 minutes more. If all the chicken pieces won't fit in a single layer with a reasonable amount of space between them, cook them in batches. (David says if you have the backbone of the chicken, add that too, since it'll add a lot of flavor to the juices later.) Transfer the pieces to a plate as they are done.

continued

4   In the same pot, fry the bacon along with the mushrooms until the bacon is crisp. If browned bits stick to the bottom of the pot, add a splash of the red wine marinade and scrape the flavorful dark bits into the mixture.

5   Add the drained vegetables and herbs from the marinade to the pot and cook until the vegetables are tender. Stir the flour into the vegetables. Add the chicken back to the pot along with the strained wine, which should come up almost to the top of the chicken pieces. If not, add a bit of water or some more red wine. Cover and let the chicken simmer over medium heat for 1 hour.

6   While the chicken is cooking, heat the remaining 1 tablespoon of oil and 1 tablespoon of butter in a saucepan. When the butter is melted, add the pearl onions, season with salt, and cook until browned, about 12 minutes. Pour the water into the saucepan along with the vinegar and season with more salt. Cover the pan and simmer for about 40 minutes, until the onions are tender. Add them to the chicken along with any cooking liquid.

7   In a small bowl, make a slurry with the cocoa powder and about $^1/_3$ cup (80ml) of the warm cooking liquid from the pot. Stir it into the chicken, letting it mix into the sauce. Cook for a few more minutes to heat everything through. You can pluck out the thyme sprigs, if you wish, before serving, although the French would just leave them in.

NOTE: To peel the onions, drop them in a pot of boiling water and let them simmer for about 5 minutes. Drain them and let cool. Trim the ends off each one, and then slip off the skins.

Chicken in red wine sauce, continued

Counterfeit duck confit

FAUX CONFIT DE CANARD

Serves 4

4 duck thighs (thigh and leg attached)

1 tablespoon sea salt or kosher salt

1 tablespoon gin

¼ teaspoon ground nutmeg

¼ teaspoon ground allspice

2 cloves garlic, peeled and halved lengthwise

2 bay leaves

The first time I tasted duck confit, I declared it the best thing in the world, a belief I stuck to for the next twenty-five years. And unless something better comes along, I'll stick to it for the next twenty-five years as well. The shattering skin, fried to a crisp in velvety duck fat and encasing tender meat that easily pulls away from the bone, is in a class by itself. Fortunately, in France, it's very easy to buy already made duck *confit* (which means "preserved") at any butcher—and even in the supermarket. To be honest, it's exactly like what you make at home, and considering how many quarts of duck fat you need to make a batch, it's easier to pick up a few preserved thighs, and fry them up whenever the mood strikes.

I've had a lot of duck confit in my life, and this counterfeit version tastes every bit as good, with a lot less fuss and no mess. Because it's not preserved for a long time, it's not a true confit, but the trade-off is that I can eat it just a few hours after I've started it. I've adapted techniques from food writers Regina Schrambling in the *New York Times* and Hank Shaw on simplyrecipes.com to come up with a new-fangled way of making this traditional dish possible with practically zero effort.

The trick to this ridiculously easy technique is to use a dish that will hold the duck thighs snugly pressed together, which allows them to "confit" as they bake. If you only have a larger dish, increase the recipe and cook extra duck legs. Note that this has to chill in the refrigerator overnight before cooking.

Traditionally, duck confit is served with Potatoes cooked in duck fat (page 220) and a green salad. But since we're already bucking tradition, you can also use the shredded duck meat in place of the bacon in a *salade lyonnaise* (page 99). And, of course, it's obligatory in *cassoulet* (page 195).

1 Prick the duck all over with a needle, making sure to pierce all the way though the skin.

2 Mix the salt, gin, nutmeg, and allspice in a baking dish that will fit the duck legs snugly, with no room around them. Rub the spice mixture all over the duck legs.

continued

179

3 Put the garlic and bay leaves on the bottom of the baking dish and lay the duck legs, flesh-side down, on top of them, making sure the garlic cloves are completely buried beneath. Cover with plastic wrap and refrigerate for at least 8 hours, or overnight.

4 To cook the duck, wipe the duck gently with a paper towel to remove excess salt, then put the duck back in the dish, skin-side up. Put it in a cold oven. Turn the oven on to 300°F (150°C). Bake the duck thighs for 2½ hours, taking them out during baking once or twice and basting them with any duck fat pooling around them.

5 To finish the duck, increase the oven temperature to 375°F (190°C) and bake for 15 to 20 minutes, until the skin is deeply browned and very crispy.

A FRENCH DUCK IN AMERICA

Duck is very easy to get in France, and most supermarkets carry it right alongside the chicken and turkey (and for some reason, rabbit is in there, too, even though I've never seen a rabbit with wings). Duck is available as fresh or preserved thighs (*confit*) packed in duck fat and as plump breasts called *magrets de canard*.

A typical *magret* (half-breast) is so meaty and rich that it's cut and fanned out into slices, and one half-breast can feed four people. The reason they are so juicy and succulent is that the breasts come from ducks bred for foie gras. *Magret* is always served very rare, meaning very bright-red all the way through, which gives visitors pause if they are not accustomed to eating the "other red meat," as it could be called in France.

Most duck in France is Moulard, a hybrid of Muscovy and Pekin, which is meaty and fatty. In America, Pekin ducks (also called Long Island ducks) are most frequently found and used in Chinese cooking, where plump meat isn't as valued as much as the fatty skin. Duck is usually sold in America at butcher shops and well-stocked supermarkets (sometimes frozen, whole), but if your community has a farmers' market, check there, as well as at Asian markets. Duck is also available online (see Sources, page 339).

Chez Marc

PEOPLE OFTEN TELL ME THAT THEY'RE AFRAID to invite me over for dinner. Some think they'll have to perform culinary backflips to impress me. Others simply apologize for never inviting me, assuming that if I were to come, I'd sit there and provide a running critique of the meal. In fact, nothing is further from the truth. Having worked in restaurants for much of my life, I'm quite happy to be invited to someone's house to relax and enjoy a home-cooked meal. No apologies necessary. And I promise, no critiques either.

I don't expect anything fancy or restaurant-quality when I dine at my friends' apartments, especially since many of them have small Parisian kitchens without the *batterie de cuisine* you'd find in a restaurant kitchen. Yet when I dine at my friend Marc's—a soft-spoken fellow who's a city planner by day—each tureen or platter of food that comes to the table is more spectacular than the one before it, many riffing on time-honored or long-forgotten classic French dishes, the kind you rarely see anymore, even in the fanciest French restaurants.

Marc might make a pristine bouillon of shellfish, carefully simmering the shells and then straining and clarifying the broth so each warm spoonful is the pure, distilled essence of sweet lobster and langoustines. If I run into him at the market during game season, he'll have a sly smile on his face, having scored some sort of elusive game bird, because Marc knows which of the vendors discreetly keep hidden a few rarities—such as *polombe* (dove) or *perdrix* (partridge)—because they're only for cooks who seek them out. And vendors will only sell them to those who know how to properly cook them. (Also, I suspect a few may not be legal.)

I love game birds, and the easiest to find is *pintade*, or guinea hen. They have a pleasant, meaty flavor that's agreeable even to those who aren't familiar with eating game birds. Most French guinea hens are free-range because they need space to forage. And because they are rather lean, they benefit from braising rather than roasting; the gentle heat tenderizes the meat while at the same time allows the meat to flavor the liquid.

Marc came over one day to make lunch for some friends with me. And this time, it was I who was intimidated . . . in my own kitchen! He's exacting and precise, and he insisted on doing the shopping. He arrived bearing perfectly ripe fresh figs, a generous bundle of thyme, a black-footed *pintade* that his butcher had wrapped in several layers of crinkly brown paper, and a suave Riesling for the sauce—as well as a bottle for drinking (which got no critiques from me.)

Braised guinea hen with figs

PINTADE AUX FIGUES

Serves 4

Figs are something I saw only once in my life before I moved to California, where they're widely available in the fall. Fortunately, we get plenty of figs in Paris during the same season, but I've made the guinea hen at other times of the year with dried figs, and it works just as well. If you're using dried figs, braise them with the *pintade*. If guinea hen isn't available where you live, you can use chicken in its place.

Serve the *pintade* over Herbed fresh pasta (page 230), Mashed potatoes (page 216), or Celery root puree (page 217).

GUINEA HEN

1 teaspoon sea salt or kosher salt, plus more if needed

Freshly ground black pepper

1 (3-pound/1.35kg) guinea hen or chicken

8 ounces (225g) fresh figs, or 10 ounces (285g) dried, stemmed and halved

1 tablespoon olive oil

1/2 tablespoon unsalted butter

2 carrots, peeled and finely diced

1 onion, peeled and finely diced

1 clove garlic, peeled and minced

10 sprigs thyme

1 bay leaf

1 tablespoon all-purpose flour

1 1/2 cups (375ml) fruity white wine, such as Muscadet, dry Riesling, or Chardonnay

1 1/2 cups (375ml) chicken stock (page 326)

Generous pinch of ground allspice

1 tablespoon dry port

Chopped fresh flat-leaf parsley, for garnish

HONEY-BAKED FIGS

1 1/2 pounds (680g) fresh figs, stemmed

2 tablespoons (40g) honey

2 tablespoons salted or unsalted butter, cold

Sea salt or kosher salt and freshly ground black pepper

1 To make the guinea hen, rub the 1 teaspoon of salt and some pepper all over the outside of the guinea hen and put four fig halves in the cavity. Warm the olive oil and butter in a Dutch oven with a cover over medium-high heat. Add the hen and cook until it's browned on all sides, about 10 minutes. Remove the hen from the pan and add the carrots, onion, and garlic. Season with a bit of salt and pepper, then cook, stirring frequently, until completely soft, about 8 minutes. Add the thyme and bay leaf and cook for another minute, then stir in the flour and cook for a minute or two.

2 Pour 1/2 cup (125ml) of the wine into the pot and stir, scraping the bottom of the pan to loosen any browned bits. Add the remaining 1 cup (250ml) of wine along with the chicken stock. Put the guinea hen back in the pot with the remaining fig halves. Bring the liquid to a boil. Decrease the heat to a simmer, cover, and cook on the stove top for 30 to 40 minutes—turning the bird midway during cooking—until the guinea hen is cooked through. It's done when the meat is no longer red when you pull the thigh meat away from the bone. If using chicken, cook for about 1 hour.

3 To prepare the honey-baked figs, mark an X with a sharp paring knife across the top of each fig, cutting about one-third of the way down each one. Arrange them cut-side up in a baking dish that will fit all in a single layer without a lot of extra room, and drizzle the honey over the figs. Cut the butter into the same number of cubes as you have figs and press a piece of butter into the center of each fig. Season with salt and pepper. Bake for 15 to

continued

20 minutes (or less, if the figs are very ripe), until soft and cooked through. Remove from the oven and cover with aluminum foil to keep warm.

4   Remove the guinea hen from the pot along with the fig halves (put them in a separate bowl), and strain the vegetables and liquid through a strainer into a bowl, pressing on the solids firmly with a spoon to extract as much of the liquid as possible. (Discard the solids.) Return the liquid to the pot and reduce it over medium heat until you have about 1½ cups (375ml).

5   While the sauce is reducing, divide the guinea hen into four pieces—two breasts (removed from the bone) and two thighs with legs attached. If using chicken, detach the wings, remove the breast meat from the bones and cut the breasts in half crosswise, then remove and separate the thighs and drumsticks. Return the guinea hen parts to the pot, along with the fig halves allspice, and port. Warm until the sauce bubbles around the guinea hen parts, turning the pieces a few times to coat them well with the sauce. Taste the sauce and season with more salt, if desired.

6   Divide the guinea hen parts among four plates and garnish with the parsley. Arrange several honey-baked figs on each plate and serve with the accompaniment of your choice (see head note).

Pork and chard sausage

CAILLETTES

Serves 4

The first time I had a *caillette* was at Le Verre Volé, many years ago, when it was one of the first somewhat funky wine bars that popped up in Paris, serving simple, rustic food. For years, everything at Le Verre Volé was cooked behind the cramped counter in a home-sized broiler not much larger than a toaster oven. There wasn't a large choice on the menu, but you could get a generous platter of charcuterie or cheese to start off with, accompanied by good baguette, which the waiter plunked down on the table—whole—expecting you to rip into it with your hands. Another do-it-yourself project during dinner was choosing the wine, which you did by picking any *vin* that looked interesting off the shelf for the price that was scribbled on the neck of the bottle with a marking pen.

185

I loved it immediately, even though the staff could be a little gruff around the edges. But living in Paris, one needs to learn to give it back. One night I left the wine choice in their hands and asked them to pick a dry white. The one they opened tasted pretty sweet to me. After a lengthy discussion, which involved polling every other diner in the restaurant (it's that kind of place), I had to stand my ground, saying "I don't know all that much about wine, but as a pastry chef, one thing I am an expert on is sweet. And that wine is sweet." I don't remember if I won my case, but I kept going back because of the *caillettes*.

The first time I saw the word *caillette* scribbled on their blackboard, I assumed it was a baby quail (*caille*). But the waiter explained that a *caillette* is a sausage originally from the Ardèche, made with greens mixed into the meat. And when my plate came out, I saw that the homemade sausage was indeed in the ovoid shape of a quail.

Eventually the wine bar got spiffed up with a real kitchen, and I started making my own *cailettes* at home. They're easy to cook at home because they're baked in the oven, not pan-fried. Normally they get wrapped in caul fat to hold them together, but that's not easy to find, so I wrap them with a tasty criss-cross of bacon.

Serve the *caillettes* with a green salad and Mashed potatoes (page 216) or Potato gratin (page 211), as winter fare.

continued

1 Season the chicken livers with ¹/₂ teaspoon of the salt and a few grinds of pepper. Heat the oil in a skillet over medium heat and sauté the onion until soft and translucent, about 5 minutes. Add the livers and cook, stirring frequently, until they are cooked through, about 5 minutes. Scrape the onion and livers into a bowl.

2 To the same pan, add the pork, garlic, and thyme. Season the mixture with the remaining 1 teaspoon of salt and some pepper, and sauté over medium heat until the pork is cooked through, about 5 minutes. Stir in the allspice and transfer the mixture to the bowl of livers.

3 Chop the tough ends off the stalks of Swiss chard and wash the leaves thoroughly, changing the water a few times if necessary, to remove any grit. Bring a pot of salted water to a boil and add the chard. Cook for 5 to 10 minutes, until the stems are tender. Drain, and when cool enough to handle, squeeze as much water from the Swiss chard as you can.

4 In a food processor, pulse the pork and liver mixture and the chard together with the parsley, egg, and lemon juice until the mixture is cohesive enough to hold together, but still chunky. (If you don't have a food processor, you can finely chop the liver and chard by hand, then mix everything together in a bowl.)

5 Preheat the oven to 350°F (175°C).

6 Oil a shallow baking dish and form the *caillette* mixture into four ovals, each roughly the size of a quail, squeezing them to compact the mixture. Place them in the baking dish as you go. Drape each sausage with a crisscross of two strips of bacon, tucking the ends under the sausages. Bake for 30 minutes until the meat is cooked through.

Pork and chard sausage, continued

4 ounces (115g) chicken livers

1¹/₂ teaspoons sea salt or kosher salt

Freshly ground black pepper

2 tablespoons olive oil

¹/₂ onion, peeled and minced

8 ounces (230g) ground pork

2 cloves garlic, peeled and minced

1 tablespoon minced fresh thyme leaves

Generous pinch of ground allspice

12 ounces (340g) Swiss chard

¹/₄ cup (15g) chopped fresh flat-leaf parsley

1 large egg

2 teaspoons freshly squeezed lemon juice

8 strips bacon (not thick-cut)

186

Caramel pork ribs

TRAVERS DE PORC AU CARAMEL

Serves 4 to 6

3/4 cup (150g) granulated sugar

1/4 cup (45g) firmly packed brown sugar, light or dark

3/4 cup (180ml) beer

1/4 cup (60ml) bourbon

3 tablespoons cider vinegar

2 tablespoons ketchup

1 (1/2-inch/2cm) piece ginger, peeled and minced

2 tablespoons soy sauce

2 teaspoons harissa (page 330), Sriracha sauce, or another hot sauce

1 teaspoon Dijon mustard

1/2 teaspoon freshly ground black pepper

4 pounds (1.8 kg) pork ribs, cut into 3- or 4-rib portions

Whenever I tell friends in Paris how great Texas is, and how friendly Texans are, they're shocked; I think they imagine that gunslingers are roaming the towns, having shoot-outs on the dusty streets of Houston and Dallas, with dastardly villains galloping away on horseback. I don't know if there are still any saloons with swinging double doors left in Texas, but I can say with certainty that the people in Texas do know how to eat. And whenever I go, I do my best to get my fill of good ol' Texas barbecue.

The French enjoy ribs just as much as their Wild West counterparts. And many cafés—albeit without swinging double doors—feature *travers du porc au caramel* as the *plat du jour* at lunchtime, which is announced on chalkboards in that decidedly French cursive writing. The ribs are a little more refined than in Texas, and you won't see anyone in Paris picking up their ribs with their hands at the table (unless they want to be seen as outlaws) as Americans do, but it's nice to know that Parisians can get down with a rack of ribs, albeit in their own way.

Americans are also known for our love of ketchup, which some people seem to put on everything. Judging from the shelves and shelves of ketchup in the supermarkets here, along with *le sauce barbecue*, it's obvious that the French are shooting down the notion that Americans are the only ones enjoying the readily available red sauce. In fact, it's been whispered that some of the great French chefs add a *soupçon* of it to sauces to give them body and flavor, as I do in my barbecue sauce.

Serve these ribs French-style with plain rice, or with Mashed potatoes (page 216) and Raw vegetable slaw (page 96).

1   Preheat the oven to 350°F (180°C).

2   Spread the granulated sugar in an even layer over the bottom of a large pot with a cover, such as a roasting pan or a Dutch oven. Cook the sugar over medium heat until it starts to melt around the edges. When the liquefied sugar just starts to darken to a pale copper color, gently stir the sugar inward and continue to cook, stirring until the sugar is completely moistened. Continue to cook the sugar, stirring infrequently, until all of it is a deep

continued

copper–colored liquid, similar in color to dark maple syrup, and smoking (but not burnt). Turn off the heat and stir in the brown sugar, then add the beer. The mixture will seize and harden, which is normal.

3   Let the mixture cool down a bit, then stir in the bourbon, cider vinegar, ketchup, ginger, soy sauce, harissa, mustard, and pepper. Put the ribs in the pot and turn on the heat until the sauce boils and bubbles up. Turn the ribs a few times in the liquid, cover, and roast in the oven for $1^1/_2$ to 2 hours, until the ribs are tender. During the roasting, remove the pot from the oven and turn the ribs over two or three times.

4   Remove the lid from the pot and continue to roast, turning the ribs a few times, for 30 minutes more, or until the juices have thickened a bit. Remove the ribs from the oven, skim any visible fat from the surface of the liquid, and serve.

Smoky barbecue-style pork

PORC FUMÉ FAÇON BARBECUE

Serves 6

One quality that Parisians have that surprises people from other places is *moderation*. There is a desire to appear not *too* excited about, well, anything, which is why the French say something is "*pas terrible*" ("not terrible") if they don't like it and "*pas mal*" ("not bad") if they do. There is also a *moderation* of flavors in cooking, which precludes seasoning foods with spices and chiles, or too much flavor, as I found out the day I was at a barbecue and jumped in to tend the meat on the grill. I noticed bunches of fresh herbs growing nearby so I grabbed a big handful, dipped them in some of the marinade, and basted the meat cooking over the fire. When big clouds of aromatic smoke billowed up, permeating the meat, the host came sprinting over, worried because I was adding "*trop de goût!*" ("too much flavor!").

Although Parisians love to smoke, they haven't developed a taste for smoky foods. (Perhaps everything already tastes smoked to them, so it's not necessary to do anything to the food?) Yet in spite of smoky food having "too much flavor," I like it. And I recreate those flavors with a combination of chile powder, paprika, and bottled barbecue sauce.

The French are fascinated with American convenience foods, particularly *la sauce barbecue*, in spite of the fact that some sauces have an alarming amount of *goût*. The one brand the French sell in supermarkets is called *Oh ouizz!*, which may be a play on an English phrase, yet sounds to me like something *not* to do with cooking or eating but other bodily functions. But I haven't checked the ingredient list. And I don't think I will.

Serve with Mashed potatoes (page 216) and Winter salad (page 98) or Raw vegetable slaw (page 96).

1 Combine the salt, paprika, chile powder, cinnamon, cumin, and cocoa powder in a large, sturdy resealable plastic bag. Put the pork shoulder into the bag and rub the spices into the meat. Seal the bag and refrigerate for 24 hours.

2 Preheat the oven to 325°F (160°C).

1½ teaspoons sea salt or kosher salt

1 tablespoon smoked paprika

1 teaspoon red chile powder, preferably chipotle, pasilla, or ancho

¾ teaspoon ground cinnamon

½ teaspoon ground cumin

2 teaspoons unsweetened cocoa powder

2½- to 3-pound (1 to 1.5kg) pork shoulder

1 cup (250ml) beer

¾ cup (180ml) barbecue sauce

2 tablespoons cider or red wine vinegar

1½ tablespoons tomato paste

2 teaspoons harissa (page 330), Tabasco, or Asian chile paste

1½ teaspoons soy sauce

3 Warm the beer, barbecue sauce, vinegar, tomato paste, harissa, and soy sauce in a large Dutch oven over medium heat. Put the pork into the sauce and turn it a few times to coat. Cover the Dutch oven tightly with the lid and cook in the oven for 2 to 3 hours, turning it a few times, until the meat pulls apart very easily.

4 Remove the pork shoulder and let it rest on a platter until it's cool enough to handle. Pull the pork into bite-size shreds and return them to the sauce. Simmer until the pork and the sauce are warmed through, then serve.

191

Cassoulet

I USED TO LIVE IN UPSTATE NEW YORK, WHERE winter temperatures could drop down to nearly -20°F (-29°C). On some days, it was so cold we had to wear suede face masks to keep our skin protected. When I headed west to California I gave away all my winter weather gear—the bulky sweaters, puffy down jackets, mittens, thermal underwear, and yes, even my suede face mask. Even though San Francisco can be damp and chilly, and the favorite sport of the natives is watching shivering tourists naïvely walking around in shorts and t-shirts, usually a jacket will do and rarely do you need gloves or scarves. (On occasion, however, face masks made an appearance at certain street fairs in the kinkier parts of town. Although they were usually made of leather, rather than suede.)

I was a naïve tourist when I moved to Paris, thinking it was eternally spring in the City of Light, and I would spend my days parked on a bench by the Seine, lapping up Berthillon ice cream *en plein soleil*. But when that first winter hit, and my rooftop apartment turned into an icebox, I spent my days under the covers bundled up with a sweater, a bulky jacket, and a scarf tied around my neck, with only my hands exposed so that I could write. It's easy to see why cafés in France have been, and still are, very popular with writers: they are the only places where your fingers can warm up enough to be able to get some work done.

Another surefire way I found to keep warm is to make cassoulet, which requires a few hours of cooking. And when there is nothing between you and the elements except a thin layer of stucco, and your oven is the sole source of reliable heat in the winter, you are happy to have an excuse to use it.

The first time I had cassoulet, I was working at Chez Panisse, and it was served at irregular intervals throughout the year in the café. And my (unofficial) job was scraping up the crispy, stuck-on bits from the cassoulet pots after the cooks had dished up the cassoulet to the customers.

People come to Paris looking for cassoulet, but it's not a dish that's easily found in Paris restaurants. True, there are a few places that serve it. But anyone from one of the villages in Gascony, the Languedoc, and other parts of the southwest of France, would not be pleased if they saw what is often called *cassoulet* in Paris. Though to be honest, most of them would not be pleased with the version served in the neighboring village.

I love the creamy beans that are slightly sticky with duck fat and garlic; the big chunks of tender, velvety *confit de canard*; and the chewy mouthfuls of Toulouse sausage; all under a thick-crusted layer of toasted bread crumbs, waiting to be broken through.

Not only because I wanted to stay warm in the winter, but also because I wanted to learn how to make one of my favorite dishes of all time, I went down to Agen and had a lesson from my friend Kate Hill, who's lived in Gascony for decades. There's a lot of discussion, and dispute, about cassoulet. Traditionally it was a peasant dish, as Kate explained to me, mostly made of beans with bits and pieces of meat and sausage. The classic beans for cassoulet are *haricots Tarbais*, stout white beans grown in southwestern France. When cooked, they take on a rich, ivory color and have a particularly creamy texture that makes a perfect binder for the other ingredients.

But times have changed, and cassoulet doesn't have to be made with duck confit and *haricots Tarbais* (which few peasants could afford at today's prices anyway). You can use dried beans, such as flageolets or borlotti, and if you have access to any of the wonderful heirloom bean varieties available, use them. However, don't use canned beans or ordinary supermarket beans, which are often old and don't have much flavor. There is a difference in quality, and you want the dominant ingredient to be the best it can be.

I'm very fortunate in Paris to be able to easily find most of the ingredients in my neighborhood shops, including jars of duck confit packed in a generous amount of its own fat. (I save the fat and use it to fry potatoes, page 220.) Sausage is as close as the charcuterie down the street, which also has *jarret de porc* (ham hock), and the *épicerie* sells bags of white beans or flageolets, ready to soak and cook.

Purists like to bicker, but like bouillabaisse, another regional French classic, cassoulet has always been made with regional ingredients that are available wherever one lives. So if you can't get duck confit, use chicken thighs. You may not be able to find fresh Toulouse pork sausage, but you can find other unseasoned, or lightly seasoned, sausages from your grocer or butcher that are similar, such as mild (or sweet) Italian sausage. Instead of the ham hock, use pork or lamb shoulder simmered on the stove top (or oven-roasted). But if you can't get bacon, well, I'm going to suggest that you move somewhere else.

Cassoulet is traditionally cooked in a *cassole* (see Sources, page 339), a dish with a wide top that helps create a browned crust and gently tapers down to a flat base, which keeps the inside juicy and moist. Kate's country kitchen is lined with gorgeous *cassoles* from a local potter, and I'm always tempted to swipe one, thinking she won't notice. Fortunately, I eventually found one at a thrift store in Paris for only €5. But if you're not so lucky, or don't have a criminal streak, a deep roasting pan works well, too.

Kate took me to the market in Agen to gather the ingredients, which we spent the better part of an afternoon preparing. She told me why browning the confit and sausage are important, even though they're going to be cooked in the beans ("For flavor!") and when she diced pork rind, she laughed—"Americans would never eat this!"—then pushed it off the cutting board with the blade of her knife right into the big pot of beans simmering away.

Of course, it would not be France unless we disagreed on something, and that was whether to top the cassoulet with bread crumbs or not. Kate was pretty adamant about not using them, saying the beans will form a nice crust on their own. And when the cassoulet is baked in her wood-fired oven outside, it does, indeed, come out with a nice crust on top. But I opt for bread crumbs at home because there are no flames roasting the top to crunchy perfection in my oven.

For my city kitchen, I made a number of other changes. I added a ham hock for flavor. I increased the amount of duck confit because I always find myself digging around the cassoulet, hoping for more of it. And I blend the garlic and onion, which makes an especially aromatic liquid.

White bean, sausage, duck confit casserole

CASSOULET

Serves 10 to 12

4 cups (2 pounds/950g) good-quality dried beans (see page 192)

2 pounds (950g) unsmoked ham hock

1¾ cups (160g) diced, thick-cut unsmoked pork belly or pancetta

2 carrots, peeled

2 onions, peeled and halved

6 cloves garlic, peeled

2 bay leaves

10 sprigs thyme

Sea salt or kosher salt

4 confit duck thighs (thigh and leg attached)

1 pound (450g) fresh pork sausage, unseasoned or lightly seasoned, such as mild Italian sausage

Freshly ground black pepper

1 cup (135g) dried or fresh bread crumbs

3 tablespoons neutral-tasting vegetable oil or walnut oil

There aren't a lot of shortcuts to making cassoulet, but the rewards are vast and will give you a few days worth of meals. One shortcut is to cook the sausage with the beans. And if you make Counterfeit duck confit (page 179), it's already cooked and you can cut it up and use it without browning. But don't give the beans short shrift; try to track down a good variety (see Sources, page 339) or scope out your local natural foods store or a well-stocked supermarket. Cassoulet lovers insist that cassoulet needs to be *rechauffé*, or reheated the next day, for the best and most authentic flavor.

1   Rinse the beans and sort for debris. Soak them overnight covered in cold water.

2   The next day, put the ham hock in a separate large pot of water, bring it just to a boil over high heat, then decrease the heat to a steady simmer, and cook for about 2 hours, until the meat is tender and pulls easily from the bone. Remove the ham hock from the water and set it on a plate. When cool enough to handle, remove the meat from the bones, shred it into large, bite-size pieces, and refrigerate it. Discard the liquid.

3   Drain the beans; put them in the pot you used to cook the ham hock and cover with cold water. Add the ham bones to the pot of beans along with the pork belly, carrots, onions, garlic, bay leaves, and thyme. Bring the beans just to a boil over high heat, then decrease the heat so the beans are simmering gently, and cook until the beans are soft and tender, about 1 hour. As the water boils away during cooking, add more water as necessary. Taste the beans toward the end of cooking, and add up to 1 tablespoon of salt, if necessary.

4   While the beans are cooking, scrape any excess fat from the duck confit pieces (save it for making Duck fat–fried potatoes, page 220) and fry the duck in a skillet over medium heat until the pieces are golden brown and crisp on both sides, 5 to 8 minutes per side. (If using the Counterfeit duck confit on page 179, the duck will already be browned and ready, so there's no need to recook it for this step.)

continued

5 Transfer the duck pieces to a plate and pour off any excess fat from the pan. Prick the sausages a few times with a sharp knife, then fry the sausages in the same pan just to brown them on the outside; they don't need to be fully cooked through. Set the sausages on the plate with the duck pieces. When cool enough to handle, cut the sausages on the diagonal into 2-inch pieces. Cut each duck thigh into three pieces; cut the drumstick off, and then use a knife to divide the thigh portion into two equal pieces, cutting it in half by holding the knife parallel to the bone.

6 When the beans are done, turn off the heat. Discard the bay leaves, thyme, and ham bone, and pluck out the carrots, onions, and garlic cloves. Cut the carrots into cubes, and mix them back into the beans, along with the shredded meat from the ham hock.

7 Puree the onion and garlic in a blender or food processor with a bit of the bean liquid until smooth. Stir the mixture back into the bean mixture, season with pepper, and taste, adding more salt if desired. (Some pork products are quite salty, so at this point, adjust the salt to your taste.)

8 Preheat the oven to 325°F (160°C) with an oven rack in the top third of the oven.

9 In a wide casserole that holds at least 8 quarts (8l) or a roasting pan, assemble the cassoulet. Ladle a layer of the bean mixture and some of the liquid into the casserole. Put half of the duck pieces and half of the sausage evenly spaced over the beans. Add another layer of beans, and then put the rest of the duck and sausage pieces on top. Add the remaining beans and enough of the liquid so that the beans are just barely floating in the liquid. (Refrigerate any extra bean liquid, as you may need it later. Or if there isn't enough bean liquid, add a bit more water, just enough to moisten the beans.)

10 Toss the bread crumbs with the oil until thoroughly moistened, then spread the bread crumbs evenly on top of the cassoulet. Bake the cassoulet for 1 hour. After an hour, use the side of a large spoon or a heatproof spatula to break the crust on top in several places. Decrease the oven temperature to 250°F (120°C) and bake the cassoulet for another 2½ hours, breaking the crust two more times while cooking. Remove the cassoulet from the oven and let it rest for 15 minutes. If you want to serve the cassoulet reheated, as many prefer it, let it cool to room temperature for 1½ hours, and then refrigerate it.

196

11 To serve the cassoulet reheated, remove the cassoulet from the refrigerator 1 hour before you plan to reheat it. Preheat the oven to 350°F (180°C). Break through a piece of the top of the cassoulet, and if you don't see much liquid surrounding the beans beneath the surface, add some of the reserved bean liquid (or warm water)—just enough to moisten the insides a little, about 1/2 cup (125ml). Bake the cassoulet for 1 1/2 hours, or until it's completely heated through. If the topping isn't crusty, turn the oven up to broil—if you're using a ceramic dish, turn the oven just to 450°F (230°C), or whatever maximum heat is indicated by the manufacturer—and watch carefully until the top is browned to your liking. Remove the cassoulet from the oven and let it rest for 15 minutes. Serve the cassoulet in its dish at the table. It requires no other accompaniment, although a glass of Armagnac after (or in place of) dessert is considered obligatory to aid digestion. As is a pat on the back for making the cassoulet.

Belgian beef stew with beer and spice bread

CARBONADE FLAMANDE

Serves 6

Although this dish originated in Belgium and is popular in France, the main ingredients—beer, beef, spice cake, and bacon—will certainly appeal to anyone anywhere who likes well-seasoned beef dishes. The first time I'd heard about this cold-weather stew, I was so intrigued by the addition of spice bread that I didn't even wait for winter to make it. I love how the mustard-coated bread dissolves into the sauce, giving it extra body and zip from the spices and seasonings. Traditionally, you are supposed to "butter" the *pain d'épices* with mustard. If you don't have *pain d'épices* on hand, try some gingerbread that's a few days old. This goes well with Mashed potatoes (page 216) or Herbed fresh pasta (page 230).

1. Pat the beef dry and toss in the seasoned flour. Shake off any excess.

2. Heat the olive oil in a large Dutch oven over medium heat. Add the chunks of meat in a single layer, in batches (don't crowd the pan), and fry until they are dark brown on each side. It's important to turn them infrequently because you want deep, dark browning, which gives the dish additional flavor. As you finish each batch, transfer the pieces to a bowl. Add more olive oil to the pan as needed to keep the beef from sticking.

3. When the beef is browned, add the onions and bacon to the Dutch oven and cook for 8 to 10 minutes, stirring occasionally, until the onions are soft and transluscent. Transfer the onions and bacon to the bowl with the beef. Add the water to the hot pan, scraping up the dark bits on the bottom, and then add the beer.

4. Return the beef, bacon, and onions to the pot and add the thyme, bay leaves, cloves, and salt. Cover and let simmer over very low heat for 1 hour.

5. Spread the slices of *pain d'épices* with a thin layer of mustard. Lay the slices on top of the stew in the pot, mustard-side up. Cover and cook for 1½ to 2 hours more, leaving the lid ajar and stirring the contents (including the bread) every once in a while during cooking, until the beef is tender. Pluck out the bay leaves and serve.

3 pounds (1.35kg) beef chuck roast, cut into 2-inch (5cm) pieces

½ cup (70g) all-purpose flour, seasoned with sea salt or kosher salt and pepper

2 tablespoons olive oil, plus more if needed

2 onions, peeled and diced

2 cups (200g) smoked or unsmoked thick-cut bacon cut into lardons (see page 15)

1 cup (250ml) warm water

3 cups (750ml) beer, preferably amber

2 teaspoons minced fresh thyme, or 1 teaspoon dried

2 bay leaves

5 whole cloves

1 teaspoon sea salt or kosher salt

4 slices (6 ounces/170g) pain d'épices (page 293)

Dijon mustard

Lamb shank tagine

TAGINE DE SOURIS D'AGNEAU

Serves 4

I started working in restaurants when I was sixteen years old, washing dishes at a local chain restaurant, known as a "sirloin pit," in a strip mall. The tables were branded (like cattle), and the waitresses wore faux-rawhide skirts made of vinyl. The macho line cooks intentionally liked to instill fear into everyone else in the kitchen by showing how much bravado it took to oversee the flaming "pit" where they charred steaks for the guests. I just kept my head down over the sudsy sink and waited for staff meal, when I could eat my fill of Texas toast: extra-thick white bread with butter that was then toasted so the crust became crunchy and, surprisingly, a little sweet (possibly because the "butter" was a yellow-gold liquid that flowed from a can).

I continued working in restaurants through college. In one job I washed beer mugs, and at another, I restocked a salad bar (and learned never to get between people and an all-you-can-eat buffet). After paying my dues, I finally ended up at Chez Panisse, which felt like heaven to me. I was surrounded by other cooks dedicated to serving good food using local ingredients. I know that might sound simplistic, but few restaurants foster the kind of camaraderie that we had at Chez Panisse. Cooks tend to work there for years (or decades), because if you're committed to cooking, there's just no better place to work.

The people I worked with were not just co-workers or even friends; we were all part of the same family, and whenever life has thrown me a curveball, I get a handwritten note from my former employers offering support. Even though I left the restaurant a number of years ago, many of the cooks remain in touch, and it's still fun to cook together when we get a chance.

One of my very good friends, another David L. who I cooked with at the restaurant, comes to visit me from Switzerland, where he works as a chef. When he's in Paris, we hit the multicultural neighborhoods in search of dim sum or Vietnamese noodles since those aren't available where he lives. But David and I also enjoy making dinner together at home. So we'll pick up spices and dried fruits, and perhaps head to a halal butcher for a cut of meat that's used less often—like lamb shanks—and collaborate on dinner for friends and family in my kitchen in Paris.

continued

It took me a while to find lamb shanks in France, where they go by the curious name of *souris d'agneau*. *Souris* means "mice," and it took a little sleuthing to learn that the name likely originated because the Latin word for mice is *mus musculus*, which is the base of the word that means the muscle where the shank is located. If you go to a French butcher and ask for four *souris*, make sure you follow it with "*d'agneau*" to avoid any odd looks.

You can also use a lamb shoulder for this tagine. If so, ask your butcher to cut a bone-in lamb shoulder into four pieces. Alternatively, cook it whole for an hour or so, until the meat is soft enough to pull from the bones, and then remove the bones, and continue cooking.

Note that this can be made a day in advance, skimmed of extra fat, and rewarmed before serving.

1 Mix 1 tablespoon of the olive oil, 2 teaspoons of salt, the cumin, coriander, paprika, cinnamon, pepper, ginger, turmeric, and cayenne in a large bowl. Add the lamb shanks and use your hands to massage the seasonings into the shanks. Put the shanks in a large, sturdy resealable plastic bag and close it, pressing out most of the air. Marinate the lamb in the refrigerator for 8 to 24 hours.

2 Heat the remaining 2 tablespoons of oil in a Dutch oven over medium-high heat. Sear the lamb shanks in a single layer (if they don't all fit, cook them in batches, adding additional oil, if necessary) so they are well browned on all sides, 10 to 15 minutes.

3 Preheat the oven to 325°F (180°C).

4 Remove the shanks from the pot, reduce the heat to medium, and add the onions, garlic, and bay leaf; season with salt. Cook, stirring up any darkened bits (adding a bit of water if they're stubborn), until the onions are soft and transluscent, 8 to 10 minutes. Stir in the saffron and let cook for another minute to release the fragrance of the saffron. Add the tomatoes and their liquid, the stock, honey, and lamb shanks, and bring to a boil.

5 Cover the pot and place it in the oven to cook for 2 hours, turning the shanks and adding half of the dried apricots and raisins midway through. After 2 hours, remove the lid and add the remaining apricots and raisins. Continue to cook, turning the shanks midway through this final cooking, until the sauce is thickened, about 30 minutes.

6 Remove from the oven and skim any fat off the surface. Serve each shank in a bowl over the couscous. Surround the shank with the dried fruit and sauce and sprinkle with parsley.

3 tablespoons olive oil, plus more if needed

Sea salt or kosher salt

1 teaspoon ground cumin

1 teaspoon ground coriander

1 teaspoon sweet or smoked paprika

1 teaspoon ground cinnamon

1/2 teaspoon freshly ground black pepper

1/2 teaspoon ground ginger

1/4 teaspoon ground turmeric

1/4 teaspoon cayenne pepper

4 lamb shanks

2 onions, peeled and diced

3 cloves garlic, peeled and thinly sliced

1 bay leaf

Generous pinch of saffron threads or powdered saffron (optional)

1 (14-ounce) can (400g) chopped or crushed tomatoes

2 cups (500 ml) chicken stock (page 326) or water

1 teaspoon honey

3/4 cup (140g) dried apricot halves, preferably from California

1/2 cup (80g) golden or dark raisins

Lemon-pistachio Israeli couscous (page 237), plain couscous, or rice, for serving

Chopped fresh flat-leaf parsley or cilantro, for garnish

Meat That Melts in Your Mouth

THE ART OF BUTCHERING IS STILL IMPORTANT in France, as evidenced by the five butchers within a two-block radius of where I live. To be honest, I'm often confused by all the different terms and cuts of beef, lamb, and pork. And I keep trying to learn what cuts correspond to those I already know—such as *palerons* of beef, which are similar to short ribs, and massive *côtes de bœuf* (bone-in roast beef). But living in France, I'm also interested in cooking less familiar cuts, such as the shoulders of lamb that are lined up in the showcases. At some point, I'll graduate from those to the pink and blood-red offal that is held in the stainless-steel bins. (Or maybe not.)

As a pastry chef for so many years, I had little experience cooking meat when I first moved to Paris. David Tanis, a terrific cook and food writer, told me about the benefits of letting meat cook at a leisurely pace: "Basically, you're just cooking the meat really, really slowly. At first it will tighten up." And as he said this, he shrugged his shoulders way, way up close to his ears to emphasize the point, scrunching up his face at the same time. Then he continued, "And after a while, the whole piece of meat will just sigh, and relax," which he illustrated by letting his whole body go limp, with his face taking on a big, happy smile. It was a visually potent lesson, and I realized then that the longer certain cuts of meat take to cook, the better they will be. (And the happier the cook will be as well.) It's definitely an easy way to master meat; buy an inexpensive cut and let it braise or roast in the oven until the meat falls off the bone. I think of David every time I put a meaty pork or lamb shoulder in the oven, then a few

hours later find myself with a pot of caramelized, tender shreds of meat that *fond dans la bouche*, or melt in your mouth.

Before Parisians had ovens at home, back in the Middle Ages, meat was roasted at the neighborhood bakery—for a fee, *bien sûr*! I sometimes wish that were still an option. But then again, when I roast a lamb shoulder and it's covered with hot, crispy skin, I always reason to myself that no one would notice if I were to pluck it right off and eat it in the privacy of my kitchen. And I wouldn't trust a stranger to keep his hands off it either.

Roast lamb with braised vegetables, salsa verde, and chickpea puffs

ÉPAULE D'AGNEAU AUX LEGUMES, SAUCE VERTE, ET PANISSES

Serves 4 to 6

ROASTED LAMB

1 bone-in lamb shoulder (about 4 pounds/1.75kg)

2 cloves garlic, peeled and sliced

3 anchovy fillets, cut crosswise into thirds

1 teaspoon sea salt or kosher salt

Freshly ground black pepper

1¹/₂ cups (375ml) dry white wine, plus more if needed

1¹/₂ cups (375ml) water, plus more if needed

BRAISED VEGETABLES

2 tablespoons unsalted butter

8 spring onions, halved, or shallots, peeled and halved

4 sprigs thyme

3 parsnips, peeled and cut into batons

2 carrots, peeled and cut into thick rounds

4 medium turnips, peeled and cut into thick wedges

8 ounces (230g) very small potatoes, halved

1¹/₂ teaspoons sea salt or kosher salt

Freshly ground black pepper

1 cup (250ml) chicken stock (page 326) or water

1¹/₂ cups (200g) fresh or frozen peas or peeled fava beans

Salsa verde (page 333), for serving

Panisse puffs (page 245), for serving

Stuffing a lamb with anchovies and garlic reminds me of Provence, which makes me think of *panisses*, deep-fried chickpea fritters. After letting the anchovies and garlic mellow in the lamb for a while, they melt into oblivion yet add a marvelous umami flavor to the long-roasted meat. If you're apprehensive, I urge you try it anyway. Or, if I haven't convinced you, use rosemary sprigs in place of the anchovies.

To braise the vegetables, cut them into cubes, wedges, slices, or thick coins. Let the shape of the vegetable determine how you cut it, respecting each one's curves and form. Just be sure to cut all of the root vegetables to approximately the same size, so they cook at about the same rate. French people don't like their vegetables crunchy, or as they often say, *California-style*. So cook the vegetables through, but not to a fare-thee-well.

I've specified vegetables for this ragout, but feel free to use others, such as rutabagas, kohlrabi, asparagus, or parsnips. You should begin with a total of about 2 pounds (1kg) of vegetables, excluding the peas or fava beans. There's no need to add a lot of seasonings; the lively salsa verde will provide plenty of flavor.

I gave *panisses* a *relooking* (makeover) as popovers that have the same flavor as the deep-fried chickpea fritters from the south of France, but that are much easier to make. The batter can be made in advance and then you just pop them in the oven, where they'll rise up on their own and make you proud, right before you're ready to serve.

1 Trim the excess fat from the lamb. Make a number of deep slits in the meat and stuff them with the garlic slices and anchovies. Rub the shoulder with the salt and pepper; cover loosely and refrigerate for at least 6 hours, or overnight.

2 When ready to roast the lamb, preheat the oven to 325°F (160°C).

3 Put the lamb in a roasting pan, fat-side up, and pour the wine and water over it. Roast the lamb for 1 hour, then turn it over so it's fat-side down, and roast for 1 more hour. During the roasting, if the pan begins to dry out, pour a good splash of wine or more water over the lamb so there is always liquid covering the bottom the pan.

continued

203

4 Turn the lamb over for the final time so it's fat-side up and roast for another 30 minutes, basting it a few times with the lamb juices in the pan.

5 To braise the vegetables, about 30 minutes before you plan to serve the lamb, melt the butter in a large skillet with a lid over medium heat. Add the onions and thyme, and cook until they brown slightly, 8 to 10 minutes. Add the parsnips, carrots, turnips, and potatoes. Sprinkle the vegetables with the salt and a few grinds of pepper and stir to make sure everything is glazed in the butter.

6 Add the stock and enough water to reach halfway up the vegetables. Cover and cook at a steady, very low boil for 20 minutes, stirring a couple of times, until the vegetables are just done; don't overcook them. Add the peas 2 to 3 minutes before the vegetables are finished cooking. When the vegetables are done, remove the lamb from the oven.

7 To serve, spoon the vegetables and their liquid into shallow soup bowls. Shred the lamb into large pieces, and put them in the middle of the vegetables, making sure everyone gets a nice piece of the crispy lamb fat. Pass a bowl of salsa verde and a basket of chickpea puffs at the table.

Roast lamb with braised vegetables, salsa verde, and chickpea puffs, continued

A Beef with America

THERE ARE PLENTY OF FRENCH PARADOXES that get bandied about, but there's one American paradox that confounds me: how we like our steaks cooked. It's hard to generalize anything about an entire country as big and diverse as America, but it's widely believed in France that Americans want steaks served with ketchup, and we like 'em well done, or as the French say—*à la semelle*, like the leather sole of a shoe. And nothing rankles Paris chefs more than when a steak is ordered *bien cuit*, or well done.

To avoid that, certain restaurants like Le Sevèro and Bistro Paul Bert, note on their menus that they refuse to cook your steak to anything past *saignant* (bleeding), citing that the quality of the meat they use is so good that to cook it to any point beyond that is unthinkable. While it's true that the French generally prefer their beef *bleu*, or so rare that it's completely raw in the center, I know plenty of Americans, and others, who argue that *well-done beef* are fightin' words.

Until I got to Paris, I had no idea that Americans were also known for a love of ketchup, which the French no longer disdain. In fact, the French like ketchup so much that the government has stepped in and a decree was issued that permitted school cafeterias to serve ketchup only with *frites*, and only one day a week.

The favorite condiment on tables in France is—and will always be—mustard. To some French people, it's just not a meal without a jar of it within reach. And while the French go through a lot of mustard, they also go through a lot of butter. Butter is not put on tables to go with the basket of bread, which always is. (I once ordered

a hamburger in a café and after bringing out my burger on a bun, the waitress also plunked down a basket of baguette slices.)

In spite of our mutual love of butter, Americans don't think of it as something to go with steak, which paradoxically, the French do. Yet do try it. One forkful will make anyone agree that nothing is as good as a pat of pungent mustard butter, melting and mingling with the warm, beefy juices of a pan-seared steak with a side of fries, which you're welcome to enjoy with ketchup—well, depending on what day of the week it is.

Steak with mustard butter and French fries

STEAK FRITES AU BEURRE DE MOUTARDE

Serves 2

To make this bistro classic in my kitchen, I use a cast-iron skillet or grill pan that I get really hot, and then I sear the steak on both sides, cooking it medium-rare, which is the way I like it. My preferred cut is *entrecôte*, or rib-eye, and I ask the butcher to cut it into steaks that aren't too thick since I like lots of surface area on my steaks. I rub them with chipotle chile powder to give them a bit of a smoky flavor.

It's difficult to say exactly how long it will take a particular steak to cook to your liking since there are so many variables, but there is actually no truth to the rumor that if you cut a steak open a little and peek inside, all the juices will come gushing out and your steak will be dry. In fact, the best way to ensure a steak is dry is to overcook it. So feel free to peek inside if you need to.

1   Pat the steaks dry and rub them with the salt, chipotle powder, and cilantro. Refrigerate the steaks, uncovered, for at least 1 hour, or up to 8 hours.

2   To make the mustard butter, in a small bowl, mash together the butter with the dry mustard and the Dijon. Form it into two mounds and chill on a plastic wrap–lined plate.

3   Heat a little oil or clarified butter in a grill pan or cast-iron skillet and cook the steaks over high heat, being sure to get a good sear on each side. For rare steaks, cook 5 to 7 minutes total on both sides, or *aller-retour* ("to go and return").

4   Remove the steaks from the pan and put on plates. Top each steak with a knob of the mustard butter and some pepper and serve with a big pile of *frites*.

2 (8-ounce/225g) rib-eye steaks

1/2 teaspoon hickory-smoked salt, sea salt, or kosher salt

1/4 to 1/2 teaspoon chipotle chile powder

1 teaspoon finely chopped fresh cilantro or flat-leaf parsley

Vegetable oil or clarified butter (page 327)

Freshly ground black pepper

MUSTARD BUTTER

2 tablespoons unsalted butter, at room temperature

2 teaspoons dry mustard or mustard powder

1 generous teaspoon Dijon mustard

French fries (page 219)

Sides

ACCOMPAGNEMENTS

To me, *les accompagnements* make the meal. Sure, the star of the dinner might be roasted chicken, a griddled steak, or a roasting pan of braised meat, but they're nothing unless they have a great side dish to accompany them. The French have some spectacular side dishes in their repertoire, most notably *gratins*. It wouldn't be a bistro meal unless there was a *plat à gratin* with cheese and cream bubbling up and filling in all the spaces between the browned potatoes.

Potatoes are so revered in France that, at most markets, there invariably are a few stands that sell potatoes, and only potatoes, organized by price, origin, and use in cooking. I never dreamed I would need a consultation before purchasing potatoes, but I've learned that there are substantial differences among the varieties, and using the right potato can elevate a creamy gratin from ho-hum to holy cow! (Or, *à la vâche!*, as they say.)

Until recently, vegetables weren't given a prominent place at the table. But some of the younger chefs in Paris are incorporating fresh vegetables into their menus, and I'm starting to see more cooks using parsnips, stinging nettles, Jerusalem artichokes, and multicolored carrots in creative ways. Root vegetables, once eschewed due to their association with wartime austerity, are making a comeback, and I cook them frequently.

While some vegetables take well to steaming and simmering, oven-roasting root vegetables concentrates flavors and browns them nicely, giving them an extra layer of taste. I mix them up in Roasted root vegetables (page 225) and in Dukkah-roasted cauliflower (page 224), which turns an overlooked vegetable into something spicy and exotic.

Grains and starches play a prominent role in salads such as Lemon-pistachio Israeli cousous (page 237) and French lentil salad with goat cheese and walnuts (page 233), and it would not be France if the beloved *haricots verts* didn't make an appearance (clipped on both ends, *bien sûr!*), which I plate up as Green beans with snail butter (page 222).

For those occasions when sides take a supporting role, *panisses* (page 245) made with chickpea flour bring the taste of Nice to my plate in Paris. Herbed fresh pasta (page 230) is fun to roll out and makes a tasty tangle underneath a saucy Chicken with mustard (page 169). And because no meal is complete in France without bread, you can bake yourself a hearty loaf of Multigrain bread (page 241) that looks as good as the one Parisians bring home from their local *boulangerie*. The French don't normally serve butter with bread, but I think with this one, you can make an exception—because even good bread deserves its own *accompagnement*.

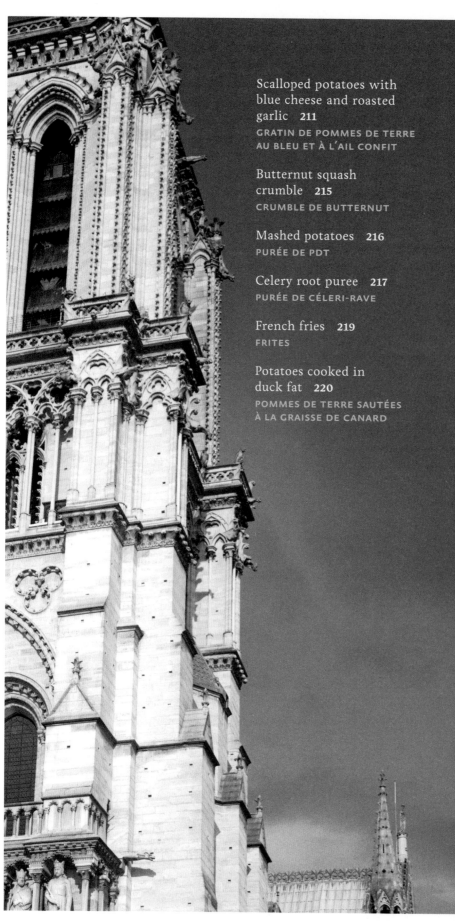

Scalloped potatoes with blue cheese and roasted garlic

GRATIN DE POMMES DE TERRE AU BLEU ET À L'AIL CONFIT

Serves 8

10 large cloves garlic

Olive oil

3 cups (750ml) heavy cream or half-and-half

2¹/₂ pounds (1.2kg) potatoes

Sea salt or kosher salt and freshly ground black pepper

¹/₄ cup (15g) minced fresh chives

1¹/₂ cups (195g) coarsely crumbled blue cheese

Although I've confessed to never being comfortable with the term *comfort food*, I'll admit it's a pretty spot-on moniker for potato gratin. Pouring cream over a dish of potatoes and adding some blue cheese and garlic, mellowed and sweetened by oven roasting, elevates a common tuber into a dish you want to snuggle up to, spooning up the long-cooked potatoes with pockets of oozing cheese between them, and not stopping until you've scraped the last browned, caramelized bits off the sides of the baking dish. Whew! Come to think of it, now I'm feeling all comfy and drowsy myself.

When assembling this bliss-inducing dish, I like to keep the cheese in fairly large chunks so it doesn't get lost among all the potato slices. As for the potatoes, a buttery-flavored potato, such as Yukon Gold, works well here. Russet potatoes are good candidates for layering in a gratin, too. Cream is traditionally used, which reduces in the oven to a rich, buttery *nappage*, but half-and-half can take its place if you're not comfortable with all that cream. Serve with *caillettes* (page 185) or with a green salad, as lunch.

1 Preheat the oven to 375°F (180°C).

2 Trim the hard stem ends off the unpeeled garlic cloves and place them on a piece of aluminum foil that's large enough to envelop them. Drizzle in a small amount of olive oil, close the foil packet securely, and roast in the oven for 45 minutes, until the cloves are lightly caramelized. (You can also do this a few days ahead when you are using the oven for something else, which is what I usually do.) Leave the oven on and move the oven rack to the top third of the oven.

3 Remove the garlic from its skins and mash the cloves in a saucepan with a few spoonfuls of the cream to make a paste. Put the saucepan over low heat and add the remaining cream; heat until warmed through and then set aside.

continued

4 Peel and slice the potatoes 1/4 inch (.75cm) thick. Generously butter a 2¹/₂-quart (2.5l) baking dish with sides at least 2 inches (5cm) high. Put one-third of the potato slices in the baking dish; season with salt and pepper. Sprinkle one-third of the chives over the potatoes followed by one-third of the blue cheese. Add another one-third of the potatoes, season with salt and pepper, and sprinkle with one-third of the chives and blue cheese. Add the final layer of potatoes, then pour the cream mixture over them and press down gently to flatten the potatoes. Season with salt and pepper, and sprinkle on the remaining chives and blue cheese.

5 Put the gratin dish on an aluminum foil–lined baking sheet and bake for 1 hour, until it's bubbling and well browned on top. The acidic cheese may cause the cream to separate a little bit, which is normal.

Scalloped potatoes with blue cheese and roasted garlic, continued

Plats à Gratin

I WAS PROBABLY TWENTY YEARS OLD WHEN I took my first trip to Paris. I had just a backpack, sturdy shoes, and a copy of *The Food Lover's Guide to Paris* by Patricia Wells, and I made a straight shot for E. Dehillerin, the famed kitchen supply shop. I don't know what took hold of me, but I ended up with a mountain of copper cookware, which included two enormous rectangular roasting pans (they were the equivalent of just $70 each at the time), a tarte Tatin mold, a nesting stack of saucepans, and two oval gratins whose shallow, gracefully sloping sides promoted evaporation of moisture, ensuring a deeply caramelized gratin.

After the shopkeepers packed it all up, they told me the price—and the shipping costs—which were exactly the same price as the cookware. Since I was on a student-travel budget, staying in youth hostels, bunking with strangers—many of whom had different ideas about personal space (and in some cases, personal hygiene) than I did—I decided that I would just carry it home myself. So I thanked them, paid, and walked out into the sidewalk with the large box.

I got ten feet out of the store and had to put the box down, certain that if I took one more step, my arm would fall off. There was simply no way I could continue to travel with this box in tow. So I dragged it with all my might onto the RER train, and left it in a locker at the airport— back in the day when they had lockers—to check it in as luggage on my way home.

Like a good investment does, this one has paid off handsomely over the years. Or at least it might have, because for the life of me, I have no idea where all those pieces of cookware are now. (And believe me, I've looked everywhere for those gratin dishes.) And to replace them today would cost the price of a *petit pied-à-terre*. So, I've been hunting down vintage *plats à gratin* at flea markets. And I now collect them in various sizes, shapes, and colors—my favorite being the bright orange

that seems to have captivated the imaginations of French cookware manufacturers during the 1970s and 80s. New ones are made of ceramic, although I find that the enameled dishes conduct heat better and you don't have to worry about breaking them.

Even though several recipes in this book call for modern-sized gratin or baking dishes, I like to use individual gratin dishes, both new and vintage, so everyone gets more of the little crusty bits that stick to the sides. (Decrease the baking time to compensate for the smaller pans.) So poke around online or in cookware shops for new ones, or at antique stores and flea markets for used ones—you never know what you'll find. Oh, and speaking of which, if you do come across two well-used copper gratin dishes for sale, and they're embossed with the E. Dehillerin logo on the side, I'd appreciate having them back.

Butternut squash crumble

CRUMBLE DE BUTTERNUT

Serves 6 to 8

The French have taken to *les crumbles*, baked dishes that Americans call *crisps*. This should not be confused with what the British call *crisps*, which are potato chips. Although I have some fond memories of long-simmered casseroles topped with shards of potato chips (or breakfast cereal), I think they'd be a tough sell with the French, so I stick with *crumble* so as not to confuse anyone around here, including me. (Thankfully, *butternut*, or *le butternut*, means the same thing in both languages.)

This savory version of a crisp—er, I mean . . . crumble—is made with sage-scented bread crumbs with bits of crackly polenta to give it a crispy/crumbly texture.

SQUASH FILLING

2 tablespoons salted or unsalted butter

2 tablespoons olive oil

4 pounds butternut squash (1.8kg), peeled, seeded, and diced into ³/₄-inch (2cm) cubes

2 teaspoons minced fresh thyme leaves

Sea salt or kosher salt and freshly ground black pepper

¹/₂ cup (60g) peeled and thinly sliced shallots

1 cup (250ml) chicken stock (page 326)

2 tablespoons finely chopped fresh flat-leaf parsley

TOPPING

³/₄ cup (105g) fresh or dried bread crumbs

¹/₂ cup (70g) stone-ground cornmeal or polenta

¹/₂ cup (1¹/₂ ounces/45g) freshly grated Parmesan cheese

1 tablespoon minced fresh sage leaves

1 teaspoon granulated sugar

¹/₂ teaspoon sea salt or kosher salt

4 tablespoons (2 ounces/55g) unsalted butter, chilled and cubed

1 large egg

1   Preheat the oven to 375°F (190°C). Generously butter a shallow 3-quart (3l) baking dish with softened butter.

2   To make the squash filling, heat 1 tablespoon of the butter and 1 tablespoon of the olive oil in a large skillet over medium-high heat. Add half of the squash and half of the thyme. Season with salt and pepper and sauté, stirring occasionally, until the squash pieces begin to brown on several sides.

3   Add half of the shallots and cook for another few minutes, until they're softened. Add ¹/₂ cup (125ml) of the chicken stock and cook for about 30 seconds, stirring, to reduce the stock a bit and heat everything through. Scrape the squash mixture into the prepared baking dish.

4   Wipe the pan clean and heat the remaining 1 tablespoon of butter and 1 tablespoon of olive oil in the pan over medium-high heat. Cook the rest of the squash and thyme the same way, seasoning it with salt and pepper, and adding the remaining shallots and ¹/₂ cup (125ml) of chicken stock, stirring. Scrape the cooked squash into the baking dish, stir in the parsley, then press the mixture into a relatively even layer. Cover the dish snugly with aluminum foil and bake for 30 minutes, until the squash is pretty soft when you poke it with a paring knife.

5   While the squash is baking, make the topping by combining the bread crumbs, cornmeal, Parmesan, sage, sugar, and salt in

continued

the bowl of a food processor. Add the butter and pulse until the mixture is crumbly and the butter is completely incorporated. Add the egg and pulse a few more times until the mixture just starts clumping together in bits. (The topping can also be made by hand in a large bowl, using a pastry blender or your fingertips to mix in the butter and egg.)

6 Remove the squash from the oven, remove the foil, and cover with the topping. Decrease the oven temperature to 350°F (180°C) and return the dish to the oven. Bake for about 20 minutes, until the top is golden brown, and serve.

Butternut squash crumble, continued

Mashed potatoes

PURÉE DE PDT

Serves 6 to 8

Most of the potatoes in France seem to end up in *purée*, which is so common that they don't bother saying *purée de pommes de terre*. It's just assumed that *purée* means "mashed potatoes." And even potatoes are so common that they're shortened to an acronym, PDT (*pommes de terre*), too.

If you have an in-house French taste-tester, like I do, he or she will probably keeping saying "*plus de beurre, plus de beurre*" between forkfuls, if you ask for advice as you're making mashed potatoes. So I keep adding more and more butter, until I fear I've gone beyond what any other person might consider rational. And that's when I know I've got it right.

1 Bring a large pot of salted water to a boil. Add the potatoes and cook until soft enough for a knife to easily pierce them, about 30 minutes.

2 Near the end of the cooking time, warm the cream in a small saucepan with the butter and salt. When the potatoes are fully cooked, drain them well and put them in the bowl of a stand mixer fitted with the paddle attachment. Add the cream and butter mixture and the white pepper and beat on medium speed until smooth. Alternatively, pass the drained potatoes through a food mill or potato ricer, add the cream and butter mixture, stirring until smooth. Taste and season with additional salt and white pepper, if necessary.

3 pounds (1.25kg) potatoes, peeled and cut into 1-inch (3cm) cubes

3/4 cup (180ml) heavy cream or whole milk

1 1/2 cups (12 ounces/340g) unsalted butter, cubed

2 teaspoons sea salt or kosher salt, plus more if needed

1/4 teaspoon freshly ground white pepper, plus more if needed

Celery root puree

PURÉE DE CÉLERI-RAVE

Serves 4 to 6

2 cups (500ml) whole milk

2 cups (500ml) chicken stock (page 326) or additional milk or water

1 bay leaf

1 teaspoon sea salt or kosher salt, plus more if needed

1½ pounds (680g) celery root

1 (10-ounce/285g) potato

1 clove garlic, peeled and thinly sliced

3 tablespoons salted or unsalted butter, at room temperature

Freshly ground white pepper

I dislike celery. It's something that I take a bite of and think, "Is there something I'm not getting about this stuff? Because that tastes like a wand of wet green string." I guess that's why so many of us slather celery ribs with cream cheese or peanut butter.

Celery root, however, is a whole different ball game, and it's one of the first things I buy when I hit the market. Not only because I don't want to forget it, but also because the celery roots in France are enormous, some almost as big as bowling balls, and I want it in the bottom of my bag so it doesn't crush everything else. In addition to *céleri rémoulade* (page 105), celery root makes a wonderful puree. It's similar to mashed potatoes, but has a richly sweet flavor that pairs very well with Counterfeit duck confit (page 179) and Braised guinea hen with figs (page 183).

Like my conversion to celery-liker (root only, please), I have become a convert to white pepper as well, ever since discovering Penja white pepper from Cameroon. It has a lively spiciness that you don't get from black pepper, and while most people use it to avoid little black flecks in their purees, the lively flavor really does add something different to this puree and to Mashed potatoes (page 216).

1 Warm the milk, stock, bay leaf, and salt in a large saucepan over low heat.

2 Peel the celery root (see step 2 on page 105). Slice the celery root about ³/₄ inch (2cm) thick, and then cut the slices into cubes.

3 Peel the potato and slice and cube it to the same size. Add the celery root and potato to the warm milk along with the garlic. Bring the liquid just to a boil, then decrease the heat to a simmer, cover, and cook until the celery root is tender (a paring knife poked into a cube should meet no resistance), 30 to 40 minutes.

4 Drain off and reserve 2 cups (500ml) of the liquid (see Note). Ladle the celery root into the bowl of a food processor (or pass it through a food mill or potato ricer) and puree it until very smooth. Stir in the butter and add a bit more of the liquid if it's too thick. Taste and season with additional salt, if desired, and pepper.

NOTE: Any leftover liquid from cooking the celery root can be used as a base for soup.

217

French fries

FRITES

Serves 4 to 6

3 pounds (1.3kg) potatoes

4 tablespoons olive oil

2 teaspoons sea salt or kosher salt

Fresh herbs, such as a big handful of sage leaves, a few sprigs rosemary or thyme, or a mixture of them

Although they didn't invent them (the Belgians did), the French love French fries. Such is their devotion that after I attempted to make them at home in a large pot of oil on the stove without a lot of success (and making a big mess), a French friend told me everyone in France has a deep-fryer at home. He was surprised when I told him that home fryers weren't so popular in America, which he thought was odd, considering how well known Americans are for liking deep-fried foods.

Equally hard to believe is that good fries in Paris are not necessarily a given. I was once so discouraged by getting yet another plate of soggy *frites* that I tied them in knots and left them on my plate, which was whisked away after I ate everything else without a word from the waiter. When I asked a restaurant owner why the fries served at his place were so soft, he said, "I used to make them crispy, but too many customers complained." Yowza. Who could complain about crisp fries?

At home, crisp fries were eluding me as well, until I switched to oven-baked fries, which are simple to make and a lot less messy. Soaking them in cold water allows them to brown up nicely in the oven and they get extra crispy on the outside. I toss in a big handful of sage leaves and some thyme sprigs—the sage leaves get crackly-crisp with the fries and they're quite tasty to crunch on, and the thyme adds an additional bit of savory flavor.

Any russet potato will make good baked French fries. I leave some of the skin on, for a more handmade look.

1 Peel the potatoes, leaving on a few strips of skin as you go. Cut the potatoes into $1/3$-inch-thick (1cm) slices. Lay the slices on a cutting board and slice them into $1/3$-inch-wide (1cm) sticks. Put them in a large bowl with very cold, lightly salted water, and let them sit for 1 hour.

2 Preheat the oven to 400°F (200°C).

3 Drain the potatoes and lay them on a kitchen towel. Rub them with the towel to dry them very well. Spray two baking sheets with nonstick cooking spray. Place the potatoes on the

continued

baking sheets. Dribble the olive oil over the potatoes and sprinkle with 1 teaspoon of the salt. Add the fresh herbs and mix everything together with your hands. Spread the potato sticks out in a single layer on each baking sheet.

4 Bake for 45 to 50 minutes, rotating the pans from front to back and top to bottom midway during baking. As they bake, stir the potatoes several times so they cook evenly. Once the fries are golden brown and crispy, remove the pans from the oven and serve.

Potatoes cooked in duck fat

POMMES DE TERRE SAUTÉES À LA GRAISSE DE CANARD

Serves 4

I've seen a lot of fad diets come and, even better, I've seen them go. In my lifetime, everything seems to have been demonized, including eggs, butter, sugar, flour, salt, and carbohydrates, which are pretty much the foundations of my diet. As as result, I've had some seriously offbeat questions put to me: I was once asked how to find low-carb chocolate, and another person expressed concern about eating grapes because they had so many calories. Not to criticize, but if you're afraid to eat fresh fruit, you might as well stick to a diet of, well . . . I'm not sure what.

Duck fat is something that's come under a lot of scrutiny, particularly regarding the cuisine of the southwest of France, where heart disease is especially low, but paradoxically, a lot of *gras de canard* is eaten. I'm not planning to write a diet book, but most signs point to duck fat as a "good-for-you" fat, and I like to keep a jar in the freezer to make these especially crisp sautéed potatoes with tender centers of high-carb potatoey goodness. And if you're worried about your health, I suppose you could skip the fresh grapes for dessert.

These potatoes are great on a cold winter night, especially with a Fresh herb omelet (page 133) or Steak with mustard butter (page 206). The gentle aroma of warm duck fat will fill your kitchen and make it smell like the French country inn of your dreams. Duck fat is generally available in specialty shops (see Sources, page 339).

2 pounds (900g) russet potatoes, or any firm-textured potatoes, such as Yukon Golds

2 to 3 tablespoons duck fat

Sea salt or kosher salt

2 cloves garlic, peeled and minced (not too finely)

1 Bring a pot of salted water to a boil. Peel the potatoes and cut them into $^1/_2$-inch (1.5cm) cubes, making them as uniform as possible. Add the potatoes to the water and cook for 4 to 5 minutes, until just tender; the point of a sharp knife should be able to pierce them, but they should not be falling apart.

2 Drain the potatoes well and blot them dry with paper towels.

3 Over medium-high heat, melt 2 tablespoons of duck fat in a large, heavy skillet, preferably cast-iron, and one that will fit the potatoes in a single, even layer. (If you don't have one large enough, use two skillets.) When the duck fat is hot, add the potatoes. Cook them for about a minute, shaking the pan or stirring them, to prevent them from sticking.

4 Cook the potatoes for 20 to 30 minutes, stirring occasionally, so they brown well on all sides. If they appear to be absorbing the duck fat or sticking, add the additional tablespoon of duck fat. Sprinkle the potatoes with salt midway through cooking. During the last minute or two, add the garlic, stirring it into the potatoes and letting it cook, but not burn. Remove from the heat and serve.

Green beans with snail butter

HARICOTS VERTS AU BEURRE D'ESCARGOT

Serves 4

Don't worry: there are no snails in *beurre d'escargot*. The name refers to butter mixed with a copious amount of garlic that is used for baking snails, those wriggly little creatures that need to be highly seasoned because I can't imagine anyone finding a platter of unadorned baked slugs all that appetizing.

At some point, *les haricots verts* will probably get some sort of national protected status in France because they are ubiquitous, and I've yet to meet a French person who doesn't love them. In fact, green beans are often served with steak *frites* in place of French fries at many bistros in Paris.

Although I've been eating the pointy tips of green beans for my entire life, it's believed in France that they are fraught with all sorts of danger: from radiation collecting in the tips to the hazard of getting the pointy tips stuck in your teeth. (I have a sizable gap between my two front teeth, so perhaps that's why I have been able to safely enjoy green beans with tips for so many years before I came to France.) So if you want to play it safe, do like the French do and trim both ends off the beans. Otherwise, you can take your chances.

1 pound (450g) green beans, tips removed

4 tablespoons (2 ounces/55g) unsalted butter

3 tablespoons minced garlic

1/2 cup (30g) finely chopped fresh flat-leaf parsley

1 teaspoon sea salt or kosher salt

Freshly ground black pepper

A few drops of freshly squeezed lemon juice

1 Fit a steamer basket into a saucepan. Add enough water to reach the bottom of the steamer basket. Cover the pan and heat until the water is at a low boil. Add the green beans and steam until just tender, 8 to 10 minutes.

2 Remove the beans from the steamer basket and set them on a kitchen towel to drain.

3 In a large skillet, melt the butter over medium-high heat. Add the garlic and cook until the garlic sizzles and begins to brown, 2 to 3 minutes. Stir in the parsley, salt, and some generous grinds of black pepper. Add the green beans and stir until the beans are completely cooked and coated with the garlicky butter. Sprinkle a few drops of lemon juice over the beans, toss a few more times in the butter, and serve.

Dukkah-roasted cauliflower

CHOU-FLEUR RÔTI AU DUKKAH

Serves 4

Americans are known to the French for the frequency with which we utter the phrase "Oh my God!" for anything we're even remotely excited about. I never really thought about it until I moved abroad, but even if a French person speaks no more than ten words in English, three of them are invariably "Oh my God!" with a pitch-perfect American accent, so there must be some truth to it.

One thing I've never heard anyone say "Oh my God!" about is cauliflower, which, I'll admit, is not the most exciting vegetable. Sure the raw florets are pretty tasty dipped in Russian dressing (a mix of ketchup and mayonnaise), but that's not going to get too many "Oh my Gods!" around here—especially from French guests.

The good thing about cauliflower, though, it that it makes an excellent vehicle for other flavors and combinations of flavors (in addition to the ketchup and mayo combo), like dukkah (page 81), the highly spiced nut mixture that I always keep on hand.

Ovens vary, but I like cauliflower well browned, even charred at the edges. The best way to tell if it's ready is to look in the oven. If the smell of the toasty, piquant spices wafting off the caramelized cauliflower engulfs you when you open the oven door, and you say "Oh my God!"—that's when you know it's done.

1 Preheat the oven to 425°F (220°C).

2 Break or cut the cauliflower apart and cut the florets into ¹/₂-inch (1.5cm) slices. Put the cauliflower on a rimmed baking sheet and drizzle over the oil. Sprinkle with salt and some pepper, and then spread out the slices in a single layer. Bake for 25 minutes, stirring once midway during roasting.

3 Sprinkle the dukkah on the cauliflower and mix it in well, coating the slices and then spreading them out in a single layer once again. Roast for another 15 to 20 minutes, until the cauliflower pieces are seared and browned. Remove from the oven and serve.

1 large head cauliflower
3 tablespoons olive oil
³/₄ teaspoon sea salt or kosher salt
Freshly ground black pepper
¹/₄ cup (30g) dukkah (page 81)

Roasted root vegetables

LÉGUMES-RACINES RÔTIS AU FOUR

Serves 6

2 large carrots

2 parsnips

1 large beet

1 sweet potato, or 8 ounces (225g) fingerling potatoes

8 ounces (225g) brussels sprouts

8 shallots

3 tablespoons olive oil

1 teaspoon sea salt or kosher salt

Fresh ground black pepper

10 sprigs thyme

After a lifetime of vegetable eating, I've concluded that there is no better way to cook vegetables than to oven-roast them. Roasting is easy and concentrates the flavor. And just a small amount of oil is needed, so they certainly fall into the "healthy" category, pushing those limp steamed veggies out of the spotlight.

I use a jumble of root vegetables—whatever I gather at the market. Long vegetables, such as carrots and parsnips, get cut into batons by peeling them and cutting them as if I were cutting carrot sticks to serve raw with a dip. Round vegetables get peeled and cut into crescents. But shallots are best just cut in half lengthwise so they hold their shape.

Additions or substitutions might include: adding leaves of radicchio during the last 10 minutes of cooking, or swapping in other vegetables; fingerling potatoes cut in half lengthwise; asparagus spears cut on the bias (or, as they say in America, "French-cut," even though no one in France that I've asked has any clue why); peeled rutabagas or turnips cut in crescents; or peeled celery root cut into whatever shapes strike your fancy, all of similar size. If you vary the mix, keep it to around 2$\frac{1}{2}$ pounds (1.25kg) of whatever vegetables you choose. You can also use different herbs, such as a scattering of rosemary leaves, sprigs of summer savory, or a big handful of sage leaves.

This is a very fuss-free recipe. The only little thing I am fussy about is making sure the shallots and brussels sprouts are placed cut-side down, so they brown nicely. Everyone's oven is different, and I usually bake these on the bottom shelf of mine, where the heat is a bit more concentrated, so they get well caramelized.

Serve these alongside Chicken lady chicken (page 173), Smoky barbecue-style pork (page 190), or a favorite roast meat or pork dish.

1   Preheat the oven to 400°C (200°C).

2   Peel the carrots and parsnips and cut them into sticks about 3 inches (8cm) long. Peel the beet and the sweet potato and cut them into batons about the same size as the other vegetables. (If using fingerling potatoes, leave them unpeeled and slice them in half lengthwise.) Trim off the tough outer leaves of the brussels

continued

sprouts and halve them. Cut the shallots in half lengthwise, and rub off any loose papery skin.

3 Put the vegetables on a rimmed baking sheet, arranging the brussels sprouts and shallots cut-side down. Drizzle with the olive oil. Sprinkle on the salt and add a few grinds of pepper; scatter the thyme over the top.

4 Roast the vegetables for 45 to 60 minutes, stirring them midway through cooking, until the vegetables are cooked through and browned on the outside. Remove from the oven and serve.

Baked Provençal vegetables

TIAN

Serves 4 to 6

Compelling evidence that the French are food-obsessed can be found in, of all places, *la Poste*. While post offices seem to be universally disliked, I've had mostly good experiences with the French post office (except for two cases of books that went astray sometime in 2004, between San Francisco and Paris, see page 148). In the past few years, *la Poste* has modernized. And now not only do my packages arrive, but *la Poste* also issues food-themed stamps, which have ranged from chocolate-scented stamps sold in a strip to resemble a bar of chocolate, to glossy portraits of the various breeds of French cattle raised for beef. And when *la Poste* issued stamps based on regional French cuisine, they were kind enough to include recipes for them, including a simple vegetable dish that I make often.

But I'm not the only who likes this dish. If you saw the film *Ratatouille*, the ratatouille that was the meal of a persnickety French food critic's dreams was actually a *tian*, a Provençal dish of baked sliced vegetables that gets its name from the dish that it's baked in. (In the film, the *tian* was also served with a bit of irony since the recipe that so won over the French food critic was designed by American chef Thomas Keller.) Another curious thing about this recipe is that it's actually better served at room temperature; baking it in advance gives the vegetables time to meld and concentrate in flavor.

continued

1 Heat 1 tablespoon of the olive oil in a skillet over medium heat Add the onion and cook, stirring occasionally, for about 8 minutes, until it starts to wilt. Add the garlic and 1 teaspoon of the thyme; season with salt and pepper. Continue to cook until the onion is soft and translucent, about 2 minutes more. Spread the onion mixture in a shallow 3- to 4-quart (3 to 4l) baking dish. (The wider the dish, the better, because the width allows the vegetables to bake rather than steam, which concentrates their flavor.)

2 Preheat the oven to 375°F (190C).

3 Trim away the ends of the zucchini and eggplant and cut them into ¹/₄-inch (.75cm) slices. Cut out the stems of the tomatoes and slice them ¹/₄ inch (.75cm) thick.

4 Arrange the vegetables in an overlapping, circular, concentric pattern, alternating the slices of eggplant, tomatoes, and zucchini, fitting all the vegetables tightly into the dish.

5 Drizzle the remaining 2 tablespoons of olive oil over the vegetables and sprinkle with the remaining 2 teaspoons of thyme. Season with salt and pepper. Cover the baking dish tightly with aluminum foil and bake for 45 minutes. Remove the foil, strew the cheese over the top, and bake for 20 to 30 minutes more, until the vegetables are completely cooked through. Serve the *tian* warm or, better yet, at room temperature the same day you make it.

228

Baked Provençal vegetables, continued

3 tablespoons olive oil

1 onion, peeled and thinly sliced

2 cloves garlic, peeled and minced

3 teaspoons minced fresh thyme

Sea salt or kosher salt and freshly ground black pepper

1 (8-ounce/225g) zucchini

2 Japanese eggplants or 1 globe eggplant, about 12 ounces (340g) total

2 tomatoes, about 12 ounces (340g) total

¹/₂ cup (1¹/₂ ounces/45g) freshly grated Parmesan, Comté, or Emmenthal cheese

Saying a Mouthful

THERE IS A LIST OF FRENCH WORDS THAT I had resigned myself to believe would remain unpronounceable to me. Yet after much diligence and hard work, I've mastered *écureuil* (squirrel), which is said to be one of the toughest French words for Anglophones to master, as well as *séchage* (dry), *moelleux* (meltingly soft), and *quincaillerie* (housewares store). After realizing that I needed to *sécher* my clothes, that I wanted my chocolate cakes to be *moelleux*, and I didn't want to continue to use the same kitchen sponge for ten years, I practiced and practiced until I got those words just right.

However the last holdout on my list is *nouilles*, or noodles, which I've stopped saying because it never fails to make French people wince (or laugh) whenever I try to pronounce it. Fortunately I've found ways to talk around the word. *Pâte* means dough or "paste" in French, and *pâte fraîche* is "fresh pasta." So I skirt the issue entirely by enjoying fresh pasta whenever I can, which keeps everyone happy.

Herbed fresh pasta

PÂTES FRAÎCHES AUX HERBES

Serves 4 to 6

Homemade pasta is fun to make and roll out. I have a pasta roller attachment for my stand mixer that makes it especially easy, although hand-cranked pasta makers are inexpensive and work well. With a little pluck, you could also roll it by hand, although the only people I know who are able to do that as well as a machine are Italian grandmothers.

Making fresh pasta is more about technique than an absolute recipe. Semolina and flour can really vary, as can eggs. So you may need to add a bit more flour as you roll it out if it's too damp and sticks to the rollers. Or moisten it with a touch of water if it's too dry and cracks when you roll it out.

My preference for fresh pasta is to use half semolina and half all-purpose flour, but pasta dough made with only all-purpose flour is fine (the pasta will be slightly more chewy than that made with semolina). Having a metal pastry scraper or spatula handy will help you in mixing the dough, too, which tends to stick to the counter.

I serve this pasta with sauced dishes that need something to soak them up, such as *coq au vin* (page 177) or *poulet à la moutarde* (page 169). It's also great cooked and tossed in some melted butter or olive oil that's had slices of fresh garlic sautéed in it just until the garlic start to sizzle, and finished with a few grinds of black pepper and plenty of grated Parmesan.

1 Put the semolina and flour, mixed with the salt and the herbs, in a mound on a countertop. Make a deep well in the center and add the eggs and egg yolks. Using your hands, stir the eggs and yolks, incorporating a little bit of the semolina and flour mixture into them as you stir them around (don't break through the sides, or you'll have a lava-like flow of eggs to deal with), gradually incorporating more of the dry ingredients as you stir. When the dough becomes shaggy, use a metal pastry scraper or spatula to knead all the ragged pieces clinging to the counter and the errant scraps into the dough.

2 Knead the dough with your hands for about 3 minutes, until it's very smooth. If it feels dry and is cracking while you knead, add a few drops of water. It's done when you can shape it into a

continued

1½ cups (270g) semolina

1½ cups (210g) all-purpose flour

½ teaspoon sea salt or kosher salt

½ cup (30g) mixed chopped fresh herbs, such as flat-leaf parsley, sage, rosemary, thyme, and oregano

3 large eggs, at room temperature

3 large egg yolks

Water (optional)

Rice flour or additional semolina, for rolling

230

disk and the sides don't crack. Pat the dough into an oval about 1 inch (3cm) thick and wrap it in plastic wrap. Let rest at room temperature for 1 hour.

3   On a lightly floured surface, divide the dough into eight pieces and flatten them into rough rectangles with your hand. Dust them lightly with the rice flour and pass the first one through the machine at its widest setting once, fold it in half, and pass it through again. If the dough sticks to the rollers or to your fingers during these passes, dust it very lightly with rice flour, and then brush away any excess.

4   Pass the dough through the machine three more times, decreasing the opening with each pass, until the pasta is the desired thickness—I like mine about as thin as a credit card. If you want to make fettuccine, run the pasta through the appropriate pasta cutter attachment that came with your machine. For thick-cut pasta, lay the rolled pasta on the counter and dust it lightly with flour, fold it over on itself two times lengthwise, and then cut off the ragged edges and make slices $1/2$ inch (1.5cm) apart. Unroll the pasta coils. If you are cooking the pasta much later, drape the pasta over a broomstick suspended over two objects to create a pasta drying rack (or use a pasta drying rack, or plastic hangers). Repeat, rolling out the remaining pieces of dough.

5   If you plan to cook the pasta right away, put it on a baking sheet dusted with rice flour and toss with rice flour so the strands don't—and won't—stick together. (It can also be refrigerated, covered with a kitchen towel, for up to 8 hours.) To cook the pasta, bring a large pot of well-salted water to a boil and add the pasta. Cook for 4 to 6 minutes, depending on the thickness. You can pluck a noodle out, run it under cool water, and take a bite to see if it's cooked to your liking. Drain and serve immediately.

232

French lentil salad with goat cheese and walnuts

SALADE DE LENTILLES AU CHÈVRE ET AUX NOIX

Serves 4 to 6

Some people only know lentils as brownish-gray disks that got boiled to a mush in those soups everyone ate during the hippy-dippy 1970s. But their reputation has suffered enough indignity, and some enterprising team decided to rescue lentils from health food store bins by rebranding fancy lentils as "caviar" or "beluga" in an attempt to elevate their status.

It seems a little silly to me to try to bestow such regal grandeur on a humble legume, but I will concede that French green lentils are worthy of caviar-like adulation for their superb flavor and texture, and their ability to hold their shape when mixed into a salad. Normally I avoid calling for very specific ingredients in recipes, but in this case, the lentils from Le Puy, cultivated in south-central France, are truly the best. I've tried using other French green lentils, and while they taste fine, they don't retain the same subtle crunch as the Le Puy lentils. They're not as hard to find as caviar, nor as expensive, and though it may take some fishing around, do try to find them. If you can't, other French green lentils will do. Just be sure to taste them before the end of the recommended cooking time, as they tend to cook faster. You want them to retain their shape in the salad and still have some bite. Don't use the large green (or other colored) lentils you might use for soup—they tend to get mushy very quickly.

This is my number-one, go-to salad, and I make it frequently because it's fast, easy, and keeps well for days. You will get to test out your knife skills when making the mirepoix, a finely diced mix of onions, carrots, and celery. In an ideal world, you want the pieces the same size as the cooked lentils.

If lentils are the caviar of the legume world, then I am going to go out on a limb and say that walnut oil is the Champagne of the oil world. It's pricier than other oils, but just a small amount permeates whatever you drizzle it into—most notably salads, infusing them with the nutty aroma and flavor of walnuts. Walnut oil is sold in small bottles because it doesn't last long. I get mine from a producer at one of the *marchés des producteuers*, where weathered farmers from across France come to sell their homegrown foodstuffs

continued

233

directly to the public. And although some people might be more interested in caviar and Champagne, I'm content to lavish lentils with freshly pressed nut oil, which get the royal treatment in this unpretentious salad.

1   Rinse the lentils and put them in a saucepan with plenty of lightly salted water, the bay leaf, and the thyme. Bring to a boil, decrease the heat to a simmer, and cook for 15 minutes. Add the finely diced vegetables and cook for another 5 to 10 minutes, until the lentils are tender; be careful not to overcook them.

2   While the lentils are cooking, make the dressing. Mix the vinegar, salt, mustard, oil, and shallot in a large bowl.

3   Drain the lentils well and mix them into the dressing while still warm, stirring to coat the lentils. Remove the bay leaf and thyme and let cool to room temperature, stirring occasionally.

4   Add a few grinds of pepper and mix in the parsley, nuts, and goat cheese. Taste, and add additional salt, if desired. I serve the salad at room temperature or warm. If served warm, omit the goat cheese, or crumble it on top at the last minute, so it doesn't melt, but just softens slightly. The salad can be made up to 2 days ahead and refrigerated. Let it come to room temperature before serving; it may need to be reseasoned after having been refrigerated.

LENTILS

1¹⁄₂ cups (270g) French green lentils (preferably from Le Puy)

1 bay leaf

5 sprigs thyme

1 carrot, peeled and finely diced

1 small red onion, peeled and finely diced

1 rib celery, finely diced

DRESSING

1 tablespoon red wine vinegar

1¹⁄₄ teaspoons sea salt or kosher salt, plus more as needed

1 teaspoon Dijon mustard

¹⁄₃ cup (60ml) olive oil, or half walnut oil and half olive oil

1 small shallot, peeled and minced

Freshly ground black pepper

¹⁄₂ cup (30g) finely chopped fresh flat-leaf parsley

1 cup (100g) walnuts or pecans, toasted and coarsely chopped

1 cup (130g) crumbled fresh or slightly aged goat cheese or feta cheese

Lemon-pistachio Israeli couscous
COUSCOUS ISRAÉLIEN AU CITRON ET AUX PISTACHES

Serves 4 to 6

1 preserved lemon

¹/₂ cup (30g) chopped fresh flat-leaf parsley

2 tablespoons salted or unsalted butter, at room temperature

¹/₂ cup (80g) diced dried fruit (any combination of cherries, cranberries, apricots, prunes, or raisins)

¹/₂ cup (65g) unsalted (shelled) pistachios, very coarsely chopped (almost whole)

³/₄ teaspoon sea salt or kosher salt

¹/₄ teaspoon ground cinnamon

1¹/₄ cups (225g) Israeli couscous or another small round pasta

Freshly ground black pepper

Every year in Menton, a city near Nice that's on the border of Italy, there's a festival celebrating the famed Menton lemons. Plump and irregularly shaped, they're seasonally available in Paris markets, with their leaves still attached. They are prized by chefs and cooks for their intense lemony flavor (without the harshness of commercial lemons), and their not-too-bitter pith, which makes them perfect for preserving.

This nutty, lemony salad makes good use of preserved lemons, which you can easily buy or make yourself (see my website for a recipe). I keep a jar on hand at all times. They take a few weeks to mellow and soften, so don't save making them for the last minute. Their flavor is incomparable, and a jar will last for months in your refrigerator. Chopped-up bits can be tossed with olives for a quick *apéro*, and they also add an assertive citrus flavor to this dish made with pistachios and Israeli couscous.

Israeli couscous are little pearls of pasta, elsewhere called pastina, which means "little pasta," and when toasted they're known as *fregola sarda*. Since they have more substance, I think they hold up a little better to North African–style braised meats, like Lamb shank tagine (page 199), than traditional couscous. (Orzo is a good substitute for the Israeli couscous.) To change things around a bit, you can vary the dried fruit or swap in fresh mint or cilantro for the parsley. Another nut, such as toasted hazelnuts or almonds or even pine nuts, could be used in place of the pistachios.

1   Trim the stem end from the lemon and cut it into quarters. Scoop out the pulp and press it through a strainer into a bowl to extract the juices; discard the pulp. Finely dice the preserved lemon rind and add it to the bowl along with the parsley, butter, dried fruit, pistachios, salt, and cinnamon.

2   Bring a pot of salted water to a boil over high heat. Add the couscous and cook according to the package instructions. Drain the couscous and add it to the bowl, stirring until the butter is melted and all the ingredients are well mixed. Season with pepper and serve.

Grenades

THE FRENCH NAME FOR POMEGRANATES IS *grenades*, and I like to think they got this moniker because their seeds provide a multitude of explosions when you bite into them. The first time I saw a pomegranate, I was in my early teens living in New England. It was so curious; a fruit with a maze of seeds running through it, clustered in ruby-red bunches and clinging tightly to the thin membranes holding the fruit together. They were exotic and tasty, but what I mostly remember is the mess. (My mother wouldn't let me forget it, either.)

Nowadays pomegranates are a lot more common, thanks to the popularity of pomegranate juice in America, which was linked to reports about the health benefits of the fruit. Those reports, coupled with a clever marketing scheme and a groovy bottle design, prompted growers in California to ramp up cultivation of the fruits.

During the winter, they're abundant at the outdoor markets in Paris, and are especially popular with the Middle Eastern community. I find a few seeds scattered in a simple green salad add a light fruitiness, as well as a brightness that's especially welcome during the gray months of winter.

My favorite, and least explosive, way to seed a pomegranate is to fill a bowl with cold water, quarter the fruit, and then submerge the sections in the water. Flex the quarters and rub the seeds away from the membranes, letting the bits of membrane float to the top. Skim off the membrane pieces and discard them, along with the pomegranate skins.

Rub the seeds under the water with your fingers to loosen any stubborn bits of membrane still attached to them. Skim those off as well, and then drain the seeds in strainer.

Wheat berry salad with radicchio, root vegetables, and pomegranate

PETIT ÉPAUTRE EN SALADE AVEC TRÉVISE,
LÉGUMES-RACINES, ET GRENADE

Serves 6 to 8

One doesn't think of Parisians as *croquant-muesli* (crunchy-granola) types. But I find some of the finest foods from France in natural food stores—an array of honeys, hand-harvested salt, cheeses from small producers, natural wines, cold-pressed oils, organic grains, and, yes, *le tofu*.

In the winter, I stock up on *petit épautre*, or wheat berries. They're similar to farro, and have a chewy texture that stands up well to flavorful root vegetables, which I perk up with slightly bitter radicchio. Although I'll often serve this as a side dish, with roasted meat, chicken, or *le tofu*, I also enjoy a big bowl of this hearty salad by itself for lunch.

1 Rinse the wheat berries. Put them in a large saucepan and cover with plenty of cold water. Add the bay leaf and bring to a boil. Decrease the heat to a simmer and cook until the wheat berries are tender, about 45 minutes. (Farro may take less time if it's been pearled.)

2 Preheat the oven to 375°F (190°C).

3 Peel the vegetables, cut them into 3/4-inch (2cm) cubes, and place on a baking sheet. Toss them with the olive oil, season with salt and pepper, and roast until tender, about 30 minutes, turning a few times. Spread the radicchio over the vegetables and roast for another 3 to 5 minutes, until the radicchio is wilted. Remove from the oven and stir the vegetables and radicchio together.

4 To make the dressing, mix together the mustard, salt, lemon juice, and honey in a large bowl. Stir in the olive oil.

5 When the wheat berries are tender, drain well and let cool to room temperature. Pluck out the bay leaf. Transfer the wheat berries to the bowl with the dressing and stir in the cooked vegetables, parsley, pomegranate seeds, and a few grinds of pepper. Taste and season with additional salt and lemon juice, if desired.

6 Serve the salad at room temperature. It can be made ahead of time and stored in the refrigerator for up to 2 days; add a few drops of lemon juice to liven it up before serving.

1 cup (170g) wheat berries or farro

1 bay leaf

2 pounds (900g) root vegetables (any combination of carrots, parsnips, beets, rutabagas, turnips) and butternut squash

2 tablespoons olive oil

Sea salt or kosher salt

Freshly ground black pepper

3 cups (150g) coarsely chopped radicchio

1/3 cup (25g) chopped fresh flat-leaf parsley

Seeds from 1 pomegranate

Freshly squeezed lemon juice (optional)

DRESSING

1 teaspoon Dijon mustard

3/4 teaspoon sea salt or kosher salt

1 1/2 tablespoons freshly squeezed lemon juice

1 teaspoon honey, or 2 teaspoons pomegranate molasses

1/4 cup (60ml) olive oil

Multigrain bread

PAIN AUX CÉRÉALES

Makes 1 large loaf

STARTER

¹/₄ cup (60ml) cold water

¹/₈ teaspoon active dry yeast (see page 243)

¹/₂ cup (70g) bread flour (see sidebar page 242)

BREAD DOUGH

1 cup (250ml) tepid water

¹/₂ teaspoon active dry yeast

1 teaspoon granulated sugar

1¹/₂ teaspoons sea salt or kosher salt

2¹/₂ cups (350g), plus 1 to 2 tablespoons bread flour

³/₄ cup (110g) whole wheat pastry flour

3 tablespoons hulled pumpkin seeds, very coarsely chopped

2 tablespoons hulled sunflower seeds

2 tablespoons millet

2 tablespoons flaxseeds

1¹/₂ tablespoons poppy seeds

People often ask me what techniques Parisians use to make their baguettes at home, or what kind of butter they use when they roll out croissants. They're invariably baffled when I respond that few in Paris would ever dream of making bread or rolling out croissants at home. Most Parisian kitchen are tiny, with miniscule counters. In fact, the oven in my first apartment in Paris was so small that when I was tempted to put my head in it after a particularly challenging visit to the *préfecture* (city hall), it barely fit.

But the main reason Parisians don't bake bread at home is that the professionals are better equipped for it. They have large counters, blazing hot ovens, and access to bags of flour bigger than the dinky kilo (2¹/₄-pound) sacks sold in French supermarkets (and that I lug home by the dozen).

Because people express frustration when they see the beautiful breads we have in France, and say that they can't get good bread where they live, here's my recipe for multigrain bread that mimics the loaves I get in Paris. It's great served with a cheese plate, or toasted for breakfast, adding a swipe of salted butter, and drizzling it with some dark honey or homemade jam.

For best results, make the starter the day before and let it rest. However if you don't want to wait, just let it rest until it starts to bubble and becomes foamy, which will take between 15 and 30 minutes.

To bake the bread, make sure your Dutch oven has a handle that can withstand the heat of the oven. I have a vintage orange *coquelle* from the 1950s designed by Raymond Loewy that was hard-won from a flea market vendor (with whom I also disputed which of us was the most stubborn), and I would flip out if anything happened to it. So I unscrew the handle and remove it before baking the bread.

1   To make the starter, combine the cold water and the yeast in the bowl of a stand mixer. Stir in the bread flour, cover the bowl with plastic wrap, and let sit overnight at room temperature.

2   The next day, make the dough. Add the tepid water to the starter in the mixer bowl. Stir in the yeast, sugar, salt, the 2¹/₂ cups (350g) of bread flour, and the pastry flour and knead with the

continued

dough hook on medium-high speed (or the highest speed the mixer will go without walking across the counter) for 6 minutes. (If you don't have a stand mixer, you can make this bread by hand, kneading it on a lightly floured surface for 6 minutes.)

3 Slow the mixer to the lowest setting, add the pumpkin and sunflower seeds, the millet, and the flaxseeds and poppy seeds. Knead for a few minutes, until the seeds are completely incorporated through the dough. When ready, the dough should be slightly sticky, but come away from the sides of the bowl. If not, knead in the additional tablespoon or two of bread flour. Cover the bowl and let rise until doubled, $1^1/_2$ to 2 hours.

4 Scrape the dough out onto a lightly floured surface and knead it into a smooth ball. Put a kitchen towel in a bowl and sprinkle the towel with a bit of flour, then put the ball of dough in it, seam side up. Sprinkle the dough with a bit more flour and draw the ends of the kitchen towel up over the dough; let it rise for $1^1/_2$ hours.

5 About 15 minutes before you are ready to bake the bread, put a Dutch oven with the lid on it (remove the handle if it's not oven safe) on the lower shelf of the oven and preheat the oven to 450°F (230°C). Have some cornmeal ready, or cut a piece of parchment paper to fit into the bottom of the Dutch oven.

6 Be very careful from this point on because the pan and cover are incredibly hot, and it's easy to forget that, especially when you remove the lid and set it aside to put the bread in the pan. Using oven mitts, remove the Dutch oven from the oven and remove the lid. Distribute an even sprinkling of cornmeal over the bottom of the pan. Flip the dough into the pan, seam-side down. The best way to do this is to open the towel and pull the edges back as much as you can, so the sides of the bread are completely uncovered, then let the dough drop into the hot pan. If it's not completely centered, don't worry about it; it'll bake up just fine. Using sharp scissors, snip a relatively deep X incision across the top of the bread. Replace the hot lid and put the Dutch oven back in the oven on the lowest shelf. Bake the bread for 30 minutes.

7 Using oven mitts, carefully remove the pan from the oven, remove the hot lid, and transfer the loaf to a wire rack to cool. If you're unsure if it's done, check for doneness with an instant-read thermometer—it should register 190°F (88°C). Cool completely before slicing.

FARINE DE PAIN

Farine de pain, or bread flour, is stronger than all-purpose flour. It has more protein and gluten, and creates a loaf with a heartier bite and a much better texture. I mix in some soft whole-wheat flour to give the bread additional depth of flavor, but don't add too much because it's hard to get a good crust with a high proportion of whole wheat flour. Spelt flour, called *farine d'épautre* in French, works well in my multigrain bread recipe as well.

In the past, I've made this bread with standard all-purpose flour and while it comes out okay, it's really worth making with bread flour. If you get a good-sized bag, you can keep it on hand and make a loaf of bread whenever you want. You can find bread flour in most supermarkets, as well as in natural foods stores and online (see Sources, page 339).

242

QUICK-RISE YEAST VERSUS ACTIVE DRY YEAST

To be completely honest, I'm cranky and old-fashioned, and I just feel like bread should take time to make. The adage that the slower the rise the better the flavor is ingrained in me. Quick-rise yeast is not widely available in France and I don't know any bread bakers who use it.

If you do want to try it, most manufacturers advise that quick-rise yeast (sometimes called "instant" yeast) can be used in the same quantity, or slightly less, as active dry yeast, and the rising time will be 50 percent faster. Follow the directions on the package, or on the manufacturer's website, for substituting whatever brand you are using for active dry yeast, if you want to go against the grain.

Panisse puffs

PANISSES SOUFFLÉES

Serves 6

2/3 cup (75g) chickpea flour

1/3 cup (45g) all-purpose flour

1 cup (250ml) whole milk

2 large eggs, at room temperature

1 large egg white

1 tablespoon salted or unsalted butter, melted, plus more for brushing the mold

3/4 teaspoon sea salt or kosher salt

1/4 teaspoon freshly ground black pepper

1/4 teaspoon ground cumin

Generous pinch of cayenne pepper

In his recipe for *panisses*, Jacques Médecin, the corrupt, long-time mayor of Nice who wrote *Cuisine Niçoise* (which some consider to be the definitive book on Niçoise cuisine), begins by saying, "Oil a dozen small saucers, and arrange them in a neat line."

I searched my kitchen for twelve *sous tasses* and realized that I didn't have twelve saucers (or twelve tea cups, either), which I took as an excuse to come up with these puffs, a nonfried riff on chickpea flour treats from Nice. A hybrid of American popovers and Provençal *panisses*, they go well with roast lamb (page 203).

Do *not* open the oven door while they are cooking; you won't be condemned to the same fate as the mayor, who fled France with embezzled public funds, but your *panisses* won't turn out well. (Of course, Médecin went on to become a public hero for beating the system; his former constituents were apparently unconcerned that he took their own taxpayer money from the public coffers by the suitcase—literally.)

Since they're very easy to make and best right after they come out of the oven, I recommend serving the *panisses* right away. A popover pan with 2¹/₂-inch-deep (6cm) molds works perfectly. You can use standard size muffin pans; the *panisses* won't rise as dramatically, but they'll still be delicious. Due to the batter's tendency to stick in muffin pans, spray the molds well with nonstick spray right before pouring the batter, or use clarified butter (page 327).

1 Preheat the oven to 425°F (220°C) with the oven rack in the middle position. Put a popover pan on the oven rack and have a baking sheet ready.

2 Combine all the ingredients in a blender until completely smooth.

3 Remove the popover mold from the oven and set it on the baking sheet. Brush the insides of the popover molds lavishly with melted butter, being careful since the pan is quite hot.

4 Quickly divide the batter among the molds, put them in the oven, then decrease the oven temperature to 400°F (200°C) and bake for 35 minutes, until puffed up and brown. Serve immediately, while warm.

The Cheese Course

When people ask me why I live in France, I simply point to the closest cheese shop. There is nothing like the feeling I get when I walk into a *fromagerie* and find myself surrounded by hay-lined shelves of ripe cheeses whose aromas defy description. I just step inside and inhale deeply, which I do often, even if I don't need to buy anything.

As much as I like going into chocolate shops, it's the cheese shops that actually excite me the most. Part of it is that I never know quite what I'm going to find. Even though many shops carry the same cheeses, there are so many variations—the ripeness, the colors, the *terroir*—all constantly changing, that make an impression on me. One of my dreams had always been to work in a cheese shop, but that was quickly vanquished when a friend who did told me about the long hours on her feet, lifting heavy wheels of cheese, and the constant cleaning.

So instead, I've decided to focus on being a good customer. And *mon dieu*, am I ever! Whenever I'm getting advice from the *fromagers* at a shop or stand at the market, I almost go into a trance, trying to focus on what they are saying, but I can't help my eyes from wandering around, taking in all the other cheeses piled up around us. And I invariably come away with more cheese than I set out to buy.

When I first started inviting friends to dinner in Paris, I'd head to the *fromagerie* and buy every possible kind of cheese that looked good to me—plus a few more just because other customers were buying them and it drove me a little batty to think that I was missing out on something.

Once home, I'd put all the cheeses out for guests. Then, at the end of the night, I'd end up wrapping the leftovers up in little packages and trying my hardest to finish them before my refrigerator reeked so strongly that everything else in there would begin to "ripen" along with the cheeses.

What changed for me was the lunch I had at Les Crayères, a multistarred restaurant in the Champagne region. Fancy restaurants like that are well known for rolling out an overloaded cheese cart at the end of the meal, and I was really (really) looking forward to it heading my way after they replaced our dinner plates with the smaller cheese plates.

Yet I had to conceal my disappointment when a cart was wheeled over bearing just a half wheel of cheese. Granted, it had been a Comté, aged for four years in the caves of Bernard Anthony, one of the most highly regarded *affineurs* (cheese ripeners) in France, but where was the variety? The waiter wielded a fork and knife with expertise on a cheese that tends to break into ragged shards rather than clean slices, and I waited patiently while he shaved off the best-looking slices one could expect. With that first bite, it immediately became clear to me why this one, singular, truly celestial cheese was chosen to be served to guests.

It was then and there that I learned, when it comes to cheese, less is more. I began to focus on just one or two (okay, sometimes three) kinds of cheeses when putting together a cheese plate, and to make sure they were the best cheeses I could find, always at their peak of ripeness.

To put together a cheese plate (or board), aim to serve cheeses that won't overwhelm your guests (this goes against the "bigger is better" ethos that we think is, indeed, better). But pile too many cheeses on a single plate, and they start to compete with each other. It's hard to focus on what makes each cheese special when there are too many of them. So it's better to have one or two examples of cheese that are the best of their genre, rather than trying to load people up on a

dozen mediocre ones. (I should probably admit that I, too, am occasionally guilty of buying too many cheeses. It's usually when I have guests from out of town who are here for just a short time and who really want to taste a lot of cheeses during their visit. So if you run into me at the market in Paris, overloaded with cheese, that's my story—and I'm sticking to it.)

To guide my selection, I insist on serving cheeses that are at their prime, which can vary by season and by shop. I also make sure the cheeses are diverse so each one has a chance to shine in its own right. A soft goat cheese from the Loire might find itself on a platter with a rectangle of aged Gruyère from Switzerland and a wedge of blue cheese from the Auvergne. Or I'll place a Roquefort Carles next to a sandy-

crusted Cantal, which will share the board with a people-pleasing, gooey Saint-Félicien. Saint-Nectaire, a top favorite with French people, might be just right next to a more challenging Bleu de Gex and an innocent little Crottin de Chavignol, named for the droppings left by the goats (*crottes*) that produce the milk for the cheese. But it's hard to get any better than a singular wedge of perfectly ripe Brie de Meaux, the center oozing its buttery lava, or a Camembert de Normandie, waiting to be sliced, its barnyard fragrance wafting forth along with the knowledge that this is one of the few cheeses that inspires a tizzy of anticipation in every single person in France.

If I'm going to serve just one cheese, I'll choose one to complement whatever main course I'm serving. Roast lamb shoulder (page 203), which is rich and flavorful, is best followed by a light goat cheese, such as Selles-sur-Cher. Or I'll ask the *fromager* for a milky wedge of Ossau-Iraty, a Basque sheep's milk cheese that is softly flavored, yet pungent enough to segue from a savory dinner to the dessert. A slab of aged Comté or a log of tangy goat cheese, on their own, makes as fine a cheese course as any. As I've learned from frequent trips to governmental offices, complicating things doesn't make them better.

The French don't feel the need to "dress up" cheeses with distracting or disparate elements like chutneys, jams, nuts, or fruit. The closest they come to gussying cheese up is to serve it with slices of bread studded with nuts and dried fruits from their corner *boulangerie*. (There is one exception: Basque cheeses are traditionally served with dark cherry jam.)

Although the cheese course is a separate course served before dessert (and I still remember the odd looks I got when I said that in America we serve cheese before dinner), sometimes I'll let the cheese course take the place of dessert. I've been know to serve slices of tangy blue cheese drizzled with good honey, or plate up a smoky Basque cheese with a contrasting dollop of sweet cherry jam in lieu of something sweeter. Another option is to make a simple green salad tossed with toasted nuts or seeds, whose natural crunchy, nutty sweetness pairs nicely with any cheese.

It's not possible to replicate the cheeses available in France. Many of the best are made with *lait cru*, and laws prohibit raw milk cheeses less than two months old from being imported into America. While you can get very good French cheeses outside of France, either made with pasteurized milk or aged enough to be imported, the quality can vary depending on a variety of factors.

But that's no reason to fret. Many cities and towns have good cheese shops, staffed by people who are both knowledgeable and passionate. (It's hard to work with cheeses all day and not become intimately connected to them because they are like children and require constant care and nurturing. In France, any *fromagerie* that doesn't sell top-notch cheese would quickly go out of business.) Natural food stores are another good source for scouting cheeses. Don't overlook supermarkets either; more and more are carrying remarkably good blue, Cheddar, dry Monterey Jack, Teleme, and goat cheeses that are made by small and large producers.

Lastly, like just about everything else in France—food-related and otherwise—there's controversy and disagreement about which is the best wine to serve with cheese. It is ingrained in most people's heads that red wine is the correct and only wine to serve with cheese. That's simply not true. There are no better pairings than a chunk of Roquefort with a glass of chilled, sweet Sauternes; a *crotte* of goat cheese from the Loire with a glass of always-elegant Sancerre; and an Arbois from the Jura, with its sherry-like taste, to quaff with batons of nutty Comté.

But in the end, it only matters what you like. Don't let "experts," or even me, tell you what to eat and drink. Find combinations you like. Experiment and take chances. After all, most wines and cheeses are the happy results of a few failures before the producer hit the right notes. And if you want to drink whiskey with Cheddar, or dip your Brie noir in a cup of strong coffee (which I learned is the way the locals eat this nearly impossible-to-eat cheese), the first third of the French national motto—*liberté*, *egalité*, and *fraternité*—gives you the indivisible right to do so.

Desserts

LES DESSERTS

ONE OF THE GREAT PLEASURES OF DINING, AND BAKING, IN Paris is that no one ever says no to dessert. Pastries and chocolates are integrated into French life, and there is a line at all hours at the more than 1,260 bakeries in Paris. I was once with a group of visitors, marveling at all the pastries in a bakery window, when someone asked, "What *do* they do with all the leftovers at the end of the day?" They were surprised when I said, "There aren't any leftovers. Everything will be gone by the time the bakery closes!"

Because there are bakeries on every street, most Parisians leave the sweets to the experts. Few home bakers have equipment like a nut *broyeur*, a machine with granite rollers to produce sheets of smooth almond paste; a *guitar*, the pricey wire instrument used for cutting *pâtes de fruits* (fruit jellies) and ganache into perfect squares; or an *enrober*, which distributes the whisper-thin layer of dark chocolate that coats the legendary confections of Jean-Charles Rochoux, Michel Chaudun, Fouquet, Jacques Genin, and Patrick Roger.

As happy as I am to support the pastry and chocolate shops in Paris, Parisians are always excited when they arrive at a dinner party to find that their host took the time to make something *à maison*. And although I don't have room for a chocolate enrober (I'm saving that for my next kitchen), I get a lot of enjoyment from making desserts at home and serving them to friends. Sometimes I make something as simple and homey as a *gâteau week-end* (page 296), giving it an herbaceous flavor with bay leaves, infusing the buttery cake with a bit of exoticism that you won't find in many bakeries. Or I'll bake up a batch of snappy Duck fat cookies (page 297), which were inspired by trips to Gascony, where every part of the duck is celebrated, including the velvety fat that gives these cookies a silky richness. And because I'm just as taken as Parisians are with *confiture de lait* (dulce de leche), I'll bake up a bittersweet chocolate crust, add a layer of the caramelized milk, and top it off with a slick of ganache. For casual dinners at home, flourless individual chocolate cakes with *confiture de lait* and fleur de sel, influenced by a favorite bistro, are simple to put together, and people like having their own individual cake, especially when it's served warm from the oven.

Lest anyone think the French are anti-American, you'll be happy to know that they love multilayered Carrot cake (page 277) as much as my fellow statesmen and women. And even *fromageries* feature their own versions of *le cheesecake* (page 302), which are a bit less rich than their American counterparts, with a little more tang. If I'm having a dinner party, my elegant Chocolate terrine with fresh ginger crème anglaise (page 287) can be made in advance, so I can spend as much time as I want with my guests lingering over the last of the wine. Or better yet, toasting the arrival of dessert with a glass of Champagne.

Coffee crème brûlée

CRÈME BRÛLÉE AU CAFÉ

Serves 4 to 6

It took a move to France to rekindle my love for crème brûlée. The dessert was, and I suspect still is, wildly popular in America. And while it gives some people great pleasure to dive into oversized pots of creamy richness, after the initial excitement, I found crème brûlée to be just too overwhelming. What made me finally fall for this classic dessert again was an adjusted caramel-to-cream ratio. In Paris cafes, crème brûlée is always served in a shallow dish, tipping the ratio in favor of more caramel, less cream.

Since admitting my love for crème brûlée, I've also developed a love of shopping at the *vide-greniers* in Paris, where I pick up small gratin dishes cast off by families cleaning their attics (hence the name *vide-grenier*, or "empty attic"). I'm happy to be part of the movement to recycle and reuse whatever I can, especially if it means I get to have stacks and stacks of vintage dishes for crème brûlée in a multitude of fabulous colors to add to my collection.

If you like crème brûlée as much as I do (again), it's worth picking up a set of shallow gratin dishes, which you can find in cookware shops or online (see Sources, page 339). For those of you who don't own gratin dishes, this crème brûlée can also be baked in six (4-ounce/125ml) ramekins. The mixture will not fill them up completely, but that is intended so you get my preferred ratio of caramel to custard.

To make coffee-flavored custards, I used to infuse coffee beans in the cream. But as the price of coffee beans climbed, and the quality of instant coffee or espresso powders improved, I switched. One caveat: instant powdered coffee or espresso varies by brand. So taste the warmed cream and milk mixture, and then add more powdered coffee, if desired.

I use some milk in place of some of the cream in this recipe because it makes a more delicate custard. Lest you think this might bother Parisians, know that I've actually had friends lift their gratin dish and lick it clean—right at the table! I also recommend using the kind of blowtorch that's available in a hardware store to create that delicious browned crust.

continued

1   Preheat the oven to 300°F (150°C).

2   Put four individual gratin dishes on a high-rimmed baking sheet or in a roasting pan big enough to hold them.

3   In a small saucepan over medium heat, warm the cream, milk, sugar, and salt until the sugar is melted.

4   In a bowl, whisk together the egg yolks. Gradually add the warm cream mixture to the egg yolks in a steady stream, stirring with the whisk (but not too vigorously; you don't want to create foam), until the cream is completely incorporated. Mix in the espresso powder and strain the mixture into a large measuring cup, or another vessel with a spout, then stir in the Kahlúa.

5   Divide the mixture among the gratin dishes. Put the baking sheet of custards on the oven rack and pour enough hot water onto the baking sheet so that it reaches at least halfway up the sides of the gratin dishes. Bake the custards for 20 to 25 minutes, or until they are just set; watch them very carefully during the final few minutes of baking. When you jiggle the pan, they should just barely quiver. Remove the custards and set them on a cooling rack. (A wide metal spatula works well for lifting the hot custards from the water; be careful, as the custards are hot.) When cool, refrigerate until ready to serve.

6   To caramelize the custards, sprinkle the tops with an even layer of sugar. It should be enough to cover the top, but not too heavily—1^1/$_2$ teaspoons for each is about right. Using a blowtorch, wave the flame over each custard, one at a time, until the sugar melts and then browns. You may need to lift and swirl the custard so that the caramel flows evenly across the top. If so, be extremely careful because the caramel is very hot and any drips will cause a painful burn. Serve immediately.

VARIATIONS: To use six (4-ounce/125ml) ramekins (or custard cups) instead of the gratin dishes, prepare the recipe as described above, snugly cover the baking dish filled with ramekins with aluminum foil, and bake the custards at 325°F (160°C) for 30 to 35 minutes, until they are just about set, but still a bit jiggly.

To make vanilla crème brûlée, replace the espresso and Kahlúa with 1 teaspoon of vanilla bean powder or paste. Using paste will make the custard a slightly tawny color. Similarly, you can split a vanilla bean lengthwise and scrape the seeds out, then place both the seeds and the pod in the warm cream for 1 hour (as indicated in step 3). Remove the pod and finish making the custard with the vanilla-infused cream.

254

1^1/$_3$ cups (330ml) heavy cream

^{2}/$_3$ cup (160ml) whole or low-fat milk

^{1}/$_4$ cup (50g) granulated sugar, plus more for caramelizing

Pinch of sea salt or kosher salt

4 large egg yolks

1 tablespoon instant espresso or coffee powder

2 teaspoons Kahlúa or other coffee-flavored liqueur

Taking the Spicy Plunge

———

ONE DAY I WAS AT THE SUPERMARKET WAITING in line to pay, when I noticed a jar on a far-off shelf whose label read *Speculoos Spread*. I was familiar with *speculoos*, the Belgian spice cookies that are similar to American gingersnaps, but I had never seen nor heard of a *pâte à tartiner* (spreading paste) made from them. I filed this information away in my brain and, like most things that get filed in there, I promptly forgot about it.

Then a few months later, I was standing in line and saw that jar again, so I let someone go ahead of me in line (which is a rarity in France; I may have made the national news that evening) to pull one off the shelf. When I got home,

I unscrewed the lid and plunged my spoon into the caramel-colored paste, breaking through the smooth surface, and scraping the thick paste onto my tongue. It was worth the wait. As the buttery, spicy-sweet *pâte* melted in my mouth, I was overjoyed to discover yet another reason to be glad that I'd moved to Europe. After polishing off the jar, I wrote about it on my site and suddenly it seemed like everyone, everywhere had to have it. It took a while, but eventually the paste made it to America, where it is sold under a variety of names, including *spiced cookie butter* and *Biscoff spread*. These custards that follow are my attempt to spread the *pâte* even further.

Spiced speculoos flan

CRÈME CARAMEL À LA PÂTE DE SPÉCULOOS

Serves 6

To make these custards, you can use either whole milk or low-fat. Whole milk will yield a more dense, rich custard, and low-fat will lighten things up just a bit. I like to use Chinese five-spice powder, which has a hint of anise in it, but pumpkin pie spice or ground cinnamon are good substitutes.

1   Preheat the oven to 350°F (180°C). Have ready six (4-ounce/125ml) ramekins or custard cups.

2   To make the caramel, spread the sugar in an even layer in a skillet. Cook over medium heat until the sugar begins to dissolve around the edges. Very gently stir the melted sugar into the center of the pan, mixing it with the undissolved sugar, stirring as little as possible. Cook the caramel, stirring only as necessary, until all the sugar dissolves and the caramel turns a dark amber color and just begins to smoke. Immediately remove the pan from the heat and add the water. The sugar may seize a bit, but stir until the caramel is smooth. (You may need to reheat it over very low heat to dissolve any stubborn bits of caramel.)

———

CARAMEL

3/4 cup (150g) granulated sugar

1/4 cup (60ml) water

1/2 teaspoon Chinese five-spice powder, pumpkin pie spice, or ground cinnamon

CUSTARD

2 cups (500ml) whole or low-fat milk

3 large eggs

2/3 cup (160g) speculoos spread (also known as spiced cookie butter)

Pinch of sea salt or kosher salt

Whipped cream (page 337), to serve (optional)

Stir in the five-spice powder and divide the caramel among the ramekins. Quickly swirl each cup to spread the caramel around the sides while it's still warm. Set the ramekins in a roasting pan or deep baking dish.

3   To make the custard, combine the milk, eggs, speculoos spread, and salt in a blender and blend until everything is well combined. Don't overdo it; you don't want it to be foamy.

4   Divide the custard mixture among the ramekins. (Due to variations in the size of ramekins, you may have a small amount left over.) Fill the roasting pan with warm water to reach halfway up the sides of the ramekins. Cover the pan tightly with aluminum foil and bake until the perimeters of the custards are just set and the centers are still slightly jiggly, about 35 minutes. If you check them and they're very close to being done, remove the pan from the oven and keep the custards covered for a few minutes; they'll usually glide to the perfect doneness out of the oven.

5   Remove the custards from the water bath and cool them on a wire rack. Once cool, chill them thoroughly in the refrigerator. To serve, run a knife around the edge of the chilled custards to release them from the molds. Turn the ramekins onto individual serving plates. One at a time, grasp each plate and the overturned ramekin on it in both of your hands, and shake it a few times until you feel and hear the custard release from the mold. Some caramel will stick to the mold, which can be scraped out onto the custards with a small flexible spatula. If desired, you can serve them with a dollop of whipped cream, as the French sometimes do with custards.

257

Salted butter caramel–chocolate mousse

MOUSSE AU CHOCOLAT AU CARAMEL AU BEURRE SALÉ

Serves 6

There's not much I can say about this. One bite will leave you just as speechless.

1 Spread the sugar evenly over the bottom of a wide saucepan. Heat the sugar over medium heat. As it begins to liquefy at the edges, use a heatproof spatula to very gently drag the liquefied sugar toward the center. Watch carefully, as once the edges start to darken, the sugar is in danger of burning. Continue to cook, stirring very gently, until all the sugar is melted and begins to caramelize.

2 When the caramel is a deep amber color and starts to smoke, wait a moment for it to smell just slightly burnt, then remove it from the heat and quickly whisk in the butter, stirring until melted. Gradually whisk in the cream and stir until the little bits of caramel are completely melted. (A few can be stubborn, so be patient. You can strain the mixture if they simply refuse to budge.)

3 Once smooth, add the chocolate, stirring gently until it's melted and smooth. Scrape the mixture into a large bowl and let it cool to room temperature. Once it's no longer warm, whisk in the egg yolks.

4 In a separate bowl, whip the egg whites until stiff. Fold one-third of the whipped whites into the chocolate mixture, sprinkling in the flaky salt. Fold in the remaining beaten egg whites just until no streaks of white remain. Divide the mousse into serving glasses, or transfer it to a decorative serving bowl, and chill for at least 8 hours. While it might be tempting to serve this with whipped cream, I prefer to serve it pure, straight up with just a spoon.

½ cup (100g) granulated sugar

3 tablespoons salted butter, cubed

¾ cup (180ml) heavy cream

6 ounces (170g) bittersweet or semisweet chocolate, chopped

4 large eggs, separated

Rounded ¼ teaspoon flaky sea salt, preferably fleur de sel

Culinary Trends Done Right

I KNOW AT LEAST THREE WELL-RESPECTED CHEFS who claim to have invented the warm individual chocolate cake with a melting center. I'm not sure whom to believe, but I think there may be a bake-off winner out there who made a tunnel-of-fudge cake back in 1966 who also has a claim.

As popular as molten-center chocolate cakes have become in America, it's nothing compared to their omnipresence here in Paris, where they're described as *branché*, which literally translates to "plugged in," but often refers to something that is trendy. It's hard to find a restaurant that doesn't have *moelleux au chocolat* on the dessert menu. And it's one trend I don't mind, because what's not to like about a warm baked-to-order chocolate cake that is perfectly sized for one person?

Another culinary *tendance* that I like is the combination of salt and chocolate. Pastry chef Pierre Hermé is credited with sparking this trend in Paris. The first time I tried it at home, however, one of my guests discreetly took me aside to mention that somehow I had gotten salt in the dessert by accident. I guess he wasn't plugged in enough to realize that I had done it on purpose.

Individual chocolate cakes with dulce de leche and fleur de sel

MINI GÂTEAUX AU CHOCOLAT AVEC UN CŒUR DE CONFITURE DE LAIT ET FLEUR DE SEL

Serves 6

2 tablespoons Dutch-process or natural unsweetened cocoa powder, plus more for the ramekins

6 generous tablespoons dulce de leche (see Note)

1 scant teaspoon flaky sea salt, preferably fleur de sel

8 ounces (225g) bittersweet or semisweet chocolate, chopped

8 tablespoons (4 ounces/115g) unsalted butter, cubed

6 tablespoons (90g) packed light brown sugar

4 large eggs

Because of the sticky dulce de leche in the bottom, I use standard 4-ounce (125ml) porcelain ramekins and serve the cakes right in the ramekins. But you can use any kind of ovenproof custard cup for this recipe; the mixture will rise a bit in the oven, but not enough to overflow.

Do be sure to let the cakes cool for at least 5 minutes before serving, and let guests know the little molds are still hot. To cool things down, serve these with a scoop of vanilla or coffee ice cream, or pass a pitcher of cold, heavy cream for guests to help themselves.

1 Preheat the oven to 400°F (200°C).

2 Butter six ramekins or custard cups. Dust each with cocoa powder and tap out any excess. Put a heaping tablespoon of dulce de leche in each cup, then divide the flaky salt among them by sprinkling it over the dulce de leche. Put the custard cups on a baking sheet.

3 In a bowl set over a pan of simmering water, melt the chocolate with the butter, stirring until smooth. Remove from the heat and stir in the cocoa powder and the brown sugar. Mix in the eggs, one at a time.

4 Divide the chocolate mixture among the custard cups and bake for 15 minutes, or until the sides are firm but the center is still shiny and quite jiggly. Let the cakes cool for at least 5 minutes before serving.

NOTE: You can find dulce de leche at well-stocked supermarkets or stores that specialize in Mexican and South American products, or you can make your own, using the recipe on my website.

261

Warm chocolate cake with salted butter caramel sauce

MOELLEUX AU CHOCOLAT TIÈDE, CARAMEL AU BEURRE SALÉ

Serves 8

I'm often asked by visitors to Paris for restaurant recommendations that invariably involve the same three requirements: great food, budget-friendly, and no tourists. I always scratch my head at the last one because it's strange for someone who is a tourist to disparage the presence of tourists in a restaurant. Paris is a small city and good places get discovered quickly by locals and tourists alike. (And when I say quickly, I mean with online bulletin boards and social media, it usually takes just a couple of days.)

Paris is the most visited city in the world, and so there are also lots of "Best of Paris" lists floating around, tallying up the latest discoveries. The lists get published, and then visitors adhere to these lists as if the "top ten" places are the only places worth visiting. Since restaurants in Paris tend to be small, those ten tables at the "hot" restaurants quickly get booked months in advance. Because no Parisian would dream of reserving a table two to three months in advance (let alone two to three weeks), you have to be remarkably lucky to find a place with no tourists in it.

On the other end of the spectrum are time-honored Parisian bistros, the kind of places where you can sit at wooden tables covered with red-plaid tablecloths and soak in the convivial atmosphere for hours. The food is rich and copious, and at most tables, you'll see Parisians digging into big platters of *frites* accompanied by a thick *pavé de rumsteak* or crisp-skinned duck confit served with potatoes browned in duck fat. People are there to eat and drink, and the house wine served by the carafe invariably has to be refilled at least once (maybe twice) before the meal is finished.

Unfortunately, over the years, eating styles have changed. People are constantly on *les régimes* (diets), lunch hours have been abbreviated, and worse, many of the great Parisian bistros have been taken over by corporations that kept the beautiful interiors (and in many cases, saved them from destruction), but stopped paying attention to the food, except to see where they could cut costs by switching to frozen or prepackaged items.

Yet some of the old faithful bistros are still going strong, saved by wise folks who understand their lasting appeal and realize that, in spite of globalization, food trends, and diets, people simply need a bistro fix every once in a while.

Restaurant Astier, located up by the Canal Saint Martin, offers an optimum bistro experience. For a few years, it had fallen into the wrong hands and was threatening to fade away, but it was taken over by a caring owner and it's now back to being one of the few—and best—classic French bistros in Paris.

The signature dish at Astier is the cheese board that's brought to your table after the main course, but before the dessert. It's huge, with a couple dozen exemplary French cheeses, each one dead ripe, at the peak of its form. It's hard not to gasp when the waiter sets it down at your table with a groan (because it's so heavy), leaving the oversized cheese board on the table for people to take as much as they want.

Yet no matter how much cheese you've had, it's simply not possible to leave Astier without having dessert, which tells you how good their dessert selection is. The most recent dessert to join the classic French canon of desserts is the *moelleux au chocolat*, which I've never been able to pronounce properly. Its literal translation is "tender chocolate"; the texture of the cake is like a baked ganache.

Astier's version comes to the table as a neat little disk. And when you break off that first forkful, a lava flow of warm, thick, dark chocolate comes trickling out, and it's impossible to stop eating until the plate is scraped completely clean. (The salted butter caramel sauce alongside helps.)

Astier chef Cyril Boulet let me come into his kitchen to learn how to make their recipe. His secret: he makes the batter a day ahead of time, which gives it time to meld, resulting in an especially dense chocolate flavor and color. When I raised an eyebrow, he made a fresh one and then pulled an unbaked one from the refrigerator and baked them off side by side to show me the difference. Or rather, to let me taste the difference. And although I've been baking individual chocolate cakes for many years, literally decades, I was surprised to find that he was right and I was happy to have discovered a way to make these classics even better.

Here's his recipe, the same one served at Astier in Paris. They serve it with a restrained dribble of salted butter caramel sauce and some ice cream, and we had a good laugh when I told him that his amount of caramel sauce wasn't sufficient for American tastes, including mine. I've increased the volume in the recipe, so you can really pour it on.

Individual chocolate cakes have become so popular in France that most supermarkets now carry small, 4-ounce (125ml) straight-sided aluminum molds. (You can find them in restaurant supply

continued

263

stores, or online, see Sources, page 339.) If you plan to make them frequently, you can get a set of similar sized individual metal cake molds. You can also bake these cakes in ramekins or custard cups, which require a little more coaxing to get the cakes out, but the duds are excellent for breakfast the next day(!).

The chef at Astier uses salted butter in the cakes. If you only have unsalted butter, add a scant 1/4 teaspoon of salt to the chocolate and butter while they're melting together.

Warm chocolate cake with salted butter caramel sauce, continued

264

8½ ounces (250g) bittersweet or semisweet chocolate, coarsely chopped

6 tablespoons (3 ounces/85g) salted butter, cubed, at room temperature

5 large eggs, at room temperature

¾ cup (85g) powdered sugar

⅔ cup (90g) all-purpose flour

Salted butter caramel sauce (page 334)

Whipped cream (page 337) or your favorite ice cream

1   Butter eight (4-ounce/125ml) individual aluminum cake molds generously, then dust them with flour or cocoa powder, tapping out any excess.

2   In a bowl set over a pan of simmering water, melt the chocolate and butter until it's just about smooth. Remove the bowl from the pan and stir until smooth.

3   In the bowl of a stand mixer fitted with the whip attachment, beat the eggs and powdered sugar on high speed until the mixture is thick enough to hold its shape when you lift the whip, about 5 minutes. With the mixer set to the lowest speed, sprinkle in the flour, beating just until it's mixed in.

4   Fold about one-quarter of the whipped eggs into the melted chocolate. Fold half of the lightened chocolate mixture back into the eggs, mixing thoroughly. Finally, fold in the rest of the chocolate mixture, just until there are no streaks of eggs visible.

5   Divide the batter among the prepared molds and refrigerate the cakes until firm, preferably for 24 hours. (But they can be baked within 3 hours.)

6   When ready to bake the cakes, preheat the oven to 350°F (180°C). Set the cakes on a baking sheet and bake for 12 to 13 minutes. The centers of the cakes should feel soft and not quite fully set when you touch them in the center.

7   Remove the cakes from the oven and let sit for 5 minutes to settle. Unmold the cakes by overturning them onto serving plates, then coax each cake out by rapping the rim of the mold against the plate. If using porcelein ramekins, you may need to run a knife around the edges to help them out. Serve the cakes immediately with a generous ladleful of salted butter caramel sauce and either whipped cream or a scoop of ice cream.

Chocolate chip, hazelnut, and dried sour cherry fougasse

FOUGASSE AUX PÉPITES DE CHOCOLAT, NOISETTES, ET GRIOTTES SÉCHÉES

Makes 2 large loaves, 12 servings

When people ask me what I want them to bring me from the States, I have to admit that at times, I get overstocked on chocolate-covered peanut butter cups (note: I did *not* say I am overstocked on crunchy organic peanut butter—so keep bringing that), chocolate chips, dried fruits, wild rice, and Sharpies. Still, people are certainly kind enough to let me know they are coming this way, in case I'm in need of anything. So I put the word out that I could use a bottle of Château d'Yquem (page 316), which they wouldn't have to schlep across the Atlantic. But oddly, the offers suddenly dried up. *Merde.*

While no one's taken me up on the bottle of Yquem, the next best thing is the bags of dried sour cherries that arrive from time to time, which I'll admit to hoarding in a nearly pathological manner. And I am always working on creative ways to make the most of those cherries, ideas that will make my cherished supply last as long as possible.

In this recipe, I knead them into a French bread known as *fougasse*, which is shaped to resemble a leaf. A number of bakeries in Paris bake little breads with dried fruits and nuts, called *pain sportif*, or sports bread, a nod to the fact that the ingredients are considered healthy. Since chocolate is often touted in France for its health benefits due to the high magnesium content, I like to think that my match of cherries and chocolate makes this a sportier snack to have around than cakes and cookies. Or chocolate-covered peanut butter cups.

1 Pour the water into the bowl of a stand mixer fitted with the dough hook. Sprinkle the yeast over the water. Add the sugar and olive oil, and then stir in 1¼ cups (175g) of the flour until a paste is formed. Let sit 15 minutes, until foamy.

2 Add the salt and the remaining 1 cup plus 2 tablespoons (160g) of flour. Attach the bowl to the stand mixer and knead on medium-high speed for 5 minutes. (You can also knead it by hand on a lightly floured surface.) Add the chocolate, hazelnuts, sour cherries, and orange zest and continue mixing for a few more minutes until everything is well incorporated. Cover the mixer bowl and let the dough rise for 1½ hours, or until doubled in bulk.

1 cup (250 ml) tepid water

1 teaspoon active dry yeast

1 tablespoon granulated sugar

2 tablespoons olive oil, plus more for brushing

2¼ cups plus 2 tablespoons (335g) all-purpose flour

1 teaspoon sea salt or kosher salt

4 ounces (115g) bittersweet or semisweet chocolate, coarsely chopped

½ cup (60g) hazelnuts, toasted and coarsely chopped

½ cup (70g) dried sour cherries, coarsely chopped

Finely grated zest of 1 orange (unsprayed)

Flaky sea salt

3 Line two baking sheets with parchment paper, or lightly oil the baking sheets.

4 Once the dough has risen, scrape it onto a lightly floured surface and knead it briefly. Cut it into two equal pieces. Use a rolling pin to roll each piece into an oval approximately 6 by 8 inches (15 by 20cm).

5 Starting 1 inch (3cm) from the edge, with a very sharp knife, slash one oval of dough lengthwise down the center, cutting all the way through the dough, stopping before you reach the other edge. Use the knife to make two nearly parallel slashes—but slightly diagonal, with the cuts starting close to the outer edge and stopping before you reach the center—on both sides of the initial lengthwise slash.

6 Transfer the dough to one of the prepared baking sheets and pull the dough out from where you've made the slashes, creating open spaces where you've slashed the dough, so the bread is about 8 by 10 inches (20 by 25cm). Repeat the process with the other oval of dough. Cover both loaves with plastic wrap and let rise for 1 hour.

7 Preheat the oven to 375°F (190°C) about 10 minutes before you're ready to bake the breads.

8 Remove the plastic and brush each bread carefully with a light coating of olive oil (try not to deflate the breads), then sprinkle each with an even dusting of flaky salt. Bake the breads for about 15 minutes, rotating the baking sheets in the oven midway during baking, until golden brown on top. Remove from the oven and slide the breads from the baking sheets onto a wire cooling rack. The *fougasse* is best eaten fresh the day it is made, but it will keep for a few days at room temperature, wrapped in a kitchen towel. You can also freeze the second loaf, well wrapped, for up to 2 months.

Almond cakes with browned butter

FINANCIERS

Makes 20 individual teacakes

Shortly after I arrived in Paris, in 2003, I discovered that there is a whole side of the city, and many neighborhoods, that never get a mention in traditional guidebooks (remember those?), or in food and travel magazines. At that time, the places that got press attention were clustered around the Left Bank or located just across the river around the Place de la Madeleine. But then, maverick chefs and bakers started striking out on their own in Paris, moving to the outer neighborhoods because they couldn't afford the rents in the more highfalutin areas.

This expansion to *les quartiers normeaux* started with the gastro-bistro movement back in the 1990s, when a number of famous chefs turned in their Michelin stars to open smaller, more convivial places where the food was stellar, but they didn't have to worry about the corners of the napkins forming perfect 90-degree angles or if the hinges on the bathroom doors were correctly polished. And eventually a generation of pastry chefs set up kitchens in the double-digit *arrondissements* as well, focusing on being a neighborhood bakery, rather than catering to an upscale clientele.

Since I had been dabbling in writing at this time, I proposed some articles to various culinary magazines profiling some of these new restaurants and bakeries. None of the editors responded (*brrmph!*), so I decided to share *mes bonnes adresses* on my blog. Of course, I can't take credit for any their successes (their superb pastries pretty much took care of that . . .), but my reward was when a baker or chocolatier thanked me because a good number of their customers were people who had read about their establishment on my site. *Fait accompli!*

Though my online persona is quite gregarious, I'm actually timid when I meet bakers, chefs, and chocolatiers whom I admire, even though most are nice people. One of the nicest is pastry chef Fabrice Le Bourdat, the owner of Blé Sucré. It's a superb bakery located far away from the Left Bank, in a lovely square where moms watch their kids playing in the park and shoppers from the nearby Marché d'Aligre take a coffee break in front of the bakery and enjoy one of the best croissants in Paris, as evident by the flurry of buttery flakes scattered all over the sidewalk in front.

Although Chef Le Bourdat has worked in some of the fanciest restaurants and hotels in Paris, he's an astonishingly down-to-earth

3/4 cup (75g) almond meal (also called almond flour or powder)

1 cup (130g) powdered sugar

6 tablespoons (60g) all-purpose flour

1/4 teaspoon baking powder (preferably aluminum-free)

1/4 teaspoon sea salt or kosher salt

8 tablespoons (4 ounces/115g) unsalted butter, cubed

1/2 cup (125ml) egg whites (from about 4 large eggs)

BROWN BUTTER

When browning butter, which the French call *beurre noisette* (literally, "hazelnut butter," but colloquially, "brown butter"), you want to get the butter rather dark, so it smells like *noisettes*. This involves cooking it until it stops sputtering and takes on the color of maple syrup. That color is the key to its flavor.

guy. When we had coffee together, he not only ran into the kitchen to bring out his book of pastry recipes (which I was tempted to swipe, sell on Ebay, and then use the money to buy one of those fabulous top-floor apartments on the Île-Saint-Louis), but he also told me that if I ever needed to borrow any equipment, to feel free and stop by.

Even though I couldn't bring myself to slip his recipe book into my bag, and I'm too shy to stop in to borrow some madeleine molds, he was more than happy to give me the recipe for his excellent *financiers*. Unlike a lot of other bakers, Chef Le Bourdat puts dark bits of browned butter into his batter, not only to add flavor, but also to give the financiers a speckled appearance. His original recipe called for 811 ounces of egg whites. Unlike the *bonnes adresses* that I shared on my site, I didn't think you would appreciate my sharing that version with you—you'd need about four hundred eggs—so I worked it down to a more manageable level. (Although I suppose if I made the full amount, I could have a bake sale on my Parisian sidewalk and make enough money for that down payment.)

1 In a bowl, whisk together the almond meal, powdered sugar, flour, baking powder, and salt.

2 Melt the butter in a skillet over medium heat. As the butter cooks, it will sputter a bit, and then it will settle down. Continue to cook the butter until it's the color of maple syrup and smells toasty. Remove the butter from the heat and set it aside to cool until tepid.

3 Stir the egg whites into the dry ingredients. Stir in the browned butter gradually, until it's fully incorporated. Cover the batter and chill for at least 1 hour, or overnight.

4 To bake the *financiers*, preheat the oven to 400°F (200°C).

5 Butter the insides of 20 indentations of a mini-muffin tin (preferably nonstick), or use a silicone mold with indentations of similar size. Fill each buttered indentation three-quarters full with batter. Rap the pan on the counter a few times, then bake for 15 minutes, until the *financiers* spring back lightly when you touch them in the center.

6 Remove from the oven and let cool for 5 minutes, then tilt the *financiers* out of the pan onto a cooling rack. Store the *financiers* for up to 5 days in an airtight container at room temperature.

Buckwheat madeleines

MADELEINES AU SARRASIN

Makes 18 teacakes

When I was making a list of my favorite recipes that I make in Paris, I noticed that an overwhelming number of them contain buckwheat. In reality, I think I may need a buckwheat intervention—or there may be a buckwheat cookbook in my future.

Buckwheat gives these madeleines a heartier flavor than their daintier, more refined white-flour counterparts. They taste healthier, which is slightly dangerous, since I'm usually tempted to eat more than I should as a result. Because of the buckwheat flour, your madeleines won't have that characteristic hump, but it's a good trade-off.

I'm often asked about future trends in baking, which always puzzles me because if I could see the future, I wouldn't be baking and washing dishes—I'd be buying lottery tickets! (Actually I'd still keep baking, but would hire someone else to do the dishes.) When pressed for an answer, I fumble around a bit, knowing that tiramisù, macaroons, and cupcakes have all had their day in the *soleil*. But one tendency I have noticed is an increased use of whole grains and various flours in baking, and sometimes in nontraditional places, such as whole-wheat bagels (um, no), cornmeal pizza dough (yes), and rye whiskey (yes!).

To find specialty flours in Paris, you need to go to the natural foods stores, and those are actually my favorite places to shop. The produce has dirt still clinging to it and the fruits and vegetables are often locally grown. I find sheeps' milk yogurt, organic goat cheeses from small farms, and non-homogenized milk with a big wad of cream clogging the neck of the bottle. And when I'm looking for something sweet, there are a variety of chocolate and nut-based spreads made from natural ingredients that give Nutella a palm kernel–oily run for its money.

One nonwhite flour that is available in French supermarkets is buckwheat flour, or *farine de sarrasin*, although it's extremely uncommon to find sweets made with it. If you ask at a *crêperie* for a dessert crêpe made of buckwheat rather than white flour, as I always do, you'll likely stump the server, as this is just not done. Yet whenever I make a dessert with buckwheat for my friends, they love it. So perhaps I'm at the forefront of a trend of my own around here.

Cocoa nibs are readily available in America (thanks to a trend of bean-to-bar chocolate makers) and aren't sweetened; they're simply ground-up roasted cocoa beans. I purchase them by the kilo

BLACK-EYED BUTTER

There's a French expression, *œil au beurre noir*, which means to have a black eye. Although it's not as odd-sounding as a "black-butter eye," *beurre noisette* or "browned butter" is a *bête noir* for a number of people. Browned butter is easy to make; it's the result of cooking the butter until the water is removed, and then continuing to cook it until the remaining butterfat takes on a rich color, flavor, and aroma, similar to a *noisette*, or a hazelnut.

The first part of browning butter can be a messy affair. Since butter is roughly 19 percent water, it will sputter when you start cooking it like when you accidentally splash some water in a pan of hot oil). But as the butter cooks down, the water boils off, and the butter will start simmering and browning.

At this point, watch it carefully; you want the butter to brown, but not burn. It will turn a rich, caramel color and smell amazing—it's tempting to think it's done at this point, especially when a bit of smoke begins to waft off the pan, but keep going (and continue to be vigilant, watching it). Then, when the liquid turns light brown, the color of weak black tea, turn it off and let it sit until tepid. Some folks will carefully strain the brown butter through cheesecloth or a fine-mesh strainer to get rid of any of the dark solids, but I don't mind them. In fact, they add a little extra flavor; just make sure you don't scrape the bottom of the pan and use too much, or the browned butter will taste burned.

8 tablespoons (4 ounces/115g) unsalted butter, cubed

²/₃ cup (105g) buckwheat flour

¹/₃ cup (45g) all-purpose flour

³/₄ cup (150g) granulated sugar

1¹/₂ teaspoons baking powder (preferably aluminum-free)

¹/₂ teaspoon sea salt or kosher salt

¹/₂ cup (125ml) egg whites, at room temperature (from about 4 large eggs)

1 tablespoons dark honey, such as buckwheat honey

3 tablespoons roasted cocoa nibs (see Note)

(2¹/₄ pounds) and add them to almost every chocolate dessert I can. They offer a marvelous crunch and you can't get a more pure chocolate flavor.

Curiously, the first time I went looking for them in Paris, I did an image search online and found the accompanying words *grue de cacao*. I've never seen the word *grue* before, and when I looked it up, I found out a *grue* is a wrecking crane, although my French dictionary also says it means "hooker." I had no idea what connection any of those had to cocoa beans, and since I've made a number of foot-in-mouth mistakes in French, I decided I couldn't go into a shop and ask for a hooker (unless I was on the rue Saint-Denis). So I asked a pastry chef friend, who explained to me that the word was *grué*, with an accent, and it is one of those words that exist in French to describe something incredibly specific. In this case, roasted and ground cocoa nibs, which is good to know . . . just in case you're looking to pick some up in Paris.

271

1   Melt the butter in a skillet over medium heat (see sidebar, opposite). As the butter cooks, it will sputter a bit, and then it will settle down. Continue to cook the butter until it's the color of maple syrup and smells toasty. Remove the butter from the heat and set it aside to cool until tepid.

2   In a medium bowl, whisk together the flours, sugar, baking powder, and salt. Stir in the egg whites and honey. Stir in one-third of the browned butter; gradually add the rest of the butter, including all the dark bits, without scraping the bottom of the pan. Mix in the cocoa nibs, stirring until the batter is smooth.

3   Preheat the oven to 400°F (200°C).

4   In two madeleine molds, brush 18 indentations with melted butter. Fill the molds three-quarters full with the batter and bake the madeleines for 9 to 10 minutes, until they spring back lightly when you touch them in the center. (Because of the buckwheat flour, color isn't a good indication of doneness.) Remove from the oven, wait 30 seconds, and then tip them out onto a cooling rack. Madeleines are best eaten warm, or the same day that they're made.

NOTE: If you can't find cocoa nibs, omit them or substitute chopped-up chocolate chips or mini chocolate chips in their place.

Madeleines: Methods and Madness

PROUST'S NAME INVARIABLY COMES UP WHENever someone mentions madeleines. Call me skeptical, but I wonder how many of those people have actually waded through the 4,000 or so pages of *In Search of Lost Time*? Nevertheless, Proust is forever associated in people's mind with these tiny scalloped cakes because they evoked memories of his childhood . . . from what I hear. (I'm not going to lie to you; I haven't read the book either.) My affection for madeleines is clearly related to the fact that I simply enjoy them for what they are: delicate buttery cakes that take me back, and back again—to the cooling rack to snack on yet another one.

I've read a few different stories about the origins of these famous teacakes. The most popular involves a young housekeeper named Madeleine who was asked to step in for a chef to prepare a royal banquet, but the only dessert she knew how to make were these little cakes. Everyone loved them so much they named them for her.

There's no information about how they came to be associated with a large *bosse*, or hump, and there are now commercial versions in French supermarkets whose hump looks suspiciously overdeveloped. I've chased that hump myself, trying various techniques to perfect it, which has been a bumpy ride of buttery highs and floury lows. My latest is one I discovered in a French culinary magazine whose recipes have unfortunately never failed to fail me. However it produced the hugest hump I've seen in a madeleine pulled out of my oven . . . although it's not guaranteed. My success rate hovers at about six out of every seven batches. And now, almost every time I make madeleines, it's hump day—except for that pesky seventh.

. . .

The hardest part about making madeleines is finding the pans. But you don't need to fly to France to pick one up—they're available online and in well-stocked cookware shops. Nonstick ones are considered the standard now; they still require buttering, but they make knocking the just-baked cakes out of the pans a snap, and also help with clean-up. Here are a few other tips:

- Because my madeleine recipes use baking powder for leavening, be sure to use aluminum-free baking powder, which doesn't leave any unpleasant aftertaste. You can find it easily in natural food stores and most supermarkets. (The most common brand is Rumford.)

- I'm normally not a dictator about vanilla, but ground vanilla beans or vanilla bean paste, rather than extract, yield a truly French-tasting cake. The French don't use vanilla extract (*aroma vanille*) to the extent that Americans do, and they generally prefer the beans. If you can't get the paste or ground vanilla beans, use good-quality extract.

- This bears repeating: For best results, use nonstick madeleine pans. I'm not particularly fond of silicone bakeware, but it has its fans, so use it if you wish. Molds made of metal attract heat better, so will give you a darker crust; the silicone molds will give the scalloped surfaces a slick, shiny finish, which I don't particularly like.

- Several prominent pastry chefs in Paris told me to use only softened butter, *beurre en pommade*, not melted butter, for greasing the pans. And I've baked off hundreds of madeleines using their method, making sure to reach into each little ridge in the scalloped pans with great care, using my fingers to create the perfect surface for the future madeleines to slide right off. One day I gave melted butter a try and found it was no different. Actually, it was better since there were no bare spots for the cakes to stick to. So now it's melted butter for me, although I find it's best to melt the butter, then let it cool, stirring every so often so the butter is still melted and soft, but re-emulsified. When you butter the pans, wipe a little extra around the upper rims of each indentation, as the individual cakes tend to stick there.

- For portioning the madeleine batter into the indentations, I use a spring-loaded ice cream scoop that makes a smaller *boule* than a regular ice cream scoop. When I scoured the cookware shops of Les Halles for the smaller ones, no one had any (when I told the clerks that they were perfect for shaping cookies, one explained that the French don't make drop-style cookies—fair enough) so I brought a collection of various sizes back from the States. The French use a pastry bag with a plain tip to fill the molds. But should you find yourself without cookie scoops or a pastry bag, two soupspoons working in tandem—one scraping the batter off the other—are fine for portioning the batter into the molds.

- Fill the indentations in the pans three-quarters full. Overfilling the indentations will cause the batter to overflow and it won't "hump" properly. The batter needs to rise just to the top during baking, which is when it peaks into a hump. It may take you a sheet of madeleines to figure it out, but if you stick with the same recipe and the same pans, it's easy to get it right.

- Once you fill the pans, place a folded kitchen towel on the counter and rap the pan a few times; this will flatten and distribute the dough evenly.

- If you just have one madeleine pan on hand, you can reuse it by cleaning it between each batch, drying it thoroughly, and then baking off the next batch. Depending on the efficacy of your buttering technique, if the pans are

pretty clean after baking off the first batch, simply wipe them clean with a paper towel, let them cool, and then butter them again to bake off the rest of the batter.

- Madeleines are thrilling to eat when warm, although they're no slouch when served at room temperature. The batter can be held in the refrigerator for up to 24 hours. You can put it into buttered pans, and then pop the pans right from the refrigerator into the oven just before serving.

- There's no exact standard size for madeleine pans, so you may get a couple more, or less, depending. You can also use mini-madeleine pans, adjusting the baking time to compensate for the smaller size.

- If you don't have madeleine pans, both of my madeleine recipes make excellent teacakes that can be baked off in mini-muffin pans, adjusting the baking time as appropriate for the size of the indentations.

- Buckwheat madeleines will not get the *bosse* (hump) that madeleines made with all-purpose flour will. Buckwheat madeleines will be more compact and dense, especially if you leave them overnight after baking.

- Lastly, I've baked a million madeleines (upon reflection, I've revised my number from the hundreds that I mentioned above, to the larger amount) and although most of the time I get a nice hump, sometimes it just doesn't happen. I've been in French bakeries and have seen everything from flat cream puffs to blackened palmiers, which was likely a sign that the baker was still working on a cigarette outside when he should have been paying attention to the oven. So don't worry if you don't get a hump; the madeleines will still taste exactly the same. And I'm fairly certain that the reason for the scalloped molds is so that you can present madeleines with their best side up, no matter which way they turn out.

Madeleines

MADELEINES

Makes 16 individual teacakes

I've spent years making these teacakes, which are a popular treat sold in most Parisian bakeries. They're usually flavored only with vanilla beans, although Fauchon, in the aptly named Place de la Madeleine, makes them in varieties that include green tea, candied orange, and honey.

These madeleines are on the less sweet side. The French don't automatically put vanilla in cookies and cakes since they prefer to let the flavors of the butter and eggs shine, but when they do use it, it's often the beans rather than the extract. So here I use some vanilla bean paste, which is made by grinding up vanilla beans, and adds a fuller vanilla flavor than extract.

1   In the bowl of a stand mixer fitted with the whip attachment, cream together the eggs and sugar on high speed until doubled in volume, 3 to 5 minutes.

2   Stir in the flour, baking powder, salt, and vanilla bean paste. Cover the bowl and let rest for 1 hour. While the batter is resting, melt the butter and honey in a small saucepan. Remove from the heat and cool to room temperature, about 1 hour.

3   Dribble the butter and honey mixture (rewarm slightly, if necessary, to liquefy it) into the batter, stirring until the batter is smooth. Cover and let the batter rest for 1 hour more.

4   To bake the madeleines, preheat the oven to 400°F (200°C). In two madeleine molds, brush 16 indentations with melted butter.

5   Fill each indentation in the molds three-quarters full with batter and rap the molds on the counter to level the batter. Bake the madeleines for 9 to 10 minutes, until they spring back lightly when you touch them in the center. Remove from the oven, wait 30 seconds, then tip them out onto a cooling rack. Madeleines are best enjoyed warm, or the same day that they're made.

2 large eggs, at room temperature

$1/2$ cup (100g) granulated sugar

1 cup (140g) all-purpose flour

$1 1/2$ teaspoons baking powder (preferably aluminum-free)

$1/2$ teaspoon sea salt or kosher salt

$1/2$ teaspoon vanilla bean paste, or $3/4$ teaspoon vanilla extract

8 tablespoons (4 ounces/115g) unsalted butter

1 tablespoon honey

274

Pour la santé

FOR MANY YEARS, I HAVE BEEN ASKED IF I AM going to open a bakery or restaurant in Paris; in fact, quite a few people think I already have one. Some have even gone so far as to send reservation requests for my restaurant in Paris via email along with their credit card numbers for a deposit.

To the people who inquired about my bakery, I used to say that the French are not all that interested in American desserts, aside from *le cheesecake*. (How could anyone not be?) As for the people who sent me their credit card number, I was tempted to do a little damage at Hermès before letting them know that, *malheuresement*, my restaurant was fully booked. But in the end, I chose honesty and valor over a closetful of belts with the letter "H" for a buckle.

My fabled restaurant aside, it's well-documented that the French are adventurous eaters: they chow down on *tête de veau* (jellied calves' brains), *rognons* (kidneys), and *boudin noir* (blood sausage), *sans problème*. But flecks of carrot in a cake? That's another story. To help my French friends overcome the shock of vegetables in dessert, knowing that most are prone to a touch of hypochondria, I often resort to a special technique: I assure them the cake is *"Très bon pour la santé."* This makes any reluctance fizzle away, and gives them permission to try something because it's good for their health. *"Ah, bon?"* they'll say, and dig right in. It works every time.

Speaking of adventurous, my friend Laurel Sanderson, who hails from Charleston, South Carolina, opened an American-style bakery and café in Paris, which she said made Paris feel a little less foreign to her—although the place is constantly full of Parisians. (Maybe because they heard somewhere that carrot cake is good for their health?) After discovering pitchers of real, honest-to-goodness iced tea brimming with ice, the next thing that got my attention the first time I entered Laurel's bakery was the towering carrot cake frosted with generous swirls of cream cheese frosting. So I invited her over to make it with me.

Laurel doesn't peel her carrots, and she bakes the cake in three layers. Although in America we eat peels of things like carrots and grapes, the French are fastidious about peeling everything, from tomatoes to nectarines. (I've been tempted to serve French friends fried potato skins just to see the reactions.)

As a confirmed lover of traditional cream cheese frosting, I was a little traumatized myself when Laurel told me she used mascarpone in the frosting. But I breathed a little easier—unfortunately, not from loosening up one of my many Hermès belts—when I tasted how the mascarpone added even more tangy richness. So someday, if I ever do open a bakery in Paris, I think this mascarpone-frosted carrot cake will be the star attraction on offer. But until I do, here's the recipe. No prescription required.

Carrot cake

GÂTEAU AUX CAROTTES

Serves 12 to 16

Since most people don't have the oven space to bake three cake pans, I adapted this recipe to be baked in two layers. It works best in 10-inch (25cm) pans if you have them, but two similar-sized springform pans will work just as well.

CAKE

5 large eggs

1/2 cup (125ml) buttermilk

1 3/4 cups (430ml) neutral-tasting vegetable oil

2 1/2 cups (500g) granulated sugar

2 teaspoons vanilla extract

1 1/4 pounds (560g) carrots, unpeeled, coarsely shredded

4 cups (560g) all-purpose flour

4 teaspoons ground cinnamon

2 teaspoons ground ginger

1 teaspoon ground allspice

1 tablespoon baking powder (preferably aluminum-free)

1 teaspoon baking soda

1 1/4 teaspoons sea salt or kosher salt

1 cup (100g) walnuts or pecans, toasted and coarsely chopped

FROSTING

16 ounces (450g) cream cheese, at room temperature

16 ounces (450g) mascarpone

3/4 cup (105g) powdered sugar

1/4 teaspoon vanilla extract

Finely grated zest of 1 lemon (unsprayed)

1 Butter two (10-inch/25cm) cake pans or springform pans and line the bottoms with parchment paper. Preheat to the oven to 350°F (180°C).

2 To make the cake, in a large bowl, stir together the eggs, butter-milk, oil, granulated sugar, and vanilla until well combined. Mix in the shredded carrots.

3 In another large bowl, whisk together the flour, cinnamon, ginger, allspice, baking powder, baking soda, and salt until there are no lumps.

4 Gradually add the carrot mixture to the dry ingredients, using a gentle folding motion, until they're completely incorporated. Finally, stir in the nuts.

5 Divide the batter between the prepared cake pans and smooth the tops. Bake the cakes for 45 minutes, until deep golden brown on top. A toothpick inserted into the center should come out clean.

6 Let the cakes cool completely on a wire rack. Run a knife around the insides of the pans to loosen the cakes, and then tip them out.

7 To make the frosting, in the bowl of a stand mixture fitted with the paddle attachment (or in a bowl, by hand with a flexible spatula), beat the cream cheese on medium speed until smooth. Add the mascarpone, powdered sugar, vanilla, and lemon zest, and beat until combined.

8 Set one of the cake layers on a serving platter and trim the top so it's flat. Spread about 1 1/4 cups (280ml) of the frosting over the top of the cake, and then set the other cake layer on top. Spread a layer of frosting around the sides, then over the top. Refriger-ate the cake if not serving it shortly after icing it; the cake will keep for up to 4 days.

Hands Off—and On

I'M NOT NECESSARILY A TOUCHY-FEELY KIND OF person, but one thing that took some getting used to in Paris is not being able to touch things in shops. You don't go into a bakery and pull a cake or loaf of bread off the shelf, or even a marshmallow lollipop, which a friend absentmindedly did (it was a gift for her son) and accidentally dropped it on a €45 tart situated just below. When she recounted the humiliating dressing-down she got, it made me realize that I was best off keeping my hands to myself.

Me? I'm still recovering from the surprise I got in the Laundromat when I accidentally opened a washing machine midcycle, causing a major *cascade* to flood across the floor. Washing machines in France are required to have a prominent *arret* button, I later learned, so apparently I wasn't the first person to make this mistake. If only I had known at the time that *arret* means "stop."

A nicer surprise is when I order a *baba au rhum* in Paris, a yeasty cake soaked with liquor, and the waiter sets a bottle of rum on the table from which I have complete liberty to pour as much as I want over the cake. Call me paranoid, but I'm sure my reputation for clumsiness (or cascading liquids) precedes me because they never bring

over a bottle that's more than 10 percent full. But there is always enough that I can completely soak the baba to my liking. I may not be so touchy-feely anymore, but when I hear there's baba for dessert, I'm all ears—and hands.

Kirsch babas with pineapple

BABAS AU KIRSCH ET ANANAS

Makes 8 individual cakes

Various muffin pans hold different quantities; use whatever is available, filling them no more than halfway. Depending on the size of your molds, you may get more or less than noted. Using 4-ounce (125ml) molds, this recipe will yield eight babas.

DOUGH

2 teaspoons active dry yeast

2 tablespoons plus 1 teaspoon granulated sugar

2 tablespoons tepid water

1/4 cup (60ml) whole milk

1 teaspoon sea salt or kosher salt

1 vanilla bean (see Note on page 280)

1³/4 cups (250g) all-purpose flour

4 large eggs, at room temperature

8 tablespoons (4 ounces/115g) unsalted butter, cubed, at room temperature

1/4 cup (40g) golden raisins (optional)

SAUTÉED PINEAPPLE

1 large pineapple, peeled, cored, and cubed

2 tablespoons light brown sugar, plus more if needed

A few drops of kirsch

SYRUP

2 cups (500ml) water

1 cup (200g) granulated sugar

1/2 cup (125ml) kirsch or rum

Whipped cream (page 337), for serving

1   To make the dough, in the bowl of a stand mixer fitted with the dough hook, combine the yeast, the 1 teaspoon of sugar, and the tepid water. Let sit for 10 minutes.

2   While the yeast is proofing, warm the milk with the remaining 2 tablespoons of sugar and the salt in a small saucepan over low heat. Split the vanilla bean lengthwise, scrape out the seeds with a paring knife, and add them to the milk. Remove the milk from the heat and let cool to room temperature.

3   Once the yeast is bubbling, stir in about a quarter of the flour. With the mixer on medium speed, add the milk mixture, and then the rest of the flour. Add the eggs one at a time. Once the eggs are fully incorporated, scrape down the sides of the bowl, then increase the speed to medium-high and beat for 5 minutes.

4   Strew the butter cubes over the dough, cover the bowl with a kitchen towel, and let rise in a slightly warm place for 1 hour.

5   After 1 hour, beat the dough on medium-high speed for about 5 minutes, until it's smooth and silky. Add the raisins during the last minute of beating. Butter the indentations of a muffin pan (see the headnote for quantities), and then fill each indentation halfway with the sticky dough. I use a spring-loaded ice cream scoop, but you can use two soupspoons, scooping the soft dough with one spoon, and using the other to scrape the dough into the indentations.

6   Let the dough rise in the molds until it reaches the top of the molds, 1 to 1¹/2 hours.

7   About 15 minutes before the dough is ready, preheat the oven to 350°F (180°C).

8   Bake the babas for 15 to 20 minutes, until golden brown on top. Remove from the oven.

continued

9 To make the sautéed pineapple, warm the pineapple in a large
   skillet with the brown sugar. Cook over medium heat, stirring occasionally, until the pineapple is softened and completely
   cooked through and juicy, about 10 minutes. Remove from the
   heat and stir in the kirsch. Taste the pineapple; it may need a bit
   more brown sugar.

10 To make the syrup, heat the water with the sugar in a saucepan
   over medium heat until the sugar is dissolved. Remove from the
   heat and stir in the kirsch.

11 While the babas are still slightly warm, remove them from the
   molds and poke each baba all over with a toothpick or wooden
   skewer. Submerge the babas in the warm syrup, a few at a time,
   tossing them around and squeezing them slightly to help them
   absorb more of the syrup, and then put them on a rimmed
   platter. Continue with the remaining babas. After all have been
   soaked and have had a few minutes rest, toss them again in the
   syrup, and then place them back on the platter and pour any
   remaining syrup over them. (The babas can be stored, covered,
   at room temperature at this point for up to a day before serving.) Serve the soaked babas with the sautéed pineapple at room
   temperature, along with a generous amount of whipped cream.
   You might also want to offer guests a bottle of kirsch to soak
   their cakes further.

NOTE: I prefer to use vanilla seeds to flavor this dough instead
of vanilla paste, which can darken the dough considerably. (Save
the scraped pod for another use.) If you prefer to use vanilla
extract, add 1 teaspoon to the dough instead of the vanilla seeds.

Merveilleux

MERVEILLEUX

Makes 10 individual cakes

If you think you don't like meringues, you haven't tried a *merveilleux*. The first time I went to Les Merveilleux de Fred, one of three shops (originally from Lille) that opened in Paris, I bought a good-sized box of them to share with a friend and took them to a nearby bench to wait for him. By the time he arrived, which wasn't that much later, I had scraped the container clean, and all I had to show him was a white cardboard box with a plastic spoon and a little bit of cream stuck in the crevasses that I wasn't able to scrape out. (I would have upended the box and licked it clean if there weren't so many people around.) Unfortunately—or fortunately, depending on how you look at it—I don't live close to Les Merveilleux de Fred, because I would be there every day. But I did go back to get some guidance on how to make them at home.

The cream they use to fill the meringues is beaten very stiff, almost to the consistency of buttercream. When I asked if there was regular butter added to the cream, the bakers shook their heads and said, "*Ni beurre, ni farine!*" (No butter, no flour!) So when you make them, it's important to beat the cream until it's as stiff as possible. A spoon should be able to stand up in the cream without wavering, and if you taste it, the flavor should be a bit "buttery" on your lips.

The meringues can be stored in an airtight container at room temperature for up to 1 week before they're filled. Once filled, the cakes will keep in the refrigerator for up to 2 days, but are best eaten within 24 hours.

1 Preheat the oven to 275°F (135°C). Line two baking sheets with parchment paper.

2 To make the meringues, in the bowl of a stand mixer fitted with the whip attachment, beat the egg whites on medium speed until foamy. Add the salt, turn the mixer to high, and whip until the egg whites are almost stiff and stand in peaks. Lower the speed and add the powdered sugar in three batches. Add the vanilla and vinegar and increase the speed to high; whip until stiff.

3 Using a pastry bag fitted with a ¹/₂-inch (1.5cm) plain tip, or an offset spatula, pipe or spread the meringue onto the baking sheets

continued

MERINGUES

¹/₂ cup (125ml) egg whites, at room temperature (from about 4 large eggs)

Pinch of sea salt or kosher salt

1 cup (140g) powdered sugar

¹/₂ teaspoon vanilla extract

¹/₂ teaspoon white or cider vinegar

MERVEILLEUX

2¹/₂ cups (625ml) heavy cream

²/₃ cup (90g) powdered sugar

2 teaspoons instant espresso powder (see Note on page 282)

³/₄ teaspoon vanilla extract

¹/₃ cup (80g) crème fraîche (page 327; optional)

About 10 ounces (285g) bittersweet or semisweet chocolate, coarsely grated

in twenty (2-inch/5cm) circles, evenly spaced, ten per sheet. Each circle should be relatively thick, at least 1 inch (2.5cm) high. Don't worry if they're not perfect; flaws will be hidden later.

4 Bake the meringues for 1 hour. Turn off the oven and let the meringues remain in there until the oven is cool and the meringues are dry and crisp.

5 To make the *merveilleux*, set out ten paper muffin cups on a small baking sheet or platter and flatten them slightly.

6 In a stand mixture fitted with the whip attachment, whip the cream at high speed until it holds its shape. Spoon in the powdered sugar, espresso powder, and vanilla. Whip at medium-high speed until very stiff. The cream is done when it hold its shape quite firmly without drooping. (If it's not stiff enough, it will seep and make the meringues soggy as they sit. So do make sure it's stiff and shiny; it should almost reach the point where it is nearly as thick as buttercream.) At the end, whip in the crème fraîche.

7 Spread a generous layer of the cream over ten of the meringues; the layer should be about as thick as the meringue. Sandwich the cream with another meringue, and then coat the outside of each cake with a layer of the whipped cream. (If it's too unwieldy to coat them with the cream, chill the meringue sandwiches, which will firm up the interior.)

8 Put the shaved chocolate on a dinner or pie plate and roll each cake generously in the chocolate, making sure all cream-covered surfaces are coated as best you can. Use a spoon to lift the cakes and place each one in a muffin paper, bottom side down. Refrigerate the cakes for at least 1 hour or until ready to serve, and serve the cakes chilled.

NOTE: I often use Via instant coffee powder (see Sources, page 339). You can also use an Italian brand of espresso powder, which is available in grocery stores. Strength does vary depending on brand, so feel free to add more or less to taste.

282

The Most Special Pastrymaker in Paris

WHEN I ONCE MADE UP A FRENCH WORD IN something I wrote, a friend was so deeply troubled that she called to let me know that it was simply *pas possible* to make up a word in French. I didn't want to get her worked up, so I didn't mention words like *bromance* (a deep friendship between two heterosexual men, and wonder if a crush on the sausage guy at my market counts?) or the rise of *cheftestants* (a mash-up that reinforces the notion that cooking is somehow competitive), a phenomenon that has spread even to France.

French people are brought up with a deep respect for their language. This is understandable because the rigorous educational system isn't known for teaching kids to be creative or think outside the box, but rather for rote memorization and absolute, strict adherence to rules and tradition. But every once in a while, a few students fall outside the system and become *freethinkers*, as we call them in English. In French, those people are referred to as *special*.

Jacques Genin is *très special*. I first met the elusive chocolatier when he was working out of a cramped, nondescript workspace whose front door was fitted with a one-way mirror. If you were deemed worthy of going inside, you'd find yourself smack dab in the midst of one of the smallest full-scale chocolate production facilities in France. The entire *laboratoire* was probably twenty feet square, with a large marble countertop in the center that had just enough room around it to accommodate the man himself and the staff who were squeezed in there with him. If someone wanted to pass by the others with, say, a sheet pan of chocolates that needed to be put in a refrigerator, everyone else had to draw in a deep breath, or risk getting a little too intimate with their coworkers.

Jacques made chocolate and caramels that were sold wholesale to the best restaurants and hotels in Paris, which in turn, would send them out to guests on silver platters. And the only way to get them was to stay in a fancy hotel or eat in a Michelin-starred restaurant—unless you were fortunate enough to pass muster with Jacques and he let you in. Depending on his mood, he might be persuaded to sell you chocolates, although he would only sell them by the kilo (2¼ pounds), and *he* decided what to put in the box. (Most of my visits to him started with me getting an earful about how hard it was to run a business, and ended with glasses of whiskey—no matter what time of the day it happened to be.)

continued

As word got out about Jacques, he had no choice but to open a much larger workshop in the Marais, with a spacious shop on the street level. The clear glass doors slide open freely and anyone can enter and buy as few, or as many, chocolates and caramels as they want. The other bonus of this generous space is a configuration of tables and chairs so guests can sample Jacques's desserts, which are even better than his caramels.

I've spent quite a few days with the mercurial Jacques Genin in his kitchen, surrounded by a larger team in less-intimate surroundings, churning out chocolates and those heavenly caramels; slender *bâtons* of rich French butter melded with burnt sugar. We're the best of frenemies (he once tried to strangle me as a joke—well, I think it was . . .), yet every time I close my mouth around one of his caramels and the buttery sweetness oozes forward, no matter how *special* he treats me, it's hard to hold a grudge against anyone who can make something that good.

There may be no better caramels in the world than those that Jacques makes, but his Paris-Brest is my favorite dessert in Paris. Like many Parisian desserts, it takes a small army of skilled pastry cooks to put it together, and each is made to order. After I took my first forkful, I wasn't sure I'd ever had a pastry so good. So in spite of any dangers, I keep going back, over and over, and ordering one just to make sure.

He's been known to go on pastry hiatus, depending on his whims. But when he makes them for his café, Jacques bakes the base for his Paris-Brest in the traditional circular shape, meant to resemble a bicycle wheel to commemorate the race between the two French cities. (You can also order one to go, in advance.) The French are pretty protective, not just with their language, but with French classic pastries, and adding anything such as a swipe of chocolate over Paris-Brest is unthinkable. So I renamed my elongated, éclair-like version Paris-Paris to mimic the route I take to Jacques's place in Paris, which, fortunately, is a straight shot from mine.

Paris-Paris

PARIS-PARIS

Makes 10 to 12 individual éclairs

While the pastry makes twelve éclair shells, and you could possibly eke out a dozen pastries with the hazelnut praline cream filling, I don't like to be stingy. So depending on how big your éclair shells turn out, you may only get ten éclairs if you fill them as generously as I do.

HAZELNUT PRALINE

1/2 cup (100g) granulated sugar

3/4 cup (100g) very coarsely chopped untoasted hazelnuts

Generous pinch of sea salt or kosher salt

PASTRY CREAM

1 cup (250ml) whole milk

3 tablespoons cornstarch

3 large egg yolks

3 tablespoons granulated sugar

4 tablespoons (2 ounces/55g) salted or unsalted butter, cubed, at room temperature

1/2 teaspoon vanilla extract

ÉCLAIR PASTRY

3/4 cup (180ml) water

2 teaspoons granulated sugar

1/4 teaspoon sea salt or kosher salt

6 tablespoons (3 ounces/85g) unsalted butter, cubed

3/4 cup (110g) all-purpose flour

3 large eggs, at room temperature

CHOCOLATE GLAZE

1 cup (140g) powdered sugar

2 tablespoons (15g) Dutch-process or natural unsweetened cocoa powder

2 tablespoons hot water

1 Lightly grease a baking sheet or line it with a silicone baking mat.

2 To make the hazelnut praline, spread the sugar in an even layer in a skillet. Heat it over medium heat until the sugar at the edges begins to melt and eventually turns a light amber color. Use a heatproof spatula to drag the liquefied sugar toward the center, and then add the nuts and a pinch of salt, stirring gently, turning the nuts in the caramelized sugar until the caramel begins to smoke. At that moment, when the hazelnuts smell very toasty, immediately scrape the nuts and the caramel onto the prepared baking sheet, spread as evenly as possible, and let cool completely. (Once cool, the nuts can be stored in an airtight container at room temperature for up to 1 week.)

3 To make the pastry cream, warm the milk in a small saucepan and set it aside. Whisk the cornstarch and egg yolks in a saucepan until smooth, then whisk in the sugar. Dribble in a little of the hot milk, whisking constantly. Gradually add the rest of the milk, whisking. Cook the pastry cream at the lowest possible boil for 1 1/2 minutes, whisking vigorously and making sure you reach into the corners of the pan with the whisk, until it's very thick, like mayonnaise. Remove from heat and whisk in the butter, a few cubes at a time, and the vanilla extract, until the mixture is smooth. Scrape the mixture into a bowl, cover, and refrigerate. (To speed things up, put it over an ice bath, stirring until cool, and then refrigerate it. It can be kept for up to 3 days.)

4 Preheat the oven to 375°F (190°C). Line a baking sheet with parchment paper or a silicone baking mat.

5 To make the éclairs, heat the water, sugar, salt, and butter in a saucepan, stirring occasionally, just until the butter melts. Immediately add all the flour and stir for a few minutes over

continued

low heat, until the mixture forms a smooth ball that pulls away from the sides of the pan. Remove the pan from the heat and let cool for about 3 minutes, stirring occasionally to cool it slightly.

6 Add the eggs, one by one, stirring briskly after the addition of each one, until the dough is smooth. (You can also use a stand mixer fitted with the paddle attachment.) Transfer the warm éclair dough to a pastry bag fitted with a 1/2-inch (1.5cm) plain tip and pipe out ten to twelve 5-inch (12.5cm) lines of dough evenly spaced on the baking sheet. (You can also use a resealable plastic bag with a corner snipped off.) With a damp finger, smooth out any spiky points you might have made from lifting the pastry bag.

7 Bake for 25 to 30 minutes, rotating the baking sheet midway during baking, until the éclair shells are deep golden brown. Remove from the oven and poke a paring knife into the side of each pastry, twisting it as you poke to help the steam escape and keep the dough crisp. Let cool completely.

8 Finish the filling by breaking up the caramelized hazelnuts and pulsing them in a food processor until they're very finely ground. Add one-third of the cooled, stiff pastry cream and pulse the processor a few times to incorporate it. Using a flexible spatula, mash the hazelnut mixture into the remaining pastry cream, just until incorporated. Avoid overzealous mixing, which can make the cream too runny.

9 Slice each éclair open lengthwise across the side with a serrated knife, cutting almost all the way through. Using either a pastry bag fitted with a plain tip, a spoon, or a resealable plastic bag with a corner cut off, fill the éclair shells with the hazelnut praline cream.

10 To make the glaze, mix the powdered sugar and the cocoa powder in a small bowl; stir in the hot water until smooth. The icing should be thick enough to spread but hold its shape pretty much when applied. If too thick, add a few drops of hot water. If too thin, add a sprinkle of powdered sugar.

11 With a spoon or a small spatula, lift each éclair and wipe a broad layer of the glaze over the top, scraping off most of the excess. Chill the glazed éclairs in the refrigerator for at least 1 hour before serving. Serve cold or at room temperature. The filled and glazed éclairs can be kept in the refrigerator for up to 3 days.

Chocolate terrine with fresh ginger crème anglaise

TERRINE AU CHOCOLAT, CRÈME ANGLAISE AU GINGEMBRE

Serves 8

I'd never bought an egg until I moved to Paris. Actually, what I mean is that I had never bought one single, solitary egg until I came here. For someone used to going through eggs by the dozen, it was interesting to see hay-lined baskets of eggs in *fromageries* that look like they were just plucked from the henhouse, where they're handled and packaged for customers in crisp wrapping paper—even if you only want one.

And when you crack a French egg, it's easy to see why they merit such attention; the yolks are an ultrasaturated, deep-orange color. Whether I am using just one, or a half-dozen, the yolks never fail to make me pause and take a look at the glossy orbs bobbing around in the bowl before I whisk them up.

Another difference between France and America is the approach to eggs: I've never met a French person who was worried about eating them undercooked, or raw. I am not sure whether there are any egg-related problems in France, but the few times I've brought it up when serving dessert, everyone looked at me like I was crazy. Then they dug right in.

Even though raw eggs are acceptable, other items that I cook or bake with sometimes stump people around here. A startled supermarket cashier had never seen fresh ginger and held the gnarly root up for inspection as if it was an alien form of life that had landed on her conveyor belt. I use a lot of fresh ginger, especially in desserts like this one, where its spicy flavor makes a nice counterpoint to an egg-rich custard sauce, and of course, the dark chocolate.

TERRINE

10 ounces (285g) semisweet or bittersweet chocolate, coarsely chopped

8 tablespoons (4 ounces/115g) unsalted butter, cubed

4 large eggs, separated, at room temperature

Pinch of sea salt or kosher salt

4 tablespoons (50g) granulated sugar

FRESH GINGER CRÈME ANGLAISE

2 ounces (60g) unpeeled fresh ginger, sliced

2 cups (500ml) whole milk

1/3 cup (65g) granulated sugar

Pinch of sea salt or kosher salt

5 large egg yolks

1 To make the terrine, melt the chocolate and butter in a large bowl set over a pan of simmering water, stirring occasionally, until the chocolate is melted and smooth. Remove from the heat and let stand until the outside of the bowl feels tepid.

2 Whisk the egg yolks into the melted chocolate mixture, one at a time, until well blended.

3 Line a 9-inch (23cm) loaf pan with a sheet of plastic wrap and smooth it to remove as many wrinkles as possible.

continued

Chocolate terrine with
fresh ginger crème anglaise,
continued

4 In the bowl of a stand mixer fitted with the whip attachment, or by hand, whip the egg whites with a pinch of salt on high speed until they start to hold their shape. Add the sugar, 1 tablespoon at a time, and continue to whip until the egg whites are stiff and shiny, about 2 minutes. Fold one-third of the beaten egg whites into the chocolate mixture, and then fold in the rest, just until there are no streaks of egg white visible.

5 Scrape the chocolate mixture into the prepared loaf pan. Rap the pan a few times on the counter to remove any air bubbles. Smooth the top. Refrigerate the terrine for at least 4 hours. (The terrine can be made up to 3 days in advance and refrigerated.)

6 To make the crème anglaise, combine the ginger slices with just enough water to cover them in a saucepan over medium heat and simmer for 2 minutes. Drain the ginger, discarding the liquid. Put the blanched ginger slices back in the saucepan. Pour in the milk, and then add the sugar and a pinch of salt. Heat until the milk is steaming. Remove from the heat, cover, and steep for 1 hour.

7 Make an ice bath by nesting a metal bowl in a larger bowl filled with ice and a little cold water. Set a mesh strainer over the top.

8 Rewarm the milk. In a small bowl, lightly whisk the egg yolks. Whisk in some of the warmed milk mixture, and then scrape the warmed yolks into the saucepan. Cook over medium-low heat, stirring constantly with a heatproof spatula, scraping the bottom, sides, and corners of the pan, until the custard is thick enough to coat the spatula. Don't let the mixture boil.

9 Immediately strain the custard through the mesh strainer into the chilled bowl. Discard the ginger in the strainer, and stir the crème anglaise with a clean spatula to help cool it down. Once cool, refrigerate until ready to serve. (The crème anglaise can be made up to 3 days in advance, and stored in the refrigerator.)

10 To serve, unmold the terrine onto a plate and remove the plastic wrap. For best results, dip a sharp knife into very hot water before cutting each slice. Serve with a pitcher of very cold crème anglaise.

VARIATION: Add 2 tablespoons of espresso or a favorite liquor, such as dark rum, Cognac, or Grand Marnier, to the chocolate once it's melted in step 1.

Chocolate–dulce de leche tart

TARTE AU CHOCOLAT ET CONFITURE DE LAIT

Serves 10

CHOCOLATE CRUST

6 tablespoons (3 ounces/85g) salted butter, at room temperature

¼ cup (35g) powdered sugar

1 large egg yolk

1 cup (140g) all-purpose flour

⅓ cup (35g) Dutch-process or natural unsweetened cocoa powder

¼ teaspoon fleur de sel or other flaky sea salt

FILLING

8 ounces (230g) bittersweet or semisweet chocolate, chopped

2 large eggs

1¼ cups (310ml) whole milk

½ teaspoon vanilla extract, or 1 teaspoon dark rum

1 cup (240g) dulce de leche

Flaky sea salt, for sprinkling over the tart

Whipped cream (page 337) or vanilla ice cream, for serving (optional)

I wasn't sure whether I was in the right supermarket aisle when I first saw sweetened condensed milk sold in tubes, like toothpaste, in France. It wasn't until a French friend told me how much she loved to put the tube right into her mouth and squeeze the contents out that I got it. (Who says the French aren't efficient?) After she explained this to me, I could see her thoughts drifting away, thinking about that *souvenir* of her childhood. I know that after I use a can of it to make my own dulce de leche, I can't resist scraping the tin clean and licking the spatula, but the idea of buying (or eating) sweetened condensed milk in a tube does sound a little more *efficace*.

Even more efficient is buying *confiture du lait*, or dulce de leche, which is sold in many cheese shops in Paris. The dense, glossy caramel paste is ladled from wide earthenware bowls, and I use it as a base for a variation on the classic *tarte au chocolat*, with a layer of bittersweet chocolate ganache concealing a layer of *confiture de lait*. There's no hiding the fact that it's one efficient way to get your fix of chocolate and caramel at the same time. Now if someone could figure out how to put both flavors into a tube so I could carry it around, that would be even more efficient than carrying around wedges of this tart, which you'll be as tempted to do as I am.

This recipe was inspired by one that originally appeared in *delicious.* magazine.

1 To make the crust, in the bowl of a stand mixer fitted with the paddle attachment, beat the butter and powdered sugar on low speed just until smooth. Add the yolk, stopping the machine to scrape down the sides of the bowl, until it's fully incorporated.

2 In a small bowl, whisk together the flour and cocoa powder. Add them to the butter mixture, mixing just until the dough comes together. Form the dough into a disk, wrap in plastic, and let rest for 30 minutes at room temperature.

3 Use the heel of your hand to press the dough into a 9-inch (23cm) tart ring with a removable bottom, getting the bottom as flat as possible and pressing the dough up the sides of the pan

continued

until it reaches the rim. Sprinkle the salt over the bottom of the dough and press it into the pastry. Put the pan in the freezer for 30 minutes.

4 Preheat the oven to 400°F (200°C). Line the chilled tart crust with aluminum foil and cover with a layer of pie weights or dried beans. Bake the tart shell for 15 minutes, remove the foil and pie weights, and then bake for 5 minutes more, until the tart shell feels set. Remove from the oven and decrease the oven temperature to 300°F (150°C).

5 While the tart is baking, make the chocolate filling. Melt the chocolate in a clean, dry bowl set over a pan of simmering water. Once melted, remove the bowl from the heat and set a fine-mesh strainer over the top.

6 Whisk the eggs in a bowl. Heat the milk in a saucepan, then gradually whisk the warm milk into the eggs. Scrape the mixture back into the saucepan and cook over medium heat, stirring constantly with a heatproof spatula, until it's steamy and thickens slightly, about 3 minutes. (If it separates a bit, remove it from the heat, and whisk it vigorously to bring it back together.) Pour the custard through the strainer into the chocolate. Add the vanilla and stir until smooth.

7 Spread the dulce de leche over the hot tart shell in an even layer, being careful as you spread to make sure you don't break the flaky bottom of the tart. (If the dulce de leche is very thick, let it sit in the tart shell for a minute or so, to let the heat soften it, which will make it easier to spread.) Set the filled tart shell on a baking sheet lined with aluminum foil, then pour the chocolate custard over the dulce de leche, smooth the top, and add a generous sprinkling of flaky sea salt.

8 Bake the tart for 20 minutes, and then turn the heat off and leave the tart in the oven with the door closed to glide to a finish, 25 minutes more. Remove from the oven and let cool before serving. Serve the tart with softly whipped cream (page 337), vanilla ice cream, or just as is.

Honey-spice bread

PAIN D'ÉPICES

Makes 1 (9-inch/23cm) loaf, 12 to 16 slices

Some people travel to sightsee or visit museums, cathedrals, or gardens. Me? I travel to eat. The times I'd traveled to Europe prior to my current long-term gig, I always wondered why people didn't travel much outside their own country, especially the French. Now I realize it's because there is so much diversity in France—from the beaches of Biarritz to the mountains of the Jura—there's not a lot of incentive to leave. (Add to that, everyone speaks your language. And in the days before the euro, you didn't even have to change money.)

With the zippy train system, it's easy to get around France, and I've been terribly remiss in not checking out all the churches and scenic vistas, which I've made up for by eating as much as I can whenever I visit a new place. One region I've not visited, though, is Burgundy, known around the world for its wine, black currant liqueur, and Dijon mustard. And some of the same spices that go into that mustard make up the spices found in *pain d'épices*.

Unlike American spice cakes, which are often buttery and moist, true *pain d'épices* is *pain*, or bread. And its texture is both chewy and dense. The best description (and advice) I've heard so far was from Montreal food writer Lesley Chesterman, whom I'd contacted when I was perfecting my recipe and who said, "It has to taste medieval."

Even though a few things went astray when I moved across the Atlantic, I managed to hold on to a *dossier* of interesting recipes that I've been gathering over the years, which I continue to add to in France. Recently added were some unusual recipes for *pain d'épices*, including one from a French honey producer that raised my eyebrows. It had only two ingredients: flour and honey. (I wasn't sure how the bread would come out, but it did seem like an excellent way for people who bought his fancy honey to blow through a lot of it.) Some recipes had rye flour, which is traditional, but can make the bread too dry for modern tastes. And another had glucose (similar to corn syrup), which for some reason struck me as the least authentic of the lot.

Lesley sent me a recipe from André Lerch, a famed baker who closed up his little shop in Paris a number of years ago. His recipe included a technique for boiling the honey to concentrate it, which

continued

I adapted to give the bread just the texture I was looking for. This loaf is aggressively spiced, but will mellow after a day or two. In fact, it improves with age.

The type of honey you use will determine the flavor of the bread. Dark honey will give the bread an assertive, deeper flavor, while a lighter honey will result in a slightly sweeter loaf.

Pain d'épices has gone through a resurgence in France, thanks to creative types who like to pair it with foie gras. It is the classic addition to *carbonade flamande* (page 198).

1 Preheat the oven to 350°F (180°C). Butter a 9-inch (23cm) loaf pan and line the bottom with a sheet of parchment paper.

2 Heat the honey, brown sugar, water, and salt in a saucepan until it begins to boil. Decrease the heat to a simmer and cook for 5 minutes. Remove from the heat and stir in 1 cup (140g) of the all-purpose flour. Let cool to room temperature.

3 In a large bowl, whisk together the remaining 1/3 cup (45g) all-purpose flour, whole wheat flour, baking powder, baking soda, anise, cinnamon, allspice, ginger, nutmeg, and cloves.

4 In a small bowl, whisk together the egg and egg yolk.

5 Stir half the honey mixture into the dry ingredients; add the eggs, then the rest of the honey mixture, stirring just until smooth. (If any bits of flour remain, whisk the batter briefly to break them up and incorporate them.)

6 Scrape the mixture into the prepared loaf pan. Bake for 35 to 45 minutes, until a toothpick inserted into the center comes out clean. Let cool for 20 minutes, loosen the sides of the cake from the pan with a knife, then tip the cake out onto a wire cooling rack and cool completely. If possible, wait a day before slicing. *Pain d'épices* will keep for at least 1 week at room temperature, if well wrapped. It can also be frozen for up to 2 months.

VARIATION: Replace 1/4 cup (80g) of the honey with mild-flavored molasses for a more robustly flavored *pain d'épices*.

3/4 cup (240g) honey

1/2 cup packed (90g) light brown sugar

3/4 cup (180ml) water

1/2 teaspoon sea salt or kosher salt

11/3 cups (175g) all-purpose flour

2/3 cup (90g) whole wheat flour

1 teaspoon baking powder (preferably aluminum-free)

1 teaspoon baking soda

1 teaspoon whole or ground anise seed

1 teaspoon ground cinnamon

1 teaspoon ground allspice

1 teaspoon ground ginger

1/2 teaspoon freshly ground nutmeg

1/2 teaspoon ground cloves

1 large egg

1 large egg yolk

294

Le week-end

As much as the powers that be have tried, there's been little progress in stopping the English language from creeping into French.

The Internet is a good example. At the risk of sounding like a cultural imperialist, many terms and websites are in English because somehow, that's emerged as the common language. So I think we can agree that we should all just say "Facebook" instead of *Livre de visage*, or *Faccia di libro*, in our respective languages, and hope that others understand. And even though Twitter has been rechristened *Tweeter* by the French, in my opinion, that's close enough to give them a pass.

But the French government has had enough and decided that the word "hashtag," which had been universally accepted, should officially be banned in France and replaced with *mot-dièse*. Of course, they didn't take into account that the new hyphenated term couldn't be hashtagged—or *mot-dièse*'d I guess I should say—because of the hyphen.

Another word they wanted to curb was *le week-end*, which has always been my ace-in-the-hole when I pull the W tile at *le Scrabble*. There is only a half page of words in the French dictionary that begin with W, and most of them have roots in English, such as *wagon, western* (used when referring to a film that takes place in the Old West, as *de l'Œustern* doesn't quite convey the same meaning), and *water-polo*. So I'm rooting for them to hold on to as many words that begin with W as possible, in hopes of one day finally winning at *le Scrabble*.

Aside from the obvious, *week-end* can also refer to a pound cake, which is sold in most *pâtisseries*, which, unlike the multitiered layered or cream-filled cakes, can be kept just fine through the three days that make up *le week-end*.

I give my pound cake a slightly herbal edge and use bay leaves as a flavoring, which pairs nicely with a few swipes of fragrant orange zest. Interestingly, many recipes advise using "Mediterranean" or "imported" bay leaves, as American bay leaves are twice as strong. That's normally good advice. But here, the full flavor of the American bay, or—if I may use another foreign language, Latin, without causing a stir, *Umbellularia californica*—works especially well. If you know someone with a bay leaf tree, by all means, raid it to make this cake. And if you can, make the cake a day before you plan to serve it—letting it mellow overnight allows the flavors to permeate the cake even more.

One professional trick I learned in France is to pipe a line of creamed butter down the center of the pound cake prior to baking, which makes an attractive decorative crack down the top. I tried to look up the official name for "line of creamed butter" in my French culinary dictionary, which labels itself "an exhaustive compilation of terms from French gastronomy," but I didn't find it. However I did notice that there was one lone entry under "W," *Waterzooi*, with *le week-end* noticeably absent. I'm not sure if there was an intervention from the French language police, but until I get a summons in the mail, I'm going to stick with calling this cake *gâteau week-end* because in the time it takes me to say "*le gâteau pour les trois jours fin de semaine: vendredi, samedi, et dimanche*," I could be pulling one out of the oven.

Bay leaf pound cake with orange glaze

GÂTEAU WEEK-END PARFUMÉ AU LAURIER,
NAPPAGE À L'ORANGE

Makes one (9-inch/23cm) cake, 12 servings

I've reversed the way pound cake is traditionally made. Melting the butter and saturating the flour results in a moist pound cake with a buttery crumb. You could substitute rose geranium or another scented leaf, making sure—of course—that whatever leaves you are using are unsprayed. To make a version that kicks up the orange flavor, see the Variation (opposite).

1 To make the cake, melt the 6 tablespoons (85g) of butter in a small saucepan. Remove from the heat and add 3 of the bay leaves. Let steep for 1 hour.

2 Preheat the oven to 350°F (180°C). Butter a 9-inch (23cm) loaf pan. Dust with flour and tap out any excess, then line the bottom with parchment paper. Dab one side of the remaining 7 bay leaves with a little bit of butter and place the leaves, evenly spaced, on the bottom of the prepared loaf pan, buttered side down.

3 In a large bowl, whisk together the flour, sugar, baking powder, and salt.

4 In a small bowl, whisk together the eggs, sour cream, orange zest, and vanilla until combined.

5 Rewarm the butter to liquefy it and pluck out the bay leaves.

6 With a rubber spatula, gently stir the egg mixture into the dry ingredients, just until the batter is smooth. Do not over-mix. Scrape the batter into the prepared pan, being careful not to disturb the bay leaves. Put the remaining 1 tablespoon of softened butter in a plastic bag and snip off a corner (or make a parchment paper cone), then draw a straight line of the butter down the center of the cake. Bake for 40 to 45 minutes, until a toothpick inserted into the center comes out clean.

7 Remove from the oven and let cool for 10 minutes. Run a knife around the perimeter of the cake and then tip the cake out onto a cooling rack and let cool completely.

8 To make the glaze, combine the powdered sugar, orange juice, and orange liqueur. Spread the glaze over the cooled cake, allowing it to drip down the sides and harden.

CAKE

6 tablespoons (3 ounces/85g) unsalted butter, cubed, at room temperature, plus 1 tablespoon butter, softened, for piping

10 fresh or dried bay leaves

1²/₃ cups (230g) all-purpose flour

1 cup (200g) granulated sugar

1 teaspoon baking powder (preferably aluminum-free)

1/2 teaspoon sea salt or kosher salt

3 large eggs, at room temperature

1/2 cup (125g) sour cream

Finely grated zest of 1 orange (unsprayed)

1/2 teaspoon vanilla extract

ORANGE GLAZE

1 cup (140g) powdered sugar

1¹/₂ tablespoons orange juice

1 teaspoon orange liqueur, such as Grand Marnier or Cointreau

VARIATION: To make an orange-scented *gâteau week-end* without the flavor of bay leaves, strip the zest of 3 oranges with a vegetable peeler. (If you use a rasp-style zester, you won't get the same amount of zest.) Grind the peels in a food processor with the granulated sugar. The sugar will turn a bright orange color from extracting the flavorful citrus oils. Use that to make the pound cake, omitting the bay leaves and substituting 2 teaspoons of orange liquor, such as Grand Mariner or Cointreau, for the vanilla in the cake batter.

Duck fat cookies

SABLÉS À LA GRAISSE DE CANARD

Makes 45 to 50 cookies

The French haven't embraced "extreme eating," and thank goodness for that. I don't have to watch perfectly normal adults turn into wide-eyed, drooling lunatics when faced with a cake festooned with strips of bacon or slamming down pork-belly and lard Jell-O shots. The only people you see in Paris squealing with delight when faced with an overloaded platter of innards are foreign chefs taping their television shows; the French are simply used to eating those things because sausages, bacon, and duck fat are just part of everyday life.

I'm not afraid of fat (if I was, I'd be out of work), and I use it when it makes something taste better. Yet even I am not immune to its less desirable effects. When I left the restaurant business years ago, I realized that because I was eating anything and everything around me, I was getting a little pork belly myself. With my restaurant years behind me, I was able to get back to fighting weight by being a little more prudent with what I eat and practicing the famed French *moderation*, a carefully calculated mindset where everything is to be enjoyed—but in moderation. (However, I don't adhere to the equally important part of the weight-loss plan that includes copious amount of tobacco.)

In the southwest of France, the locals are famous for enjoying abundant amounts of duck fat, which some speculate is the reason they so are long-lived. I can't say eating cookies will make you healthy, but if you're looking to get a little more duck fat into your diet, this is a pretty delicious way to do so.

continued

1 In a small saucepan, heat the currants over low heat with the Armagnac until the liquid is completely absorbed. Remove from the heat and set aside to cool to room temperature.

2 In the bowl of a stand mixer fitted with the paddle attachment, or by hand in a bowl, cream the duck fat, butter, and sugar on low speed just until well combined. Mix in the vanilla.

3 In a small bowl, whisk together the flour and salt. Add it to the fat mixture, stirring until the dough comes together. Then mix in the currants.

4 On a lightly floured surface, knead the dough briefly until smooth. Shape it into a rectangle, and cut the dough in half lengthwise. Roll each piece of dough into a log 6 inches (15cm) long. (If the dried fruit makes the dough crumble a bit, stick your thumbs into any fissures to seal them, pressing the dough back together, then continue to roll it into cylinders.) Wrap each log in plastic and refrigerate until firm, at least 30 minutes. (The dough can be made up to 3 days in advance and refrigerated, or frozen for up to 2 months.)

5 Preheat the oven to 350°F (180°C) and line two baking sheets with parchment paper or silicone baking mats.

6 To bake the cookies, slice the dough into $1/4$-inch (.75cm) rounds and set them on the baking sheets, evenly spaced. Bake the cookies, rotating the baking sheets midway through, for 12 minutes, until golden brown on top. Remove the cookies from the oven and cool on the baking sheets until crisp. The cookies can be stored in an airtight container at room temperature for up to 3 days.

1/4 cup (30g) dried currants or chopped dried cherries

1 tablespoon Armagnac, Cognac, or brandy

6 tablespoons (85g) chilled duck fat

4 tablespoons (2 ounces/55g) salted or unsalted butter, at room temperature

3/4 cup (150g) granulated sugar

1/2 teaspoon vanilla extract

1 1/4 cups (175g) all-purpose flour

3/4 teaspoon sea salt or kosher salt

Buttermilk ice cream with olive oil and fleur de sel

GLACE AU LAIT RIBOT, HUILE D'OLIVE ET FLEUR DE SEL

Makes about 1 quart (1l)

1¾ cups (430ml) heavy cream

½ cup (100g) granulated sugar

3 tablespoons (60g) light corn syrup

1¼ cups (310ml) buttermilk

Fruity, extra-virgin olive oil

Flaky sea salt, preferably fleur de sel

France is a paradise of fermented dairy products. Of course, there are luscious French cheeses, and other farm-fresh goodies, such as *fromage blanc*, *faiselle* (drained cheese), and *crème fraîche* aplenty. But it's hard not to be impressed by the supermarket yogurt aisles as well, which are the longest ones in the store.

Buttermilk, however, seems to be the lost cousin of the lot. It makes an appearance most notably in bowls in *crêperies* served as a drink—although looking around, I always seem to be the only one sipping it.

So I was surprised to see *glace au lait ribot* (buttermilk ice cream) on the menu of a hypertrendy restaurant in Paris recently. The presentation was lovely, but the flavor didn't have the tang of dairy that I was expecting, so I bought a bottle of *lait ribot* to churn up my own later that week. When it was ready to serve, I drizzled it with some extra-fruity olive oil, dusted it with a flurry of fleur de sel crystals, and happily dug in.

This tangy ice cream is terrific with sugared strawberry slices, nectarine slices, or blueberries instead of the olive oil and salt, or with Apricot crumble tart (page 309). It also pairs well with fruit compotes (see sidebar) where its tartness offsets the sweetness of fruits and berries.

Because buttermilk is low in fat, this ice cream becomes hard after a day or so in the freezer. Hence the corn syrup, which helps keep it scoopable. If you'd prefer to leave the corn syrup out, substitute mild honey or add an additional ¼ cup (50g) of granulated sugar. Take it out of the freezer about 10 minutes before serving for easier scooping.

UNE AUTRE IDÉE

One of my favorite compotes is made with plums and raspberries. To make it, preheat the oven to 375°F (180°C). Halve 1½ pounds (680g) of Italian prune plums (or quarter regular plums), pluck out the pits, and put the plums in a baking dish. Toss them with ½ vanilla bean split lengthwise, ¼ cup (60ml) of white wine (dry or sweet), and 2 tablespoons of sugar. Cover the pan snugly with aluminum foil and bake for 25 minutes, or until the plums are cooked through. Remove the plums from the oven, add 4 ounces (115g) of fresh raspberries, replace the foil, and let the compote cool with the berries. Mix everything together gently before serving with the ice cream.

1 In a small saucepan, warm the cream over low heat with the sugar and corn syrup, stirring occasionally, until the sugar is completely dissolved. Chill the mixture thoroughly, at least 8 hours.

2 Stir the buttermilk into the chilled sweetened cream and freeze in an ice cream maker according to the manufacturer's instructions. Once churned, transfer the ice cream to a container and freeze for a few hours, until firm enough to scoop.

3 To serve, scoop the ice cream into bowls. Drizzle each serving with olive oil and sprinkle with a flurry of sea salt.

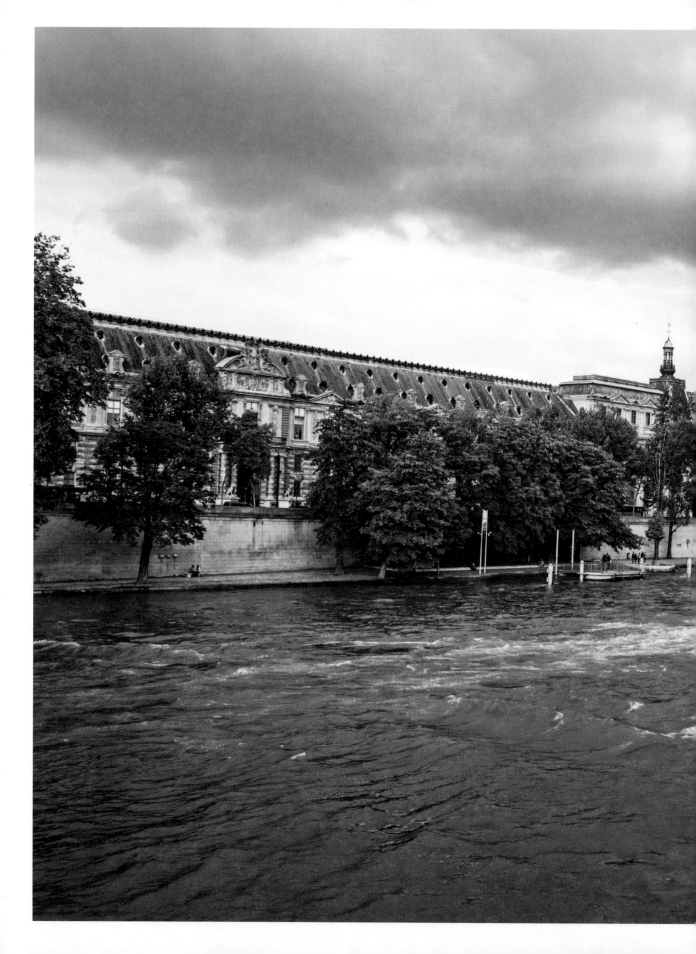

French cheesecake

TORTEAU FROMAGER

Serves 10 to 12

"What's that burnt thing?" people ask me, pointing to a charred, puffed-up disk at the *fromagerie*. At a glance, it's easy to see their bewilderment, until I tell them that underneath the exceptionally thin layer of black is an egg-lightened cheesecake made with goat cheese. I remember the first time I bought one out of curiosity, and how relieved I was to discover that the inside was nowhere near what the charred exterior suggested, which is similar to Paris, where things are not always what they seem to be.

This phenomenon, which the Japanese have dubbed the "Paris Syndrome," is a troubled psychological state that people find themselves in when they learn that Paris is not necessarily the city they see on postcards or in the movies. I, myself, may have experienced this syndrome from time to time. The worst was when my combined Internet and telephone service went off for three months, and I couldn't get in touch with the company that provided it because—of course—my Internet and telephone didn't work. I don't know if this is a symptom of the syndrome, but after yet another exasperating visit to their office, where they assured me for the fourteenth time that the problem would be fixed the next day, I literally stood in the middle of my apartment and screamed. (An image I doubt you'll ever see on any postcards of Paris.)

A few weeks later, I was asked to speak at Bloom Where You're Planted, a seminar for newcomers to get adjusted to the peculiarities of the city. So I decided my topic was going to be ways to "cope" with the oddities of life in Paris and to help the people in my seminar recover from various experiences. One had been traumatized by a supermarket checker who refused to give him a bag for a single banana (I kind of sided with the cashier on that one). Another was scared to go into her bank because they didn't want to give her any of her money when she wanted to withdraw some, which led to my explanation of why sales of home safes are so brisk in France. The most important piece of advice that I left them with was if it gets overwhelming, take a trip out of Paris.

People forget that France is a diverse country, and Paris is just one specific part of it. (Note that it's called the Paris Syndrome, not France Sydrome.) Aside from enjoying the slower pace of life outside of the French capital, the other reason to visit various regions is to learn about regional cuisines by sampling the local specialties.

(Sampling the wine also helps overcome post-traumatic, internet-service-provider symptoms, such as hollering like a maniac in your apartment.) My favorite part of any road trip involves stopping at service stations on the *autoroute* where I'll find a selection of regional confections, liqueurs, and even recipe books, like the cookbook on the cuisine of the Poitou-Charentes I picked up at a gas station.

Tourteau fromager is a specialty of that region, and something that's definitely not what it seems like, until you peer under the surface. The blackened crust hides a cake with the unique flavor of a dense American cheesecake, but with the light sponginess of a Japanese cheesecake. The baking is traditionally started off in a very, very hot oven to get the dark crust on top, and then the temperature is reduced to get the inside cooked. Yours may or may not end up looking like the blackened version that you get in France, but it's not something to scream about if it doesn't.

CRUST

1½ cups (210g) all-purpose flour

2 teaspoons granulated sugar

¼ teaspoon sea salt or kosher salt

8 tablespoons (4 ounces/115g) unsalted butter, chilled and cubed

1 large egg

2 tablespoons ice water

FILLING

10 ounces (285g) fresh goat cheese

2 tablespoons sour cream or crème fraîche

1¼ cups (250g) granulated sugar

1 teaspoon vanilla extract

1 teaspoon Cognac or brandy

5 large eggs, separated, at room temperature

Scant ½ cup (60g) all-purpose flour

Honey, for serving (optional)

Fresh berries tossed with sugar, for serving (optional)

1   To make the crust, in the bowl of a stand mixer fitted with the paddle attachment (or in a bowl, by hand), combine the flour, sugar, and salt. Add the chilled butter and beat on low until the butter is crumbled and the mixture resembles cornmeal. Add the egg and ice water and beat until the dough comes together. Gather the dough and shape it into a flat disk. Wrap the dough in plastic and refrigerate for at least 30 minutes or up to 1 day.

2   Preheat the oven to 450°F (230°C).

3   Remove the dough from the refrigerator and roll it out on a lightly floured surface into a 15-inch (38cm) circle. Fit the dough into a 9- to 10-inch (23 to 25cm) springform pan, lifting the sides of the dough and releasing it to ease the dough into the corners of the pan without stretching it, then press it gently to adhere it to the sides. Trim any overhang with a sharp knife.

4   To make the filling, in the bowl of a stand mixer fitted with the paddle attachment (or in a bowl, by hand), beat the goat cheese with the sour cream, half of the sugar, the vanilla, and the Cognac on medium speed until well combined. Replace the paddle attachment with the whip attachment and add the egg yolks. Beat on medium-high speed (or use a sturdy whisk and whip by hand) until smooth, then mix in the flour.

continued

5 In a separate bowl, whip the egg whites on medium-high speed until they hold their shape. Add the remaining sugar and whip until the whites hold their shape when you lift the whip attachment. Fold one-third of the whites into the goat cheese mixture, and then fold in the remaining whites in two batches, just until you no longer see any streaks of egg whites in the batter.

6 Scrape the batter into the dough-lined pan and smooth the top. Bake for 20 minutes without opening the oven door. Decrease the oven temperature to 400°F (200°C), and continue to bake for 15 minutes. Let the cake cool completely on a wire rack, and then carefully remove the sides of the springform pan. Slice, and serve the cake at room temperature. Traditionally, *torteau fromager* is served without accompaniment, but it's good with a drizzle of honey or a mixture of sweetened fresh berries.

304

Oh-la-la!

I OFTEN VIEWED *LE TARTE TROPÉZIENNE* WITH A little trepidation. It's called a tart, but is actually closer to a cake, with its lofty height and a creamy filling as thick as the spongy cake layers surrounding it. Somehow it always seemed out of place in Paris pastry shops alongside the sleek, slender cakes covered with shiny chocolate ganache or decorated with fanciful swoops of cream and chocolate curls. It wasn't until I was on the Île du Levant, also known as Héliopolis, an island off the southern coast of France, that I had one that excited me.

Héliopolis was a community founded in 1931 by two French brothers, both doctors. For health reasons, they advised people to eat a vegetarian diet, not to drink alcohol or smoke, and to reject medicine. Oh, and not to wear any clothes.

Consequently, the island became a *naturiste* preserve with people wandering around soaking up the sunshine or going about their daily business with nothing on but a layer of sunscreen. The island has a year-round community, and there's not much in the way of services, except for a small grocery store, *a boulangerie*, and a handful of places to eat.

At the restaurant Le Gambaro, located at the port—one of the only two areas where clothing is required—we had remarkably fresh seafood, which, probably due to all the hooks involved, was sold by fully clothed fishermen who pulled up to the docks each morning. After an excellent bouillabaisse, a multicourse meal made of fish served from a steaming cauldron, I ordered the *tarte tropézienne* on a whim even though I

was stuffed. After one forkful, I was immediately sorry that I'd only ordered one to split with my tablemate. It wasn't the mosquitos buzzing in my ear that kept me awake later that night; it was that *tarte tropézienne*. And the next morning we went back and ordered two more (no more sharing!). The French waiter didn't quite know how to handle the request; French people just don't order desserts at 10:45 a.m. But we persisted and two more were found, and enjoyed.

The connection with Saint Tropez, which is just a short boat ride away, is rather curious. When Brigitte Bardot was filming *And God Created Woman* in Saint Tropez, she was so charmed by the local pastry that she dubbed it *la tarte tropézienne*. From the look of her in that film—*oh-la-la!*— it's hard to believe that she ate even one bite of this rich cake, filled with more custard than I've ever seen in a French dessert. But since everyone knows that French women don't get fat, she probably enjoyed her fair share.

When I got back to Paris, I set to work recreating that tart at home. Remembering that the tart filling had the richness of buttercream and the eggy flavor of pastry cream, I made a batch of both, and then mixed the two together. It took me more tries than I care to recount to get the right balance, but I was happy when I finally got it. So now, when I'm in the privacy of my kitchen in Paris, longing for the days of resting at a beachside café overlooking the Mediterranean, I can enjoy a slice of my very own custard-filled *tarte tropézienne*, no matter what I'm wearing. Or not.

St. Tropez tart

TARTE TROPÉZIENNE

Serves 12

The original recipe for this tart is a closely guarded secret. So I polled the bakeries in my neighborhood to ask the bakers what they use as a filling and was told everything from pastry cream lightened with whipped cream to whipped cream with warm butter to make crème mousseline. I settled on making a quick, unfussy "express" butter-cream and folded that into pastry cream, which works great. The brioche dough is somewhat sticky, which is why I recommended that you use a stand mixer to make it.

The pearl sugar is obligatory (check Sources, page 339). But if you're in a pinch, crush some sugar cubes in a sturdy resealable plastic bag with a rolling pin until they are crumbled into pieces the size of very large bread crumbs.

1   To make the brioche, stir together the eggs, milk, sugar, yeast, and 1/2 cup (70g) of the flour in the bowl of a stand mixer fitted with the paddle attachment. Let sit for 10 to 15 minutes, until bubbles start to appear on the surface. Gradually stir in the salt, and the remaining 1 1/4 cups (175g) flour. Attach the bowl to the mixer and mix on medium-high speed for 8 to 10 minutes, until the dough is smooth and silky.

2   Decrease the speed to medium and, with the mixer running, add the soft butter, cube by cube, making sure each one is incorporated before adding the next. Once all the butter is mixed in, beat on medium-high speed for 5 minutes. Remove the paddle, cover the bowl with a kitchen towel, and let the dough sit in a warm place until it doubles in volume, about 1 1/2 hours.

3   Once the dough has risen, run a flexible spatula around the outside of the dough to fold it into the center. (The dough will be sticky and a bit wet.) Chill the dough in the refrigerator for 1 hour.

4   To make the pastry cream, whisk together the cornstarch and egg yolks in a saucepan until smooth, and then whisk in the sugar. Dribble in a little of the warm milk, whisking constantly. Gradually add the rest of the milk while whisking to avoid lumps. Add the vanilla bean and, whisking constantly, heat the mixture over medium heat until it begins to boil. Cook the pastry cream at the lowest possible boil for 90 seconds, whisking vigorously and making sure you reach into the corners of

BRIOCHE

3 large eggs, at room temperature

2 tablespoons whole milk

2 tablespoons granulated sugar

2 teaspoons active dry yeast

1 3/4 cups (245g) all-purpose flour

1 teaspoon sea salt or kosher salt

10 tablespoons (5 ounces/140g) unsalted butter, cubed, at room temperature

PASTRY CREAM

3 tablespoons cornstarch

3 large egg yolks

1/3 cup (65g) granulated sugar

1 1/4 cups (310ml) whole milk, warmed

1/2 vanilla bean, split lengthwise

2 tablespoons unsalted butter, cubed, at room temperature

BUTTERCREAM

1 tablespoon granulated sugar

2 tablespoons hot water

1 large egg yolk

6 tablespoons (3 ounces/85g) unsalted butter, cubed, at room temperature

2 teaspoons orange-flavored liqueur, such as Grand Marnier or Cointreau

the pan with the whisk, until it's very thick, like mayonnaise. Remove from the heat and whisk in the butter, a few cubes at a time, until the mixture is smooth. Scrape the mixture into a bowl, cover, and refrigerate. (To speed things up, put it over an ice bath, stirring until cool, and then refrigerate it.)

5   To make the buttercream, bring the sugar and hot water to a boil in a small saucepan. The sugar will not quite be dissolved, but remove the pan from the heat and very quickly—without any hesitation—whisk in the egg yolk, and then whisk in the butter and liqueur, until smooth. Cover and chill.

6   To make the syrup, bring the sugar and water to a boil in a small saucepan and heat until the sugar is dissolved. Remove from the heat and let cool. Stir in the liqueur and set aside.

7   Remove the dough from the refrigerator. Butter a 9- to 10-inch (23 to 25cm) springform pan. Scrape the dough into the pan, and then use your hands to coax the dough to the sides of the pan, trying to keep the top as smooth as possible. If the dough is too sticky, dampen your hands slightly. Cover the pan with a kitchen towel and let rise 1 1/2 hours.

8   About 15 minutes before you're ready to bake the dough, pre-heat the oven to 375°F (190°C).

9   To make the glaze, mix the egg yolk with the milk in a small bowl, then brush it over the top of the brioche. Sprinkle the pearl sugar over the top and press it in lightly. Bake for 20 minutes, or until the brioche is golden brown on top and springs back lightly when you touch it in the center. Remove from the oven and let cool for a few minutes, then run a knife around the edge of the pan and remove the sides of the springform. Cool completely.

10 To assemble the tart, remove the vanilla bean from the pastry cream. In the bowl of a stand mixer fitted with the paddle attachment, beat the pastry cream with the buttercream on medium speed until smooth. Split the brioche in half horizontally. Remove the top and carefully turn it over. Brush both of the cut sides of the cake with the syrup. Spread the filling over the bottom half of the brioche, then carefully replace the top. Because of the filling, *tarte tropzeienne* is always kept in the refrigerator. Take it out of the refrigerator shortly before you plan to serve it, so it's not too cold.

SYRUP

2 tablespoons granulated sugar

1/4 cup (60ml) water

1 tablespoon orange-flavored liqueur, such as Grand Marnier or Cointreau

GLAZE

1 large egg yolk

1 teaspoon whole milk

1/3 cup (50g) pearl sugar

Apricot crumble tart

TARTE CRUMBLE AUX ABRICOTS

Serves 8 to 10

DOUGH

6 tablespoons (3 ounces/85g) unsalted butter, chilled

1/2 cup (100g) granulated sugar

2 large egg yolks

1 1/4 cups (175g) all-purpose flour

1/2 teaspoon sea salt or kosher salt

CRUMBLE TOPPING

3/4 cup (75g) whole almonds

1/2 cup (70g) all-purpose flour

1/3 cup (60g) packed light brown sugar

1/2 teaspoon ground cinnamon

1/2 teaspoon sea salt or kosher salt

6 tablespoons (3 ounces/85g) unsalted butter, chilled and cubed

FILLING

2 pounds (900g) ripe, fresh apricots, pitted and quartered

3 tablespoons granulated sugar

1 tablespoon cornstarch

1 teaspoon vanilla extract

1/4 teaspoon almond extract

Whipped cream (page 337), vanilla ice cream, Apricot kernel ice cream (page 312), or Buttermilk ice cream (page 299), to serve

One of the secrets of French home "bakers" are rolls of tart dough that are sold in supermarkets in boxes that look similar to those containing rolls of aluminum foil. When you want to make a tart, you simply unroll the dough, line a tart pan, and—*voilà!*—you're set to go. It's a good idea, until you taste the dough (and read the ingredients), and realize that bakeries needn't worry about the competition.

One dessert that's easy to make at home, which the French have adopted from the English, is *le crumble*. Because I am a home baker, I don't have any problem turning this into a tart with homemade dough when fresh apricots from Provence become abundant in the Paris markets each summer.

The first time I saw a fresh apricot (I had only known the dried ones) was when I was baking in upstate New York in the 1980s. Someone brought me a small basket containing just six fruits, which I carefully sliced up to make one tart for eight fortunate customers. So I'm thrilled that I can now get them by the bag load. Still, I do take the time to treat the apricots right, rolling out a tart shell (that I make with pure butter), packing them into the filling, and topping it all with a crunchy topping of nuts and a dusting of cinnamon.

I fit right in with the French because I'm hopelessly *radin* (cheap) and can't bear to throw anything away, so I also use the apricot pits to flavor Apricot kernel ice cream (page 312), which is exactly what I want melting alongside, or on top of, this tart.

1   To make the dough, remove the butter from the refrigerator 10 minutes before you plan to use it and let it soften slightly in the bowl of a stand mixer fitted with the paddle attachment. Add the sugar and beat on medium speed just until no visible lumps of butter remain. Add the egg yolks, then the flour and salt. Mix until the dough comes together. (You can also make the dough in a bowl using a spatula and a little moxie.)

2   Coat the bottom and sides of a 9- to 10-inch (23 to 25cm) springform pan with nonstick spray. Use the heel of your hand to press the dough over the bottom of the pan, and a little less

continued

than halfway up the sides. Try to get the bottom as even as possible, not because anyone will see it, but so it bakes evenly. Put the pan in the freezer for 30 minutes.

Apricot crumble tart, continued

3   To make the crumble topping, pulse the almonds, flour, brown sugar, cinnamon, and salt in a food processor until the almonds are broken up into very small pieces. Add the butter and pulse; after a few moments, the mixture will look sandy. As you continue to pulse, pieces will just start clumping together. Stop pulsing at that point and chill the crumble topping. (If you don't have a food processor, you can make the crumble topping by chopping the almonds finely and mixing the topping with a pastry blender or by hand.)

4   Preheat the oven to 375°F (190°C).

5   Line the chilled tart crust with aluminum foil and cover with a layer of pie weights or dried beans. Bake the tart shell for 20 minutes, remove the foil and pie weights, and then bake for 5 to 10 minutes more, until the tart shell is browned. Remove from the oven.

6   To make the filling, in a bowl, mix the apricots with the sugar, cornstarch, and the extracts. (Do not make the filling too far in advance because the apricots may become too juicy.)

7   Transfer the filling to the tart shell and even it out. Strew the crumble topping evenly over the apricots. Bake the tart for 50 minutes, until the crumble topping is nicely browned. Let cool on a wire rack for a few minutes, then run a knife around the outside of the tart to separate it from the pan. Let rest for 30 minutes, then remove the sides of the springform and let the tart cool. The edges may look rather dark, but should taste fine, not burnt. Serve warm or at room temperature with whipped cream or ice cream.

310

Apricot kernel ice cream

GLACE AUX NOYAUX D'ABRICOTS

Makes about 1 quart (1l)

50 apricot kernels
³/₄ cup (150g) granulated sugar
1 cup (250ml) whole milk
2 cups (500 ml) heavy cream
Pinch of sea salt or kosher salt
5 large egg yolks

There is an interesting tradition of gleaning in France. Someone who gleans is called a *glaneur*, and forages for fruit and vegetables left over after the farms finish their harvest. (In America, we call it "scrounging," which sounds less romantic.) There aren't any farms in the city of Paris that I know of, but people do like rummaging through cast-offs of various sorts, including showing up after the outdoor markets close, when the vendors are packing up, hoping to glean leftover fruits and vegetables.

I don't get down on my hands and knees and go through the piles of discarded boxes, but I do get a *bon marché* (good deal) from the vendors who are happy to get rid of a case or two of very ripe produce for a few bucks when the market is close to ending.

But I don't just make this ice cream because I can't bear to see anything thrown away either; I make it because it's absolutely delicious in the summertime served with anything made with summer fruits and berries, including Apricot crumble tart (page 309). Guests are often surprised when I tell them that the strong almond flavor in the ice cream is actually made from apricot kernels. My *invitées* in Paris love it, and lick it up, while my guests from America express reservations because the kernels might be toxic. *Quelle difference!* (Without getting too technical, apricot kernels contain amygdalin, which is something that shouldn't be consumed in very high quantities.) I tuck the pits in an old, folded-over kitchen towel that I don't care about anymore, and whack each one with a hammer until I hear a snapping sound, which indicates the shell hiding the kernel has been broken. I try not to use too much force, since it's easier to pluck out the kernel if it's still whole.

If I don't have enough apricot kernels, I will crack them and freeze the kernels until I have enough. Otherwise I'll make just half a batch of ice cream with what I have (in that case, use three egg yolks).

1 Grind the apricot kernels and the sugar in a mortar and pestle or mini food processor, until the kernels are finely chopped into tiny pieces, about the size of grains of rice.

2 Warm the milk and 1 cup (250ml) of the cream in a saucepan with a pinch of salt. Stir in the apricot kernel mixture, remove from the heat, cover, and steep for 1 hour.

3 Rewarm the apricot kernel–infused mixture.

4 Pour the remaining cream into a large bowl set over a larger bowl filled with ice, and set a mesh strainer over the top.

5 In a separate bowl, whisk together the egg yolks. Slowly pour the warm apricot kernel–infused mixture into the egg yolks, whisking constantly, and then scrape the warmed egg yolks back into the saucepan. Stir the mixture constantly over medium heat with a heatproof spatula, scraping the bottom as you stir, until the mixture thickens and coats the spatula. Pour the custard through the strainer, into the cream. Discard the apricot kernels and stir the custard with a clean spatula, until cool.

6 Chill the custard thoroughly in the refrigerator, then freeze in an ice cream maker according to the manufacturer's instructions. The ice cream will keep for up to 2 months in the freezer.

313

Très New York

ANY YEARS BACK, I WAS AT AN ART OPEN-ing in a scruffy area of the city and began a conversation with a Frenchwoman. As we talked, I could have sworn I detected a hint of New York in her speech. When I inquired about that, she immediately switched to perfect English, saying, "I'm from New York!"

Dee Goldberg moved to Paris in 1959. Back then, the locals weren't so used to having for-eigners around, and she had a difficult time adjusting. But through networking she hooked up with other women who'd moved to France. (Nowadays, anything and everything that is even remotely associated with New York, from brick walls in cafés to *le pop-up* restaurants, makes a place *très Brooklyn*, and Dee's pedigree may have made her *la première hipster* in Paris.) When they first started meeting up, one of their primary activities was to exchange recipes because so many of them craved a taste of home every now and then. And one of the most popular recipes was for New York cheesecake.

Dee did some searching around and baked up her cheesecake with the ingredients she could find, which at the time were Jockey (a brand of *fromage blanc*, somewhat similar to sour cream, but more tart) and Kiri, a French-style *pâte à tartiner* that's sold in single-serving squares, eight to a pack, and is similar to cream cheese. She had to do a bit of math, but figured out that twenty-two of them could substitute for the pound of cream cheese. Her two daughters, whom I'm now friends with as well, love her cheesecake and have fond memories of their mom handing them the two squares of Kiri that were left over to unwrap and eat on their own.

Since then, cream cheese is now sold by the brick, *très Brooklyn*-style, and has become widely available in France because the French like it just as much as Americans do, though Dee has stuck with those Kiri squares. And now that her daugh-ters are grown up and have left the house, she was coy when I asked what she did with the two leftover squares of Kiri. She gave me her recipe for *le fabuleux cheesecake* (pronounced *fabu-loo*), which truly lives up to its name. When I make it, I use regular cream cheese because I don't trust myself with any extra blocks of cream cheese lying around either.

Dee's fabulous cheesecake

LE FABULEUX CHEESECAKE DE DEE

Serves 10 to 12

2 (8-ounce /450g) packages cream cheese, at room temperature

2 cups (480g) fromage blanc

1½ cups (300g) granulated sugar

4 large eggs, at room temperature

3 tablespoons all-purpose flour

3 tablespoons cornstarch

1½ teaspoons freshly squeezed lemon juice

1 teaspoon vanilla extract

8 tablespoons (4 ounces/115g) unsalted butter, melted and cooled

2 cups (480g) sour cream

Fromage blanc is a fresh cheese in France that is sold in most supermarkets. If you can't find it, puree full-fat cottage cheese in a food processor until completely smooth. Do be sure to wrap the springform pan well. When Dee came over to make it, that step was somehow forgotten, and the mixture ran out all over my oven. Perplexed, I had to call the repairman because I couldn't figure out how to enable the "easy clean" feature stamped inside the door of my new oven. It turns out *entretien facile* means that you can remove the entire oven door for "easy cleaning." And I spent the next day doing just that, ending with a call to the repairman to get it back on—but the cheesecake was worth it!

1 Preheat the oven to 325°F (170°C). Butter a 9- to 10-inch (23 to 25cm) springform pan and wrap a large sheet of aluminum foil around the bottom and up the outsides of the pan to catch any leaks. (Use several sheets if your foil isn't wide enough.) Set the cake pan on a baking sheet.

2 In the bowl of a stand mixer fitted with the paddle attachment (or in a large bowl, by hand), beat the cream cheese and *fromage blanc* on high speed until smooth and creamy. With the machine running, add the sugar and then the eggs, one by one, stopping the mixer to scrape down the sides, until the eggs are completely incorporated. Reduce the speed to low and add the flour, cornstarch, lemon juice, and vanilla. Finally, add the melted butter and sour cream, mixing just until smooth.

3 Pour the batter into the prepared pan and bake for 70 minutes. Turn off the oven and let stand in the turned-off oven for 1½ to 2 hours; check at the 1½-hour mark and take it out when it appears almost set in the center but still jiggles slightly. Remove the cheesecake from the oven and let cool completely. Chill in the refrigerator for up to 3 days until ready to serve.

VARIATION: I once brought half of this leftover cheesecake to my local *crêperie* where I was having dinner. The waiter sent a few slices back to the kitchen, and within minutes, the crêpemaker (his wife) came running out of the kitchen to give me a hug. I suggested we try it with some of the Salted butter caramel sauce (page 334) that they keep in a pot by the stove, which elicited even more squeals of delight.

The Sweetest Sip

Many years ago, when I was making desserts professionally, we had a famous guest, actor Danny Kaye, come to the restaurant for dinner. Mr. Kaye let us know in advance that he was bringing in a rare, eighty-year-old bottle of Château d'Yquem (see page 266) and asked for a dessert that would pair nicely with it. So we made *blancmange*, a wobbly custard flavored with hand-squeezed bitter almond milk, which I surrounded with ripe mango slices. It was the perfect match, and he was so delighted that he sent a small glass of Yquem to me back in the kitchen.

As you can imagine, pastry people are the last folks in the kitchen to go home. I'd never tasted the famed wine, and remember being alone after everyone had left for the night. It was just me, in the now-quiet kitchen, holding a glass that contained a small sip of slightly syrupy, cool amber liquid pooled in the bottom. I took a tentative sip, knowing that this wine I'd heard so much about was something to savor, not swill. Shortly after it passed through my lips, flavors of ripe apricots, buttery brioche, vanilla, honey, and a hint

of mangoes unraveled in my mouth. By the time I put the empty glass down, and savored the last of the sticky wine lingering on my lips, I realized that I had passed an important milestone in my life. One, unfortunately, I would not be able to repeat on a regular basis.

Château d'Yquem is considered by many to be the finest wine in the world. And it's priced accordingly: you'd be hard-pressed to find a regular-sized bottle of it for less than $200. A bottle from 1811 set a world record as the most expensive bottle of white wine ever sold at an auction, for a record $123,000. When a bit was tasted by wine critic Robert Parker, he said it tasted like "liquefied crème brûlée."

Fortunately you don't need to forego your next mortgage payment to sip this silky-sweet elixer because you can get your hands on a very nice bottle of French Sauternes for about the price of a decent white wine. Due to the modest consumption of dessert wines in France, prices remain within reach and French Sauternes remains one of life's great, yet affordable, luxuries.

Tangerine-Champagne sorbet

SORBET À LA MANDARINE ET AU CHAMPAGNE

Makes 1 quart (1l)

3 cups (750ml) freshly squeezed tangerine juice from 4 pounds (1.9kg) tangerines

²/₃ cup (140g) granulated sugar

1 cup (250 ml) Champagne or sparkling wine

Most people associate Christmas in Paris with *luxe* items, specifically oysters, foie gras, Champagne, and chocolate. But no feast is complete until the clementines come out: shiny bowls of little orange citrus, often festooned with their leaves.

From the start of clementine season, which begins in late fall, Parisians make the rounds of the outdoor markets, going from stand to stand, tasting the samples that vendors peel and put on plates to find the sweetest specimens out there. Most vendors use their fingers to peel the tangerines, but a few use their teeth to rip away the skin. (I avoid tasting those particular ones.) Of all the things people associate with winter in Paris—the lavish department store windows, people buying Champagne by the case, lugs of fresh oysters sold on the sidewalks, butchers offering creamy slabs of *pâté de foie gras*—I look forward to those clementines the most. And it's impossible not to get caught up in the fruit frenzy at the market, with shoppers and vendors loading up big bags to carry home, and no one leaves with less than a few pounds.

Of course, my responsibility every year for Christmas is the final course, and one year I made a dessert that had everyone stunned: a Champagne jelly with *suprêmes* (carefully cut sections, with no membranes) of pink grapefruit, tangerines, navel oranges, and thin strips of candied orange peel, festively served in Champagne glasses with a scoop of icy-cold tangerine-Champagne sorbet perched on top. It's a wonderful do-ahead dessert that goes especially well after winter dishes like *cassoulet* (page 195) or Counterfeit duck confit (page 179).

1   In a large saucepan over low heat, warm ¹/₂ cup (125ml) of the tangerine juice with the sugar, stirring until the sugar is dissolved. Remove from the heat and stir in the remaining 2¹/₂ cups (625ml) of tangerine juice. Add the Champagne. Transfer to a container and chill thoroughly.

2   Freeze in an ice cream maker according to the manufacturer's instructions. Note that this will not freeze as hard as other sorbets because of the alcohol in the Champagne. However, it will make it more scoopable once fully frozen.

continued

VARIATIONS: If you wish to serve this with Champagne gelée, soften 2 envelopes (14g) of unflavored gelatin by sprinkling over 1/2 cup (125ml) of cold water in a very large bowl and letting sit for 5 minutes. In a small saucepan, heat 1/2 cup (125ml) of water with 1 cup (200g) of sugar until the sugar is dissolved, then pour it over the gelatin and stir well. Add 1 bottle of Champagne or sparkling wine (it will foam up, so pour it slowly) and a squeeze of lemon or lime juice. Pour the mixture into a smaller container and chill until firm, at least 6 hours.

To serve, spoon some of the chilled gelée in wine goblets, breaking it up into bite-size mounds. Garnish with fresh orange, tangerine, or grapefruit segments, or a combination of them. Top with a scoop of tangerine-Champagne sorbet. Duck fat cookies (page 297) make a snappy accompaniment.

Tangerine-Champagne sorbet is also good with a spoonful of warm sabayon, made with either Champagne or a sweet dessert wine, such as Sauternes. Make the sabayon by whisking together 2/3 cup (165ml) of Sauternes with 1/3 cup (60g) of sugar and 6 large egg yolks in a large bowl set over a saucepan of simmering water. Continue whisking until the mixture becomes foamy. Keep whisking until it thickens; when you lift the whisk, the mixture should hold its shape when it falls back onto the surface.

Christmas cake

BÛCHE DE NOËL

Serves 12 to 16

Every year, as Christmas approaches, we bakers roll up our sleeves to engage in the global ritual of holiday baking. A few weeks leading up to the holiday, I get requests for a *bûche de Noël* recipe, including one last year from a major food magazine. But they weren't interested in mine.

They asked me if I could find a French grandmother who made *bûche de Noël* at home and would make one for them. I think I caught them by surprise when I replied that I couldn't think of anyone in Paris who made his or her own *bûche*.

Pressed for an explanation, I told them that there are so many excellent bakeries in Paris vying for customers, that there's literally competition in the windows of the pastry shops to catch the eye of discriminating *bûche* buyers. The swankiest places make the biggest splash with their *bûches de Noël*, spraying them with everything from green tea powder to pure gold dust, or wrapping their *bûches* in marzipan with edible bows to look like packages from Père Noël himself.

One year, I saw a racy cake that was tied up with chocolate "leather" straps, which might scare many French children who will be reminded of Père Fouettard, the fabled hooded man who pays a visit during the month of December and whips (*fouetter*) children who have been bad. I also imagine few French grandmothers would be interested in creating a leather-bound *bûche*, although I'm certain they'd be popular back in San Francisco.

I'm no French grandmother, nor do I want to get punished, so I spend every year in Paris trying not to be a bad boy. The only thing I do that's even remotely naughty is make a mean *bûche de Noël*.

I veer from both the French classic and those new-fangled versions. Instead of a dense, buttercream filling, I roll up my genoise with a lightened mixture of ricotta with crunchy chopped-up chocolate and bits of candied orange, to give it that festive, holiday touch. My frosting is a slick of bittersweet chocolate, swirled over the cake to replicate bark. And instead of leopard prints or leather and lace, I stick with enchanting, magical mushrooms. Which, of course, might also make this popular with people back in my hometown of San Francisco. But this recipe pleases friends and family here in Paris, too.

continued

1 Preheat the oven to 350°F (175°C). Make an X with some soft butter on a jelly roll pan or a rimmed baking sheet (9 to 12 inches by 18 inches/23 to 30cm by 45cm). Line the pan with a sheet of parchment paper.

2 To make the genoise, in the bowl of a stand mixer fitted with the whip attachment, beat the eggs, sugar, and salt on high speed until they hold a thick ribbon when you lift the whip, about 5 minutes. Whip in the vanilla.

320

3 Remove the bowl from the mixer and using a fine-mesh sieve, gradually sift the flour over the beaten egg yolks while folding it in with a rubber spatula. Drizzle the room-temperature, but still liquid, butter over the batter, folding it in gradually; do not overfold.

4 Scrape the batter onto the prepared baking sheet and spread it in an even layer. Bake for 12 to 15 minutes, or until it's golden brown and feels just done in the center; it should spring back lightly when you touch it. Remove from the oven and let cool for 5 minutes.

5 Lightly sift some powdered sugar over the top of the cake. Lay a kitchen towel on the countertop. Run a knife around the edge of the cake to loosen it from the pan and overturn the pan onto the towel. Then lift off the pan and peel away the parchment paper. Starting on one of the two longer sides, roll the cake up in the towel and let cool for 1 hour.

6 To make the filling, mix together the ricotta, candied orange peel, chocolate, sugar, and liqueur in a bowl. Set aside.

7 To make the syrup, heat the sugar and water in a small saucepan until the sugar is dissolved. Remove from the heat and add the liqueur. Set aside.

8 Unroll the cake and spread the filling over the cake, leaving a 1-inch (3cm) edge on each of the longer edges. Roll the cake back up, wrap it in plastic, and place it seam-side down in the refrigerator to chill for at least 1 hour. (The cake can be assembled and chilled up to 2 days in advance.)

9 Preheat the oven to 225°F (110°C). Line a baking sheet with parchment paper or a silicone baking mat. To make the meringue mushrooms (see page 322), in the bowl of a stand mixer fitted with the whip attachment (or in a large metal bowl, by hand), whip the egg whites with the salt on high speed until they form soft peaks. Continue whipping, adding the sugar a tablespoon at a time, until the meringue is very stiff and glossy. Whip in the cinnamon.

continued

GENOISE

4 large eggs, at room temperature

2/3 cup (125g) granulated sugar

Pinch of sea salt or kosher salt

1 teaspoon vanilla extract

1 cup (125g) cake flour

4 tablespoons (2 ounces/55g) unsalted butter, melted and cooled to room temperature

Powdered sugar

FILLING

1 1/2 pounds (680g) ricotta cheese

1/2 cup (110g) finely chopped candied orange peel

3 ounces (85g) bittersweet chocolate, finely chopped

6 tablespoons (90g) granulated sugar

1/4 cup (60ml) orange liqueur, such as Grand Marnier or Cointreau

ORANGE SYRUP

1/4 cup (50g) granulated sugar

6 tablespoons (90ml) water

2 tablespoons orange liqueur, such as Grand Marnier or Cointreau

10 Transfer the meringue to a pastry bag fitted with a ¹/₂-inch (1.5cm) plain tip (or scrape it into a sturdy resealable plastic bag and snip off a corner with scissors), then pipe 22 round mushroom "caps" in 1-inch (3cm) mounds. Pipe the 22 "stems" by making a base that's slightly thicker, tapering the meringue as you pull the bag straight up, leaving a pointed top. Smooth the tops of the round mushroom caps with a finger dipped in water, and then bake the meringues in the oven for 1¹/₂ hours. Let cool completely.

11 To assemble the mushrooms, take a sharp paring knife and carve a small hole in the underside of each mushroom cap, large enough to fit the points of the stems.

12 Melt the chocolate in a clean, dry bowl set over a pan of barely simmering water, stirring until smooth. Dip the pointed tips of the mushroom stems into the chocolate and press each one into the hole on the underside of the mushroom cap. Set on a rack to cool, and then transfer the mushrooms to an airtight container until ready to use. (The mushrooms can be made up to 1 week in advance and stored at room temperature.)

13 To make the chocolate icing, melt the chocolate with the coffee in a heatproof bowl set over a pan of barely simmering water, stirring until smooth. Remove the bowl from the heat and stir in the butter. Once the mixture is smooth, let the icing sit until it's thick enough to spread.

14 For a tree branch–shaped *bûche de Noël*, trim off both ends of the cylinder of cake, making diagonal slices. Set the long center section on a serving plate or tray, and place one of the lopped-off pieces with the diagonal end against the cake and the flat end facing up. Attach the second piece to the other side, creating another "branch." (You can also affix it to the top, although you may need to use a toothpick to keep it in place. But if you plan to carry it through Paris on the métro, forget it.) Use a thin metal spatula to frost the cake with the chocolate icing. Once it's iced, make lengthwise grooves on the center section of the "log" with the spatula to mimic bark, and then make shorter grooves on the smaller "branches." Arrange the mushrooms around the cake then sprinkle with powdered sugar. Slice and serve. The cake can be assembled up 1 day in advance. Let it come to room temperature before serving.

VARIATION: For a richer filling, substitute mascarpone for the ricotta in the filling.

Christmas cake, continued

MERINGUE MUSHROOMS

2 large egg whites, at room temperature

Pinch of sea salt or kosher salt

¹/₂ cup (100g) granulated sugar

Generous pinch of ground cinnamon

1¹/₂ ounces (45g) bittersweet or semisweet chocolate, chopped

CHOCOLATE ICING

5 ounces (140g) bittersweet or semisweet chocolate, chopped

¹/₄ cup (60ml) coffee or water

6 tablespoons (3 ounces, 85g) unsalted butter, cubed, at room temperature

Powdered sugar, for decorating the cake

Pantry

INGRÉDIENTS
DE BASE

THIS IS MY *MÉLI-MÉLO*, OR AN assortment of things, which are part of my pantry and I like to keep on hand in the refrigerator or freezer.

Chicken stock

BOUILLON DE VOLAILLE

Makes about 6 cups (1.5l)

The number one question I am asked by Americans who have just landed in France to live is, "Where can I find canned chicken stock?" Unfortunately, it doesn't exist here. Grocery stores do sell powdered cubes (which are, for some reason, popular), but I can't abide them. So I make my own stock, which is very easy and tastes much, much better.

Many *volaillers* will have chicken carcasses on hand, which are great for making stock, or I sometimes might just buy a bag of wings and use those. But if making something like Chicken pot Parmentier (page 166), I'll pull the whole chicken out of the stock after an hour or so, let it cool a bit, remove the meat to use in the casserole, and then return the bones to the pot for finishing.

If using a whole chicken, be sure to trim any excess fat from the bird, and check inside for any giblets or other innards, which will make the stock bitter. Because stock freezes very well, if you have a large enough pot, feel free to double the recipe and freeze extra, to have stock on hand.

1   Put the chicken in a large pot or Dutch oven along with the water. Add the onion, carrot, celery, bay leaf, parsley, thyme, salt, and peppercorns. Bring the pot to a boil, decrease the heat to a gentle simmer, and let the stock cook at a bare simmer for 2 1/2 hours. As the stock cooks, skim off any foamy scum that rises to the surface and discard it. Add a small amount of water as it cooks, if necessary, so the chicken remains submerged.

2   When the stock is ready, strain it through a fine-mesh strainer and discard the solids. Use the stock as it is, chill it in the refrigerator, or freeze it until ready to use. The stock will keep for up to 3 days in the refrigerator, or 2 to 3 months in the freezer.

1 chicken (2 to 2 1/2 pounds/about 1kg) or chicken carcasses or wings of equal weight

3 quarts (3l) cold water, plus more if needed

1 onion, unpeeled and quartered

1 carrot, unpeeled, cut into 8 batons

1 rib celery, cut into 4 pieces, with leaves attached

1 bay leaf

A few sprigs flat-leaf parsley

4 sprigs thyme

Generous pinch of sea salt or kosher salt

10 whole black peppercorns

Clarified butter

BEURRE CLARIFIÉ

Makes a scant ¹/₂ cup (125ml)

Crêpe-makers in France brush their griddles with *saindoux*, or cooking lard, which has a higher burning point than butter. I prefer clarified butter, which has similar properties to lard, but tastes better to me. It's not always imperative that you use it, but you'll find it doesn't smoke like regular melted butter when you fry it at a high temperature. It'll keep for at least 1 month in the refrigerator.

8 tablespoons (4 ounces/115g) unsalted butter

1 Cut the butter into cubes and melt it in a small saucepan. Let simmer for about 1 minute. When the froth rises to the top, remove the pan from the heat. With a spoon, scrape off the foamy solids on top of the butter.

2 Strain the butter through cheesecloth or a fine-mesh sieve. Clarified butter will keep for at least a month in the refrigerator, or 2 months in the freezer.

Crème fraîche

CRÈME FRAÎCHE

Makes 1 cup (240g)

All *fromageries* in France—and even supermarkets—sell squat tubs of *crème fraîche*, a marvelously thick, rich, sweet cream that you can stand a spoon in. I use it to enrich the cream filling in Merveilleux (page 281), and to add a dollop to soups. If you can't find it in a store near you, you can make a reasonable facsimile at home.

Note that this needs to rest for 24 hours to thicken. Like heavy cream, crème fraîche can be whipped. If whipping it, make sure the finished crème fraîche has ample time to chill thoroughly in the refrigerator before taking a whisk to it.

1 cup (250ml) heavy cream
2 tablespoons buttermilk

1 In a small glass or metal bowl, stir together the cream and buttermilk. Cover, and let stand for 24 hours at room temperature, to culture and thicken.

2 Refrigerate until ready to use. Crème fraîche will keep in the refrigerator for about a week.

Hard-cooked eggs

OEUFS DURS

Makes 6 eggs

The French revere eggs so much that they are featured front-and-center in one of their most beloved dishes, *œufs mayo* (page 103). I also serve them as part of *le grand aïoli* (page 145) with strips of anchovies draped over them, or chopped into bits and strewn over leeks vinaigrette (page 88).

This method will yield cooked eggs with slightly soft yolks. Very fresh eggs will be harder to peel, but, of course, taste better. I usually do a few more than I need in case any give me trouble when I'm removing the shells.

6 large eggs, at room temperature

1   Fill a saucepan half-full of water, enough to cover the eggs, and bring to a moderate boil.

2   Using a slotted spoon, carefully lower the eggs into the water.

3   Decrease the heat so the water is at a low, rumbling boil and cook for 9 minutes.

4   Just before the eggs are finished cooking, prepare an ice bath by filling a bowl three-quarters full with ice and cold water. When the eggs are done, remove them with a slotted spoon and drop them into the ice water. Wait about a minute, and then take a spoon and tap each egg lightly a few times to crack it, and then put them back in the ice water to cool completely. Once cool, remove the eggs from the ice water and peel them, rinsing them under running water to remove any bits of shell. Hard-cooked eggs, unpeeled, will keep in the refrigerator for up to 2 days.

Poached eggs

ŒUFS POCHÉS

Makes 2 eggs

2 large eggs
1 teaspoon white vinegar

I'm a rather hearty eater and find that a poached egg floating in a bowl of soup, resting on top of a mound of Buckwheat polenta with braised greens, sausage, and poached eggs (page 158), or broken in half with the warm yolk mingling with the dressing in *salade lyonnaise* (page 99) can make a filling meal. I've tried some of the myriad of ways to poach eggs, including creating a vortex by stirring the water briskly before adding the egg, to straining the egg before poaching, and had mixed success. So I keep going back to the basic way of doing it.

1   Bring a saucepan or skillet of water to a gentle boil with the vinegar.

2   Crack 1 egg into a teacup or small bowl. When the water is at a low boil and small bubbles are vigorously rising to the surface, hold the teacup with the egg it in next to the surface of the water and gently slide the egg into the simmering water. Repeat with the second egg. Let the eggs poach for $2^{1}/_{2}$ to 3 minutes, until cooked to your liking.

3   When the eggs are done (the yolks should be very soft and jiggly), lift them out of the water with a slotted spoon, blot excess water off each egg with a paper towel, and serve.

NOTE: You can poach the eggs in advance and slide them into a bowl of ice water after they are cooked. (They can be kept that way, chilled, for a few hours.) To reheat and serve, slide them into hot water and let them simmer for about a minute to warm them through.

Harissa

HARISSA

Makes 2 cups (480g)

Harissa is Paris's answer to hot sauce. With its complex, beguiling flavor, it's not just hot—it's on fire! Harissa is often sold in tubes, like toothpaste, so you can squeeze as much or as little as you want, whenever you need a dab.

It's easy to make, and when I'm in California, I stock up on dried chiles, which from the way I revere them, you would think that I'd won a bidding war for them at Drouot auction house. But I also find dried chiles in Paris at Arabic *épiceries*, where they are simply labeled *piment fort*. The variety is never mentioned, which makes chile aficionados a little crazy, but I'm just happy to be able to have a jar of harissa in my refrigerator at all times.

So you can use any dried chiles, as I do. Harissa is meant to be hot, and it's impossible to go too far. The tiny bit of rose or orange flower water was a tip given to me by Gregory Marchand, the chef and owner of Frenchie restaurant, and provides an elusive counterpoint to the fiery chiles.

Mix a dab into egg salad to give it some color and zip, toss pasta with it (adding some oil to tame it), use is as a condiment to fire up a Lamb shank tagine (page 199), or make a quick spicy, dipping sauce when added to mayonnaise for *merguez boulettes* (page 74).

2 ounces (55g) dried red chiles

1 fresh red bell pepper

1 clove garlic, peeled and minced

1/2 teaspoon sea salt or kosher salt

1/2 teaspoon smoked paprika

1/4 teaspoon ground cumin

2 tablespoons olive oil

1 teaspoon red wine vinegar or cider vinegar

1/8 teaspoon rose or orange flower water (optional)

1 Bring a pot of water to a boil. Stem the chiles, slice them lengthwise, and remove the seeds. (I recommend wearing rubber gloves to handle the chiles.) Put them in the boiling water, decrease the heat, and simmer for 2 minutes. Turn off the heat. Put a small plate on the chiles to keep them submerged, and let sit for 30 minutes.

2 Place the red pepper directly on the gas flame on your stovetop and cook it, turning it as it blackens on each side, until it's completely charred and soft, 10 to 15 minutes. When done, put the red pepper in a bowl and stretch a piece of plastic wrap over the top; let stand until cool. Once cool, remove the stem, open the pepper, and remove the seeds, and then rub off all the skin. (If you have an electric stovetop, stem and seed the pepper, then slice it and fry the slices in olive oil, until very soft.)

3 Drain the chiles and squeeze the excess moisture out of them. (Don't forget the rubber gloves!) Put them in a blender along

with the roasted red pepper, the garlic, salt, paprika, cumin, olive oil, vinegar, and rose water and blend until the harissa is a very smooth paste. Depending on the peppers, if the skins don't break down in your blender enough to make a smooth paste, you can press the mixture through a coarse strainer with a rubber spatula or pass through a food mill. Scrape the harissa into a jar and refrigerate until ready to use. Harissa will last 1 or 2 months in the refrigerator. Adding a little layer of olive oil on top will help preserve it.

Mayonnaise

MAYONNAISE

Makes about 1 cup (240g)

Mayonnaise can be made in a bowl with a whisk, using a mortar and pestle, or in a blender. Here I give instruction for a whisk or mortar and pestle, but if using a blender, you can add the whole egg if you wish. If you want to flavor the mayonnaise with a dab of Dijon mustard, add it at the beginning because it helps emulsify the sauce.

I use a combination of olive oil and neutral-tasting vegetable oil; using all olive oil can be overwhelming, even to those of us who love the flavor of olive oil. Feel free to adjust the ratio to your liking.

6 tablespoons (90ml) olive oil

6 tablespoons (90ml) neutral-tasting vegetable oil

1 large egg yolk, at room temperature

1/2 teaspoon sea salt or kosher salt

Freshly squeezed lemon juice

1   Pour the oils into a measuring cup with a spout.

2   Set a bowl on a damp kitchen towel rolled up to hold the bowl in place, or have someone hold it for you to keep it steady, and whisk the egg yolk well. Very, very slowly, adding it drop by drop, whisk in a little bit of the oil. Continue to add the oil slowly, whisking all the while, until it begins to thicken and emulsify.

3   In a steady stream, whisk in the rest of the oil a little more quickly, until all the oil is incorporated. Stir in the salt and a good squirt of lemon juice. This will keep for 2 to 3 days, covered, in the refrigerator.

NOTE: If the mayonnaise "breaks," and turns watery, the oil was likely added too fast. To fix it, whisk another egg yolk in a clean bowl and slowly drizzle the broken mayonnaise into the egg yolk, starting off drop by drop, then increasing the flow, which should bring the mayonnaise back.

Rosemary oil

HUILE D'OLIVE AROMATISÉE AU ROMARIN

Makes ¹/₂ cup (125ml)

This recipe makes a vibrant, green-colored oil, and will yield a bit more than you'll need for garnishing the Artichoke tapenade (page 53), but any extra can be used to spoon over grilled chicken breasts or fish, or drizzled over the Cherry tomato crostini (page 110) or even a Fresh herb omelet (page 133). Feel free to use another herb in place of the rosemary; tarragon, sage, or even fresh mint work well in this herbaceous oil.

¹/₂ cup (125ml) olive oil

Generous pinch of sea salt or kosher salt

¹/₂ cup (5g) flat-leaf parsley leaves

¹/₃ cup (4g) rosemary leaves

1 Bring a small pot of water to a boil; have a bowl of ice water ready.

2 Heat the oil and salt in another small saucepan until warm, but not boiling. Remove from the heat and set aside.

3 Add the herbs to the boiling water and cook for 10 seconds; drain, and add the herbs to the ice water.

4 Once the herbs are cool, lift them out with your hand and press them in a paper towel until very, very dry, and then add them to the oil. Let the herbs infuse for 15 minutes.

5 Blend the herbs and oil in a mini-chopper or food processor for 30 seconds, then strain the oil through a fine-mesh strainer if you don't mind a few bits of greenery in the oil. If you want to be especially persnickety and get every bit of the herbs out, strain it through a few layers of cheesecloth. The rosemary oil can be kept for a few days at room temperature in a closed container, or for up to 1 month in the refrigerator; let it come to room temperature before using.

Salsa verde

SAUCE VERTE

Makes about ³/₄ cup (180ml)

You can use any mix of herbs you want. I like to use at least one that's sharp—such as tarragon or mint—especially if serving with roast lamb (page 203), which tends to be rich and full-flavored, and can stand up to strong flavors.

Other herbs that can be used include flat-leaf parsley, basil, oregano, marjoram, sage, chervil, rosemary, and thyme (though go easy on the rosemary and thyme as they can be overwhelming). Sometimes I use some chopped radish leaves, which add a distinct peppery note.

2/3 cup (50g) coarsely chopped fresh herbs

6 tablespoons (90ml) olive oil, plus more if needed

10 green olives, pitted and chopped

1 tablespoon capers, rinsed, squeezed dry, and chopped

1 teaspoon peeled and minced garlic

1 small shallot, peeled and minced

Finely grated zest of 1 lemon (unsprayed)

1/2 teaspoon sea salt or kosher salt

Freshly squeezed lemon juice (optional)

1 Combine all the ingredients in a small bowl at least 1 hour before serving. The salsa verde should be a thick, but runny, paste. If necessary, add more olive oil and perhaps a few drops of lemon juice.

2 The flavors get better as it sits, so it can be made up to 8 hours ahead. Salsa verde will keep for up to 2 days in the refrigerator. Bring to room temperature before serving.

333

Salted butter caramel sauce

CARAMEL AU BEURRE SALÉ

Makes 1¹/₂ cups (375ml)

Salted butter caramel took Paris by storm, and nowadays it's become one of the most popular treats, not just in France, but around the world. Caramelized sugar with a pat of butter swirled in, bubbling up, then smoothed out with a pour of heavy cream: honestly, what's not to like? This sauce is adapted from the one served at Restaurant Astier, where they serve it with Individual chocolate cakes (page 261), but it also makes a good accompaniment to Dee's fabulous cheesecake (page 315) and can be served warm as a sauce with your favorite ice cream.

1 cup (200g) granulated sugar
¹/₂ cup (125ml) water
6 tablespoons (3 ounces/85g) salted butter, cubed, at room temperature
¹/₂ cup (125ml) heavy cream
Sea salt or kosher salt (optional)

1   Spread the sugar in a large skillet or wide saucepan and pour the water over it. Heat the sugar over medium heat, swirling the pan very gently, just enough to moisten the sugar evenly with the water.

2   Once the sugar is moistened and starting to cook, swirl the pan only if there are dry spots of sugar that aren't melting. Continue to cook the sugar until it begins to darken. Watching carefully, gently swirl the pan, only if necessary, so it cooks evenly. (If the sugar starts to crystallize, continue cooking, stirring only if you see very dark or burnt spots appearing, and the crystals should eventually smooth out.)

3   When the caramel is a deep amber color and begins to smoke, remove the pan from the heat and drop in the cubes of butter. Stir the butter in with a whisk until it's completely melted, then gradually whisk in the cream, stirring until the sauce is smooth. If there are stubborn bits of caramel stuck to the bottom, loosen them with a wooden spoon, and stir them in. If they refuse to melt, rewarm the sauce over low heat, which should do the trick. Once the sauce is cool enough to taste, you may want to add a bit of salt. The sauce will keep for up to 2 weeks in the refrigerator and can be reheated before serving. If cooled and rewarmed, it may need to be thinned with a bit of cream or milk.

Shallot marmalade

CONFITURE D'ÉCHALOTTES

Makes 2 cups (500g)

Although I love all kinds of charcuterie, especially chicken liver pâté and Duck terrine with figs (page 113), what makes them even better is a jar of *aigre-doux* shallot marmalade served alongside. Its sweet-sour taste is a wonderful counterpoint to the richness of the meat.

2 tablespoons neutral-tasting vegetable oil

1 pound (450g) shallots, peeled and sliced

Generous pinch of sea salt or kosher salt

Freshly ground black pepper

1/4 cup (50g) packed dark or light brown sugar

2 tablespoons honey

1/3 cup (80ml) cider vinegar

1/3 cup (85g) raisins, coarsely chopped

1   Heat the oil in a skillet over medium heat and sauté the shallots for 10 to 12 minutes, stirring frequently, until they're completely soft and wilted.

2   Stir in the salt and a few grinds of pepper, the brown sugar, honey, vinegar, and raisins. Continue to cook, stirring often, until the liquid becomes thick and syrupy, 10 to 12 minutes. Scrape into a jar and let cool. The marmalade will keep for up to 6 months in the refrigerator.

Vinaigrette

VINAIGRETTE

Makes 1/3 cup (80ml), enough for 2 to 3 salads

A lot of people talk about the importance of oil in a vinaigrette, which I'll get to in a minute, but to me, just as much attention should be paid to the vinegar. All vinegars are not alike, and it wasn't until I had a job making hundreds of salads almost every night for two years, that I learned a lot about making a good vinaigrette.

The word *vinaigre* is a mash-up of two words; *wine* (*vin*) and *sour* (*aigre*), which is what naturally happens to wine that's left to stand uncorked. Like wine, vinegar varies in quality, and I use either red wine vinegar or sherry vinegar for almost every vinaigrette I make. Despite its popularity, I avoid commercial balsamic vinegar because I find it to be too sweet in salads. Sherry vinegar is my preferred choice when I want a mellower flavor, and red wine vinegar is what I use when I want the dressing to have a bit more pizzazz.

I used to always choose extra-virgin olive oil to make dressing for green salads, but since moving to France, I've tasted salads

continued

with neutral-tasting salad oil in the vinaigrette and realized that olive oil can be a little overly assertive in a dressing. So I sometimes use a cold-pressed oil, such as sunflower, safflower, or *colza* (rapeseed or canola) oil, which I get from local producers. Do try it the next time you make a vinaigrette; you might be as surprised as I was!

I almost always add shallots to vinaigrette, which impart a wonderful, slight oniony sweetness to a simple *salade verte*, or green salad. Other ways to elevate a simple green salad are to add chervil, an underused herb in America, or cut some razor-thin slices of fresh fennel from a trimmed bulb, or red radishes, and toss them with the salad greens.

Like the French, I don't make dressing in advance in large batches, but mix the dressing in a large salad bowl and pile the leaves and other ingredients on top of it, then cover it with a clean linen towel. When it's time to *fatiguer* the salad, as the French say, I toss the ingredients in the dressing—along with freshly ground black pepper, a few flakes of sea salt, and perhaps some just-chopped herbs—and serve.

This amount makes enough to dress 6 cups (100g) of torn lettuce leaves, enough for two to three servings of salad. It can be increased to serve more. If using more delicate greens, like mâche, arugula, or mesclun (baby salad mix), add it to taste, as they may require less dressing than sturdier leaves like romaine or butter lettuce.

1 Use a fork to mix together the vinegar, salt, shallots, and mustard in a *saladier* (large salad bowl), stirring until the salt is dissolved. (French people like a lot of mustard in their dressing; I suggest that you start with 1 teaspoon and add more to taste.)

2 Stir in the oil briskly until fully mixed. I try to make the dressing within a few hours of serving.

1 tablespoon best-quality red wine or sherry vinegar

1/4 teaspoon sea salt or kosher salt

2 teaspoons minced shallots (optional)

1 to 2 teaspoons Dijon mustard

1/4 cup (60ml) olive, sunflower, or safflower oil

336

Whipped Cream

CRÈME CHANTILLY

Makes 2 cups (500ml)

1 cup (250ml) heavy cream
1 tablespoon granulated sugar
½ teaspoon vanilla extract

If you're shopping for cheese on a weekend in Paris, you'll likely find a line of shoppers at *fromageries* that offer small tubs of Fontainebleau, which is freshly whipped cream enriched with fromage blanc. It's so luscious, and so fragile, that it's wrapped in gauze to preserve it. For that reason, *Fromageries* only produce it on certain days of the week, mostly weekends, when demand is highest. I highly recommend seeking it out, especially if you have some ripe strawberries or *fraises des bois* (wild strawberries) to serve with it. Topped with a sprinkle of sugar, it's creamy, dreamy nirvana.

Its cousin is *crème chantilly*, or whipped cream, which you can make easily at home. For the best-tasting whipped cream, try to find heavy cream from a local dairy that hasn't been ultra-pasteurized (UHT). The heat treatment that conserves the cream for several months also removes a lot of the flavor. It also makes it more stubborn to whip. Use a stand mixer fitted with the whip attachment, or whip the cream by hand. Either way, chilling the bowl and the whisk before starting will make it whip faster.

1   In the bowl of a stand mixer fitted with the whip attachment (or in a metal bowl, by hand), whip the cream on high speed until it begins to hold its shape.

2   Add the sugar and the vanilla and continue to whip until the cream forms soft, droopy peaks. Avoid overwhipping, which can make the whipped cream grainy. The whipped cream can be used right away or covered and refrigerated for up to 24 hours. It will likely need a light whipping just prior to serving if refrigerated for any length of time.

Sources

AMAZON
www.amazon.com
Aluminum foil baking cups, chocolate, cookware and bakeware, Dijon mustard, duck fat, French cheeses, salt, gratin dishes, lentils from Le Puy, J. Leblanc nut oils, olive oil, pearl sugar, and piment d'Espelette.

BOB'S RED MILL
www.bobsredmill.com
Bread flour, buckwheat groats, buckwheat flour, chickpea flour, vital wheat gluten, wheat berries, and other grains and seeds.

BRAM CASSOLES
www.bramcookware.com
French-inspired baking dishes and casseroles, including cassoulet dishes and tians.

CLAY COYOTE
www.claycoyote.com
Cassoulet dishes.

CHEFSHOP
www.chefshop.com
Anchovies, chickpea flour, dried beans, French honey, olive oil, salt, lentils from Le Puy, and vinegars.

D'ARTAGNAN
www.dartagnan.com
Duck fat, duck confit, fresh duck, cassoulet dishes, and haricots tarbais (cassoulet beans).

FORMAGGIO KITCHEN
www.formaggiokitchen.com
Dijon mustard, French cheese, olive oils, salts, and J. Leblanc nut oils.

FRENCH SELECTIONS
www.frenchselections.com
Dijon mustard, duck confit, duck fat, nut oils, olive oil, piment d'Espelette, salt, and vinegar.

KALUSTYAN'S
www.kalustyans.com
Chickpea flour, harissa, preserved lemons, pomegranate molasses, sumac, spices, and tahini.

KING ARTHUR FLOUR
www.kingarthurflour.com
Bread flour, cake flour, buckwheat groats, buckwheat flour, cake flour, vital wheat gluten, and pearl sugar.

LA TIENDA
www.tienda.com
Anchovies, salt cod, paprika, and Spanish sherry vinegar.

LE FANION
www.lefanion.com
French pottery: cassoulet and gratin dishes.

PENZEYS
www.penzeys.com
French salts, sumac, and other herbs and spices.

PHIPPS COUNTRY STORE AND FARM
www.phippscountry.com
Heirloom dried beans.

RANCHO GORDO
www.ranchogordo.com
Heirloom dried beans, including American-grown cassoulet beans.

SALTTRADERS
www.salttraders.com
French salts.

STARBUCKS
www.starbucks.com
Instant powdered coffee (VIA).

SUR LA TABLE
www.surlatable.com
French cookware, baking dishes, and other equipment.

THE MEADOW
www.atthemeadow.com
French salts.

THE SPANISH TABLE
www.spanishtable.com
Anchovies, clay gratin and crème brûlée dishes (cazuelas), salt cod, paprika, and sherry vinegar.

TRADER JOE'S
www.traderjoes.com
Dijon mustard, European-style dairy products and butter, French lentils, nuts and dried fruits, and speculoos cookie butter.

WILLIAMS-SONOMA
www.williams-sonoma.com
French cookware, baking dishes, and other ingredients.

ZINGERMAN'S
www.zingermans.com
Anchovies, farro, French honey, salt, and olive oil.

First and foremost, thanks to the readers of my blog, who have patiently (and sometimes with great embarrassment) followed my ups and downs as a foreigner in a quirky, beautiful, complicated, and tasty city. It was you who prompted me to hit the bakeries, restaurants, and markets, and come up with recipes in my Paris kitchen to share.

To my friends who are great cooks and chefs, who graciously shared their recipes: Cyril Boulet, Paule Caillat, Marc Desportes, Dee Goldberg, Anissa Helou, Fabrice Le Bourdat, David Leite, Marion Lévy, David Lindsay, Seen Lippert, Beena Paradin, and Laurel Sanderson.

Appreciation to Lesley Chesterman, Dianne Jacob, Shauna James Ahern, Dan Lepard, Alec Lobrano, Michael Ruhlman, Hank Shaw, David Tanis, and Regina Schrambling, for their professional advice, and to Elise Bauer and Deb Perelman for sharing laughs. To Alice Waters and Lindsey Shere, for giving me such a strong foundation. Thanks to Mara Goldberg for her help with translations as well as assistance with the nonculinary challenges of living in Paris. To Kristin Beddard for getting kale to Paris. And to Jeanette Hermann for making it extra fun to show folks my favorite places in this tasty city.

Always happy to visit Fouquet chocolates, Breizh Café, Candelaria, La Graineterie du Marché, La Grande Épicerie, Poilâne, and Jean-Charles Rochoux, and Restaurant Astier, who are kind enough to let me in behind the scenes.

To Susan Friedland, thanks to her keen eye, strong guidance, friendship, and encouragement, I made it to the finish line in the best shape possible.

Big thanks to Cindy Meyers, who did a super job testing many of the recipes in this book in the United States. Her notes and tips were invaluable.

To the wonderful folks at Ten Speed Press, who truly make every book I do with them a pleasure. Special thanks to Julie Bennett for being such an understanding editor when the less interesting aspects of life in a foreign city tried to pull me away, and from that first foggy day we met in San Francisco to the day the book landed on my door-step, for getting behind the project and enthusiastically guiding me—and the book—to completion. To Betsy Stromberg, for the gorgeous design; and Kristin Casemore and Michele Crim, for their publicity and marketing acumen. And to publisher Aaron Wehner for suggesting that *My Paris Kitchen* become a book.

To my agent, Bonnie Nadell, and her assistant, Austen Rachlis, who continue to take care of the details so I can bake and write.

It was amazing to work with photographer Ed Anderson, who came to Paris and captured everything I love about the city and the food so brilliantly—thanks, Ed! And stylists Valerie Aikman-Smith and Ethel Brennan, who shopped up a storm at the markets of Paris with me, then dished up the food so beautifully. (And thanks to the team for helping with the excess of iced rosé left over after the photo shoots.)

And lastly, *merci mille fois* to my other half, Romain. When I introduced him to some friends just after we met, one pulled me aside and said, "How did you find such a good one?" After all these years, I still don't know. But I'm glad I did.

Acknowledgments

Index

343

344

345

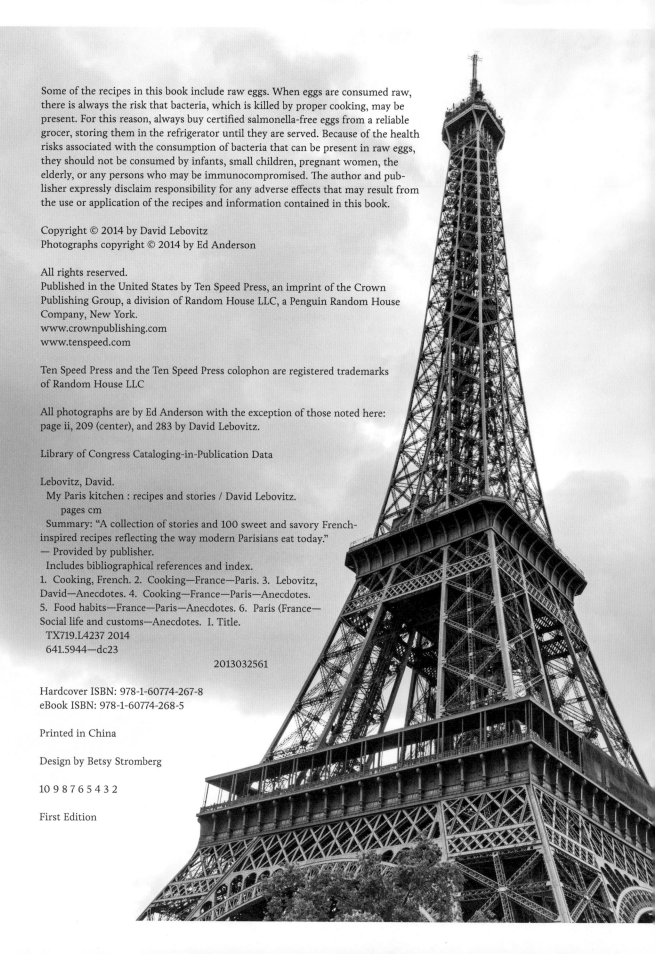

Published in the United States by Ten Speed Press, an imprint of the Crown Publishing Group, a division of Random House LLC, a Penguin Random House Company, New York.
www.crownpublishing.com
www.tenspeed.com

Ten Speed Press and the Ten Speed Press colophon are registered trademarks of Random House LLC

All photographs are by Ed Anderson with the exception of those noted here: page ii, 209 (center), and 283 by David Lebovitz.

Library of Congress Cataloging-in-Publication Data

Lebovitz, David.
    My Paris kitchen : recipes and stories / David Lebovitz.
        pages cm
    Summary: "A collection of stories and 100 sweet and savory French-inspired recipes reflecting the way modern Parisians eat today."
— Provided by publisher.
    Includes bibliographical references and index.
1. Cooking, French. 2. Cooking—France—Paris. 3. Lebovitz, David—Anecdotes. 4. Cooking—France—Paris—Anecdotes.
5. Food habits—France—Paris—Anecdotes. 6. Paris (France—Social life and customs—Anecdotes. I. Title.
    TX719.L4237 2014
    641.5944—dc23
                                2013032561

Hardcover ISBN: 978-1-60774-267-8
eBook ISBN: 978-1-60774-268-5

Printed in China

Design by Betsy Stromberg

10 9 8 7 6 5 4 3 2

First Edition